Railway & Maritime Operations
Lancaster - Morecambe - Heysham

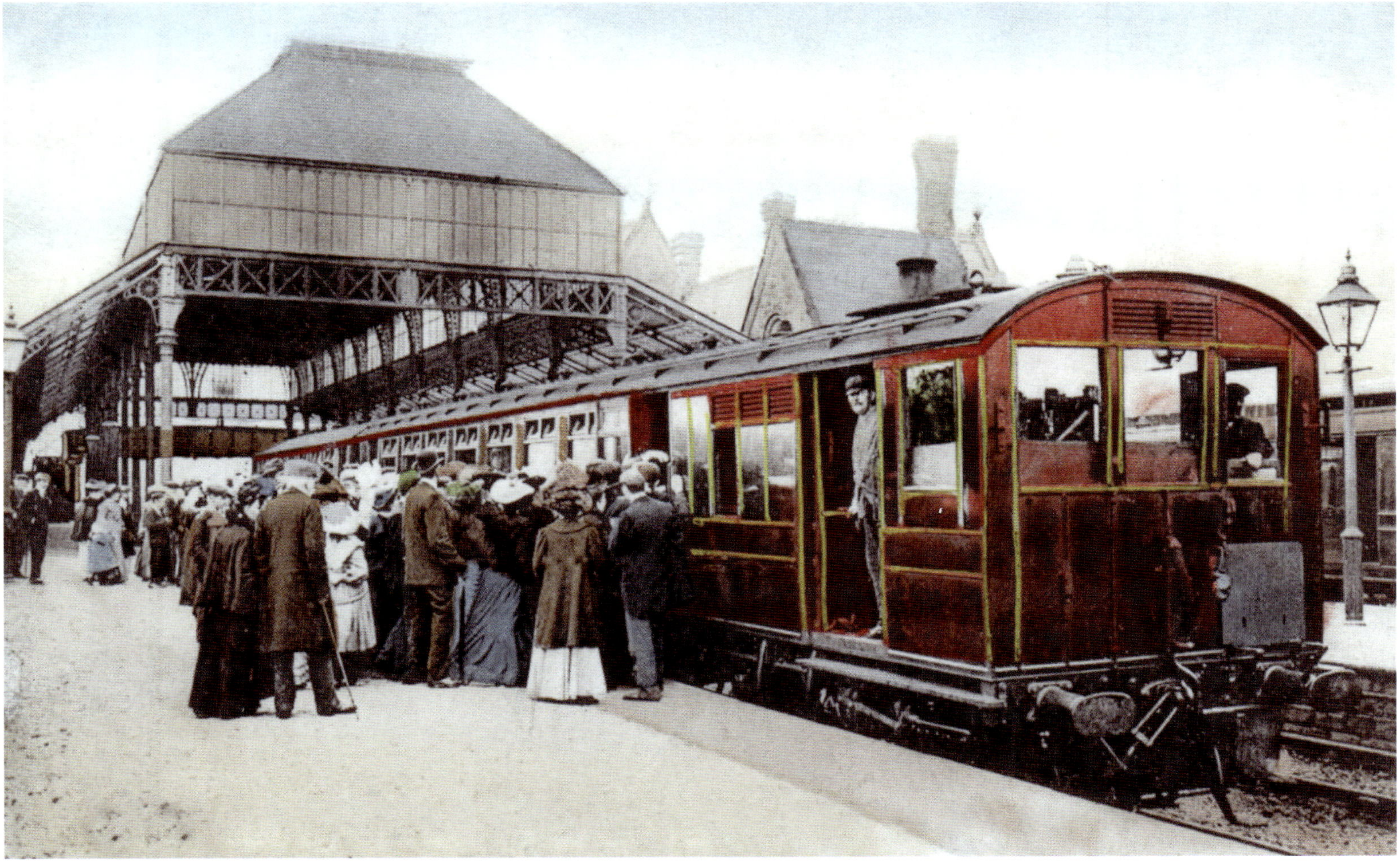

Willowherb Publishing

First published 2019

Willowherb Publishing
www.willowherbpublishing.co.uk

Printed in the UK by:
The Amadeus Press
Cleckheaton
BD19 4TQ
ISBN: 978-0-9935678-5-8

Front Cover

Having arrived at Morecambe Promenade from Lancaster, driving trailer 29021 awaits its next turn of duty. Built for the London & North Western Railway in 1914, these three-car electric units served Lancaster, Morecambe and Heysham from 1953 up to the first weekend of 1966. Their legacy is having pioneered high voltage railway electrification at industrial frequency. *(D. J. Mitchell)*

Frontispiece

A steam railmotor and trailer at the pre-1907 Morecambe Station in Northumberland Street, looking towards the Harbour. Two railmotors - Nos 2233 and 2234 - were built at Derby in 1904, specifically to work between Morecambe and Heysham. They were not successful, running for less than a year up to June 1905. 2233 was then reboilered and did see further passenger work elsewhere. But in 1907, 2234 was converted for the use of Cecil Paget upon his appointment as General Superintendent of the Midland Railway. Its power plant was removed in 1917 but it continued in use as an inspection coach until 1968. It is now in the custody of the National Railway Museum in unrestored condition. *(Martin Bairstow collection)*

Rear Cover

Duke of Argyll berthed alongside Heysham Station in 1962. Behind is the cargo vessel *Slieve Bawn* whose outpouring of smoke appears not to have been eased by the previous year's conversion from coal to oil. Further along is *Slieve Bearnagh* which was the mainstay of the Heysham to Belfast cattle and cargo trade. Beyond are the tugs *Fishershill* and *Ramsden.* *(Peter Sunderland)*

Introduction

This book is dedicated to photographer Peter Sunderland who died in January 2019. He was an early connoisseur of railway excursions to Morecambe, including some which ran through from his native Worth Valley above Keighley. In the late 1940s, these could involve non-corridor coaches hauled by a 3F goods engine with poor quality coal. If the train had stalled on the gradient from Bentham to Clapham, it could well do the same on the steeper climb between Ingrow and Oakworth – so near to home but still a way to go.

In 1947, Peter set out on the same route but travelled much further when he accompanied his parents on a part business, part holiday trip to Portrush in Northern Ireland. His memories from this included a journey on the Giants Causeway Tramway and the practice of his parents always to book Second Class rail/ First Class steamer.

There were printed Edmondson card tickets for this as there were sufficient customers who found First Class rail an extravagance but Saloon on the steamer a dire necessity. Peter found out why when he once travelled Second Class throughout with a friend on a tight budget. If you didn't feel sick when you set off to the Second Class toilet, you soon would after navigating through people actually being sick.

From these early experiences, Peter developed a life-long interest both in the railways and their associated marine operations. In time, it was the shipping which began to predominate. For nearly 40 years, I have worked with Peter's black and white photos. I knew he also had some colour but had no idea how much until I found myself one of his executors charged with the task of clearing his house.

There are plenty of railway subjects amongst his colour slides but far greater emphasis is devoted to shipping. Not deep sea or Trans-Atlantic, nor yachts or fishing boats but railway ferries, steam packets and lake steamers. Coverage extends beyond our shores to the Netherlands, Germany and Scandinavia. But the location which predominates is the port of Heysham.

Opened in 1904, Heysham gave the Midland Railway the route to Belfast which it had been seeking for over 50 years. It helped the Midland obtain the greatest foothold in Ireland of any English company with its purchase of the Belfast & Northern Counties and half share in the County Donegal.

The 'Little' North Western Railway had opened between Lancaster and Morecambe in 1848. By 1851, it was at the end of a through route from Leeds and was soon absorbed by the Midland. Morecambe Station was on the site of the present day terminus in Northumberland Street and there was an extension on to the harbour where part of the earlier Pier Station still survives. The Midland Railway operated steamers to Belfast but Morecambe was far from ideal as a cross channel port. Timetables were tidal and there would never have been scope for the larger ships which were to follow.

So, jointly with the Furness Railway, it built the line from Wennington to Carnforth which opened in 1867. This allowed Midland boat trains to reach Piel Pier, near Barrow, to which the Belfast steamers were transferred. The Furness Railway continued its development of Barrow and, from 1881, trains were able to meet the steamers at a deep water berth at Ramsden Dock.

But the Midland still wasn't satisfied. In 1896, it obtained powers to build Heysham Harbour, along with a connecting railway from Lancaster and Morecambe

Morecambe had remained a port after the loss of the Belfast sailings in 1867. Laird Line still operated to Dublin and to Londonderry but it transferred to Heysham in 1904. For the next quarter century, Morecambe Harbour was a scrap yard disposing of everything from Trans-Atlantic liners to warships. This can't have done much for the town's image as a holiday resort, unless visitors were actually drawn to the yard. In summer 1914, the White Star Liner *Majestic* was a pay-to-view tourist attraction while it waited for demolition to commence.

Passenger traffic outgrew the two-platform Morecambe station which was replaced in 1907 by the larger sea front facility which was eventually named Morecambe Promenade. By this time, a number of railways were experimenting with electric traction and the Midland selected Lancaster – Morecambe – Heysham for its first venture into the new motive power.

The Midland electrics lasted until 1951 and were then replaced in 1953 by a second generation of units as British Railways conducted experiments which were to lead to the adoption of high voltage a.c. as the standard for main line electrification.

Colour photography doesn't go back far enough to have recorded the first generation electrics, nor the first hundred years of steam operation, nor even the 25 years that Morecambe Harbour was a scrapyard. But thanks to Peter Sunderland, David Mitchell and others, we have a record of both railway and steamship operations starting in the mid-1950s, some ten years before the devastating changes of 1966.

Coverage begins at Wennington where trains from Leeds used to split into Morecambe and Carnforth portions. First we follow what was the main line - the Midland to Lancaster Green Ayre, Morecambe and Heysham. From there, we continue with the railway steamers to Belfast and sail with the Isle of Man Steam Packet Company to Douglas.

We then take a detour on London & North Western Railway territory along the branch line to Glasson Dock where we stumble on two Isle of Man steamers which hadn't really intended to be there. Finally, we return to Wennington and follow the post-1966 route to Lancaster, Morecambe and a much changed Heysham.

A Midland Railway Outpost? Surely it was part of the main line from London St Pancras to Belfast and beyond, not to mention the growing seaside resort of Morecambe. Yes, but the Belfast trade was just one overnight sailing and Morecambe was highly seasonal. It was certainly an outpost when the Midland was looking for somewhere to experiment with electric traction. And it is even more of an outpost today – at least from a railway viewpoint. Heysham Harbour is busier than ever before but not in the way the Midland would have foreseen.

Martin Bairstow, August 2019

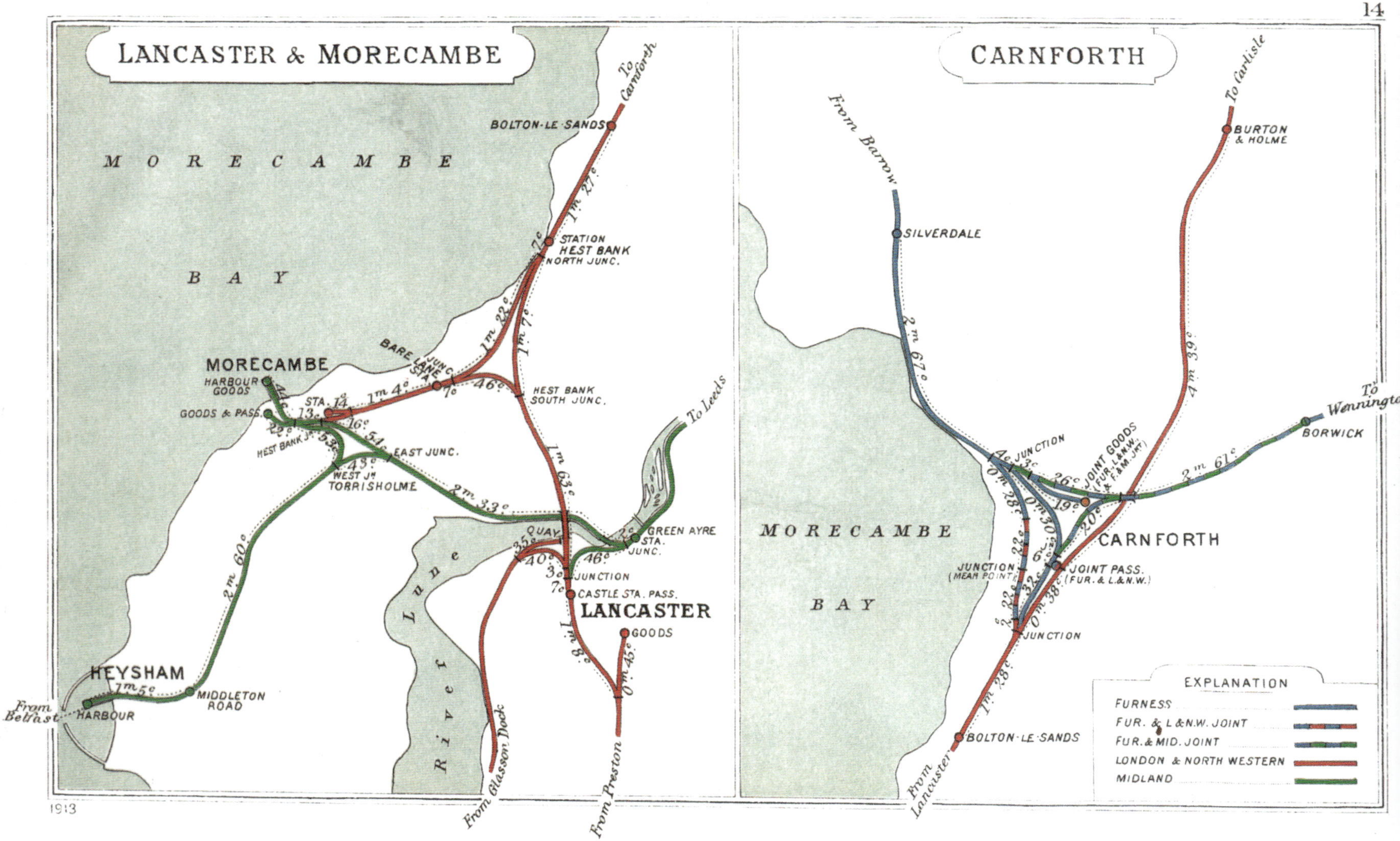

Railway Clearing House Map of 1913

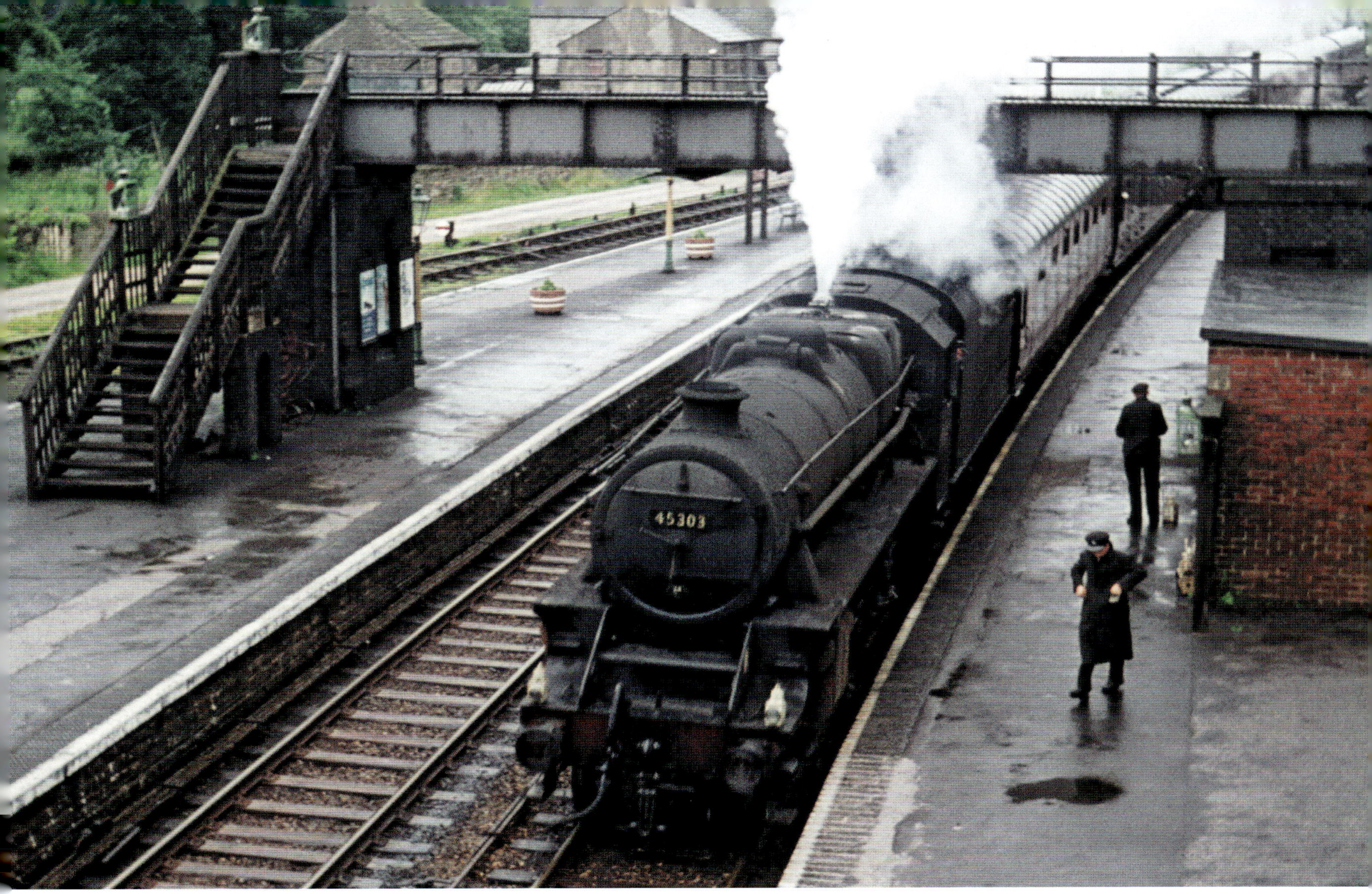

'Black Five' 4 – 6 – 0 No. 45303 arrives at Wennington from Leeds on 28 June 1963. It will detach the rear carriages for Morecambe before going on to Carnforth where it was allocated at the time. Wennington Station opened in 1849 with buildings in the same Mock Tudor style as others on the 'Little' North Western, parts of which can still be seen at Gargrave and Clapham. Those at Wennington were the first to disappear when the station was rebuilt to reflect its status as a junction after 1867. In the Leeds-bound direction, one portion would set back into the bay platform on the left to await arrival of the main train. *(D. J. Mitchell)*

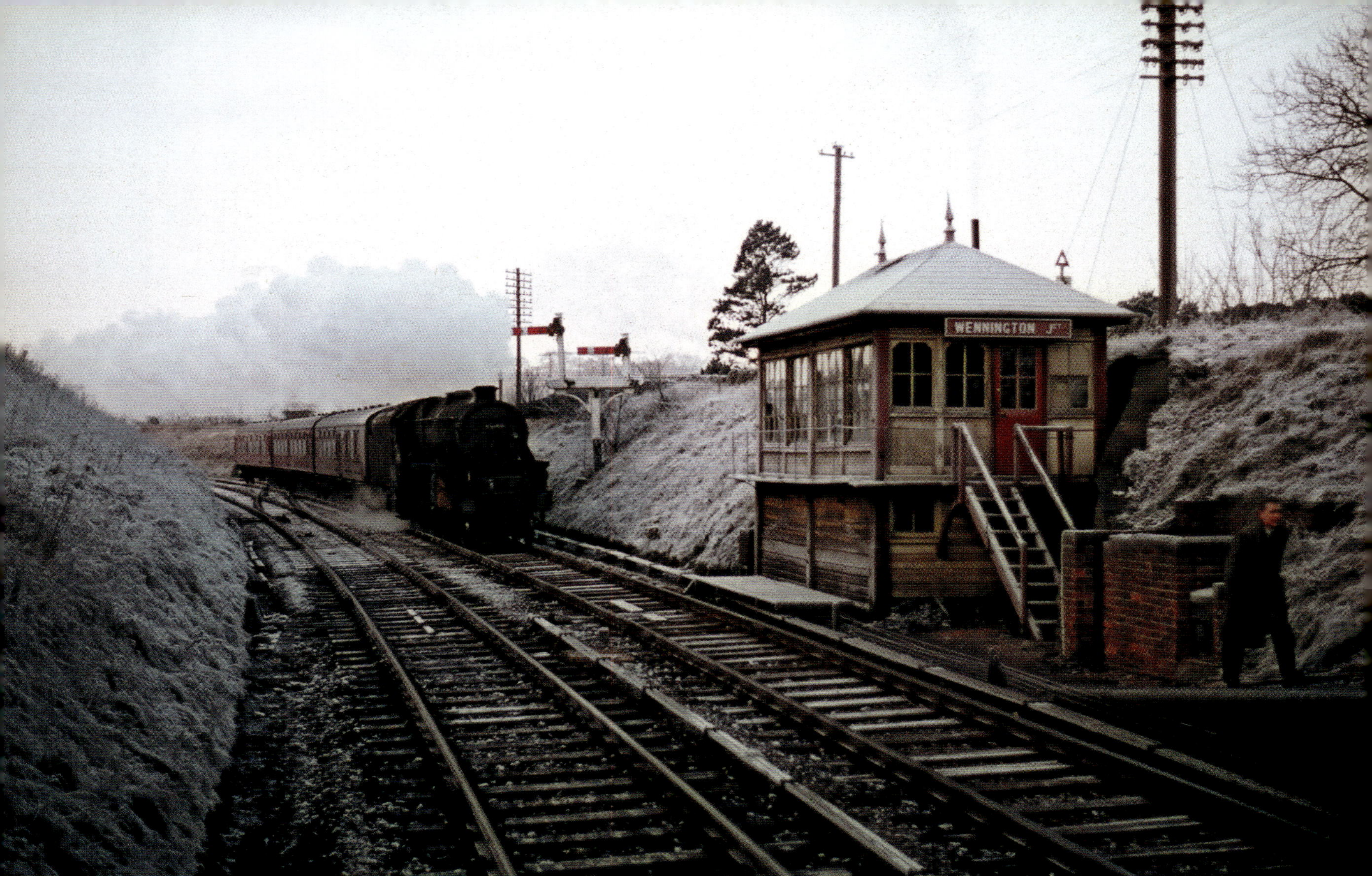

The lines for Morecambe and Carnforth diverged just beyond Wennington Station where a 'Black Five' is approaching from Morecambe in November 1965. The junction signal confirms that Morecambe was regarded as the main line and Carnforth the branch. Wennington Junction box opened in 1890. The frame was extended to 27 levers in the 1940s when additional sidings were laid. It ceased to be a junction in 1967 but remained open, with most of the levers spare, just to split the block between Settle Junction and Carnforth. It was switched out almost permanently from 1988 but not disposed of until 2006. *(D. J. Mitchell)*

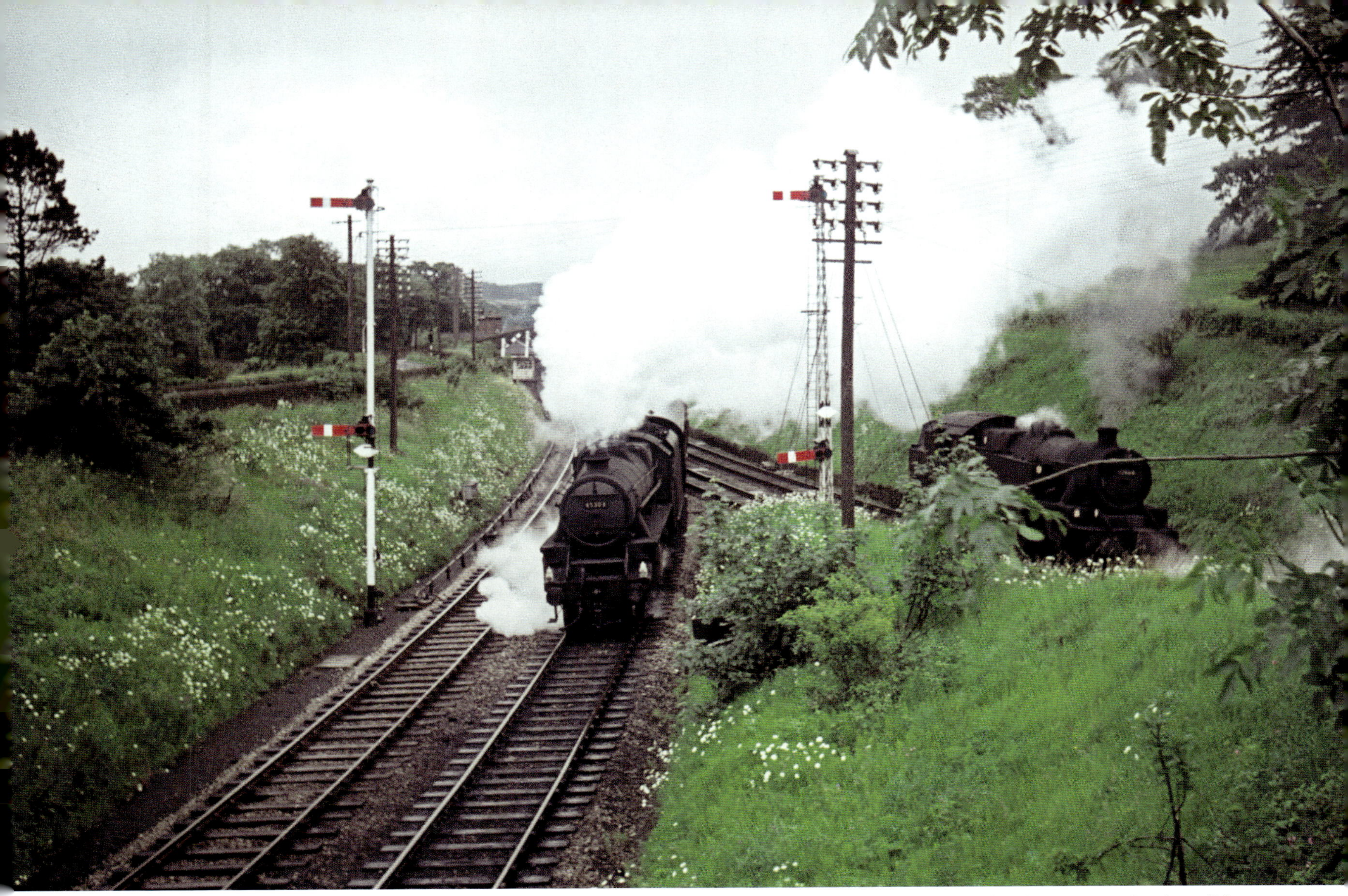

45303 heads away from Wennington with the train seen on Page 5 while Stanier 2 – 6 – 4T No 42464 waits to back on to the Morecambe portion which will depart six minutes later. The 1.54 p.m. from Leeds was the only train which split this way. The more common procedure was for the main engine and front portion to go to Morecambe, leaving the rear coaches to wait for a tank engine to take them on to Carnforth. 42464 was built in 1936 and scrapped in 1965. It was one of a class of 206 locos, none of which has been preserved. *(D. J. Mitchell)*

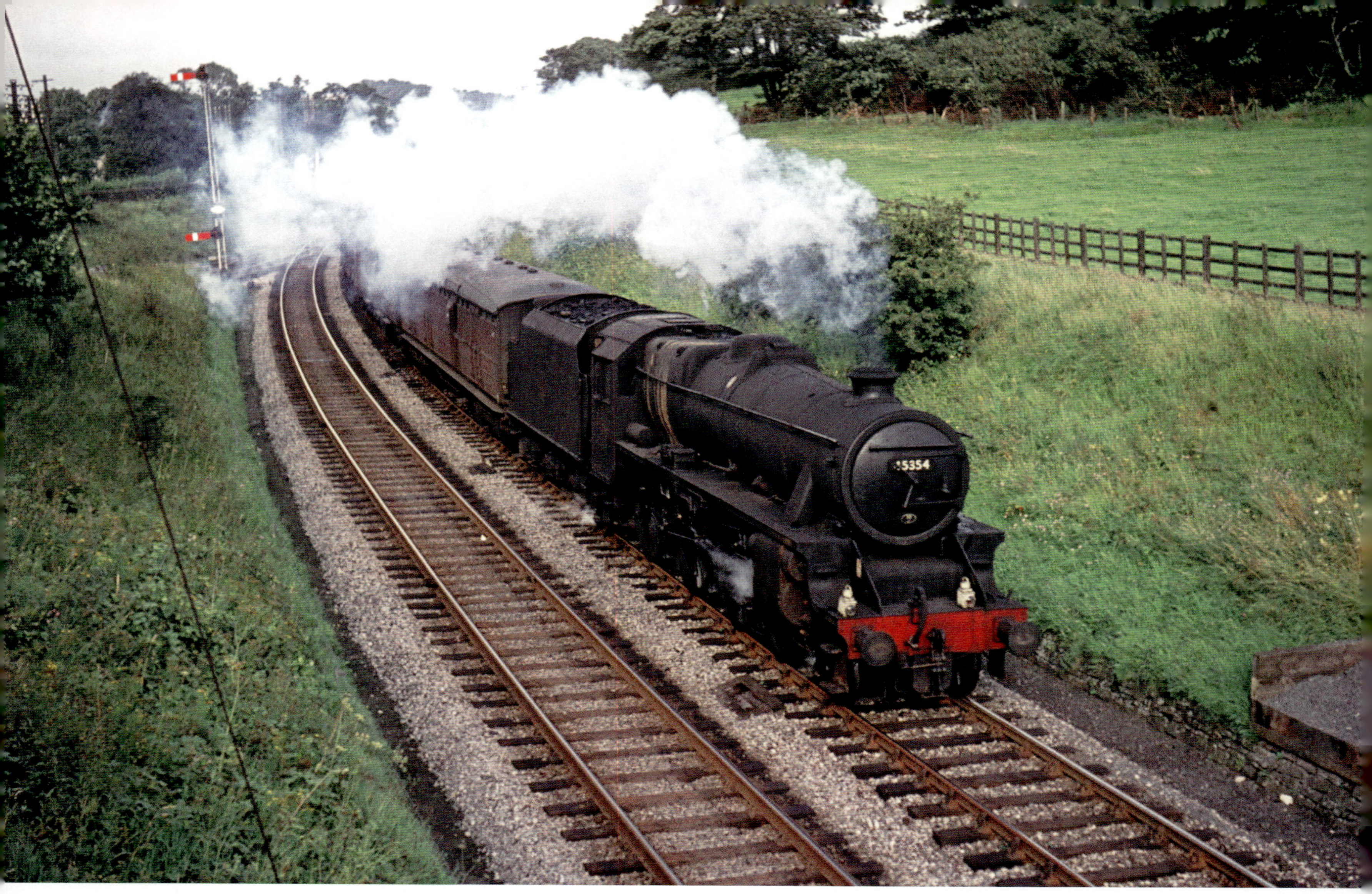

Another 'Black Five,' this time No. 45354, pulls away from Wennington towards Lancaster Green Ayre and Morecambe in August 1964. The Up Home signals, both from Lancaster and from Carnforth, have two arms to aid sighting from a distance and close up. They are too near to the junction to protect it so there are also Outer Homes on both routes ¼ mile further back. Thanks to these, the Wennington signalman could accept a train from either Hornby or Melling whilst the junction was blocked. 45354 was a Lancaster-based engine at this time and a regular on the Leeds passenger services. *(D. J. Mitchell)*

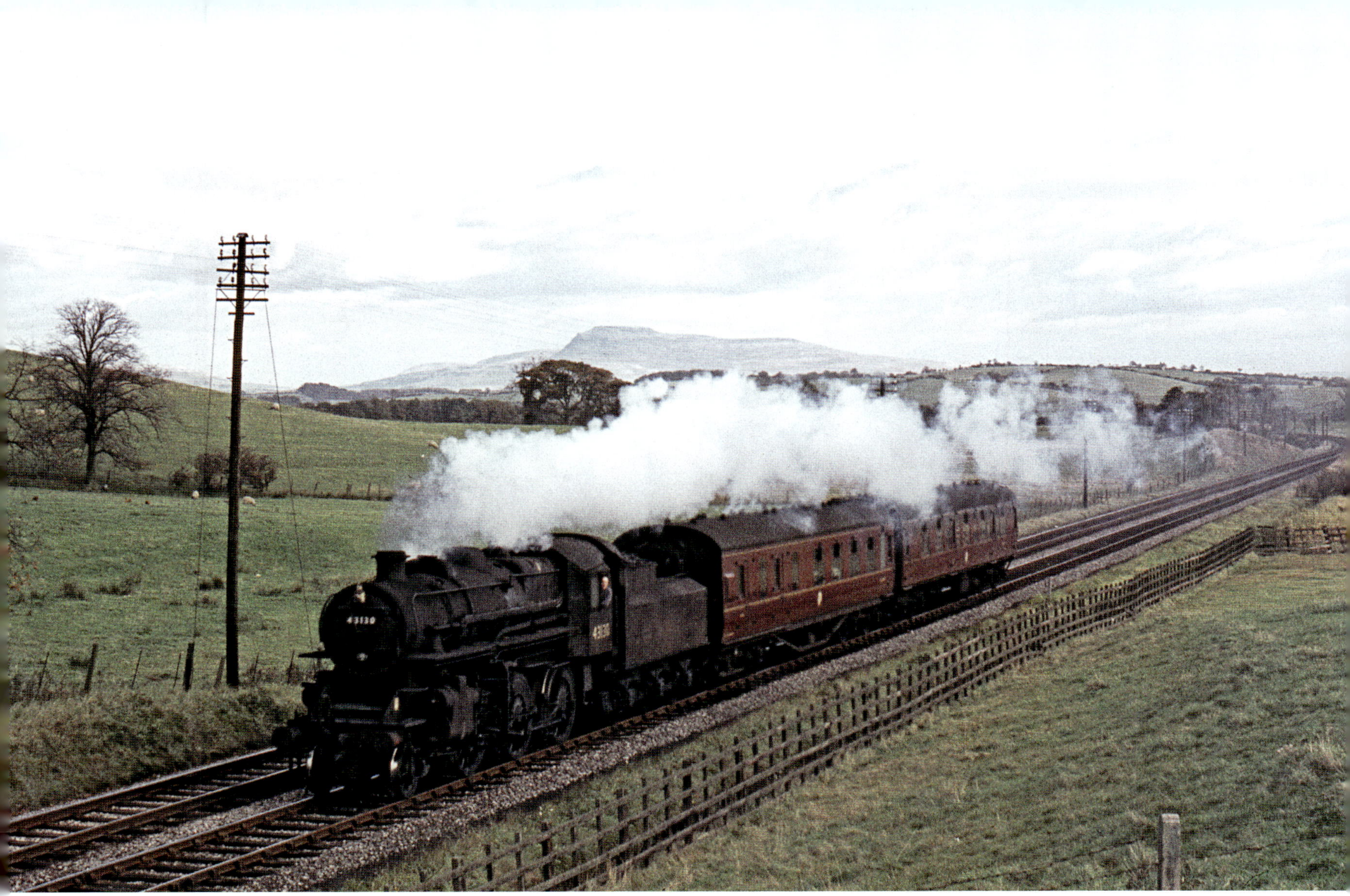

Ivatt 2 – 6 – 0 No. 43130 is seen approaching Hornby in 1965 with the Morecambe portion of the 1.54 p.m. from Leeds. Hornby Station closed in September 1957 and the only surviving relic is the hand crane from the goods yard which has been restored on the site of Lancaster Green Ayre. The loco was built in 1951, one of a class of 162 'Moguls' designed by H. G. Ivatt. It was shedded at Leeds (Holbeck) from 1957 until withdrawal for scrap in June 1967. No. 43106 on the Severn Valley Railway is the only member of the class to have survived. *(Colour-Rail)*

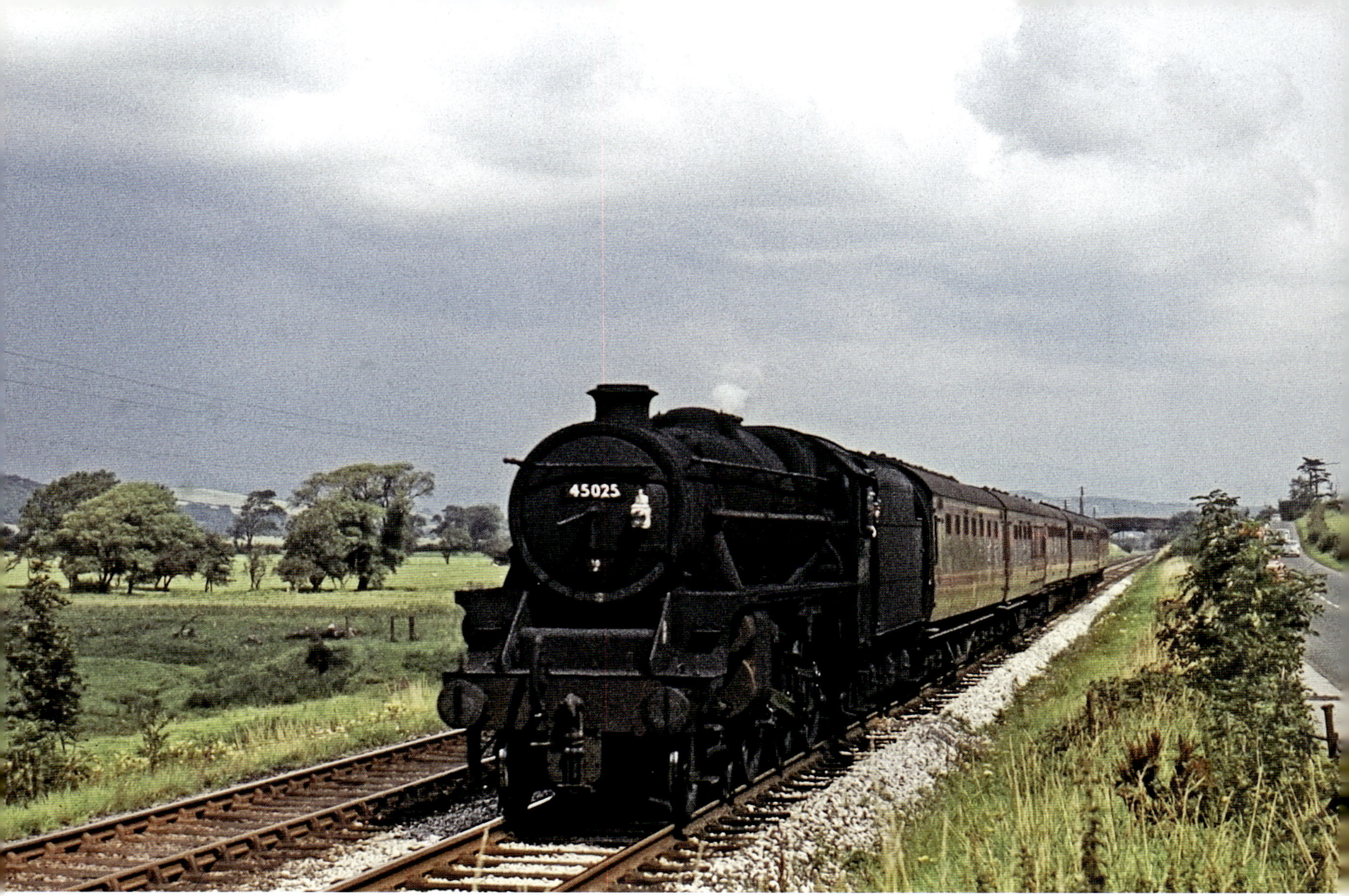

'Black Five' No. 45025 approaches Caton with a Leeds to Morecambe train on 7 August 1964. Built in 1934, the loco was shedded at Lancaster Green Ayre between 1963 and 1966. After that, it worked out of Carnforth until the end of steam in August 1968. It was acquired for preservation on the Strathspey Railway but spent the years 1969 to 1974 on the Keighley & Worth Valley until the Strathspey was ready to receive it. Out of traffic since 1994, No. 45025 is undergoing a major overhaul at Aviemore and should eventually resume operation. *(Colour-Rail)*

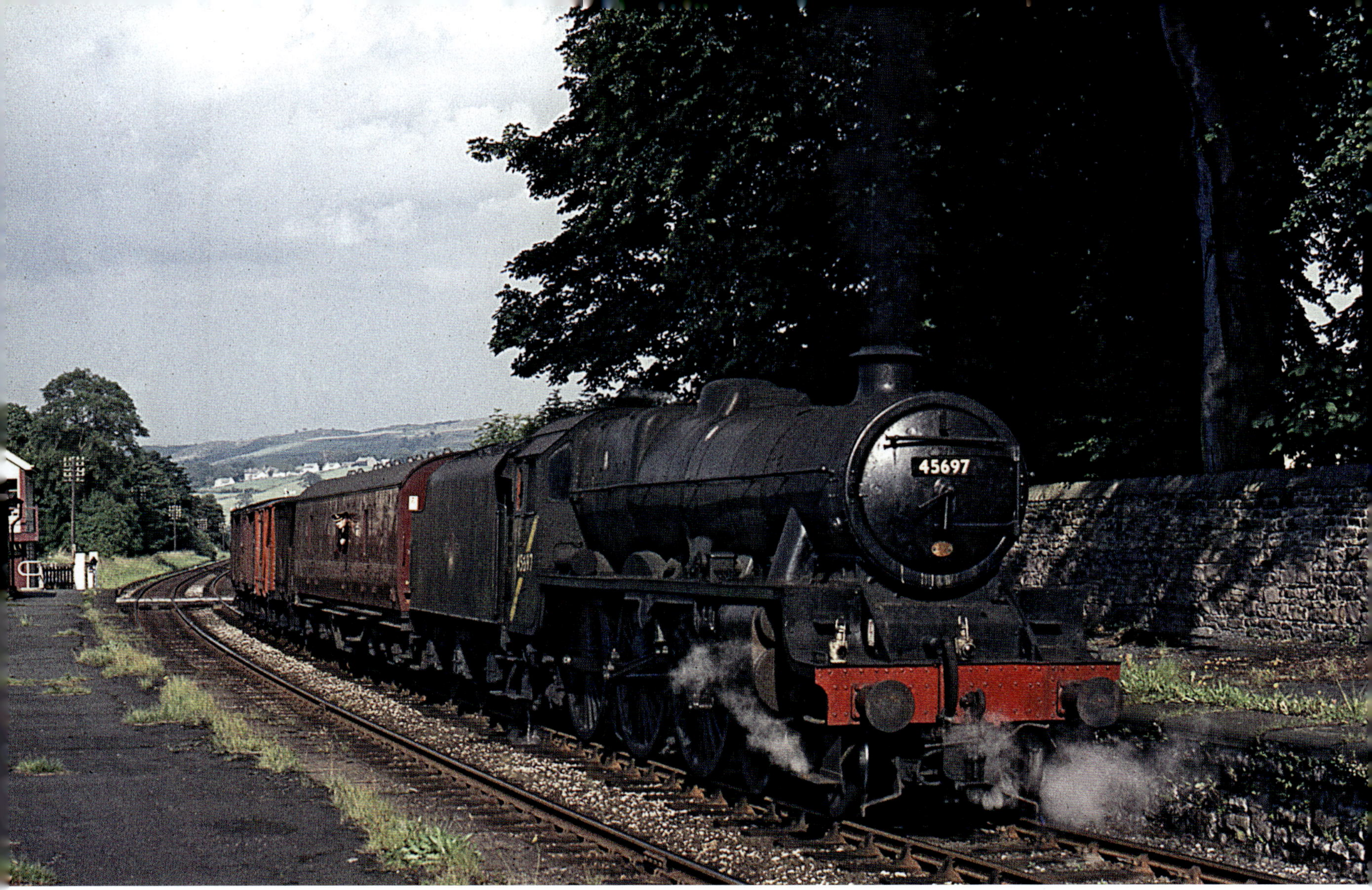

'Jubilee' Class No. 45697 *Achilles* passes Caton with a westbound freight on 16 July 1965. The station had closed in 1961. The two headlamps on the loco denote that the train is a Class 3 conveying parcels, fish, livestock or perishables and conforming to passenger train standards. All vehicles are fitted with continuous automatic vacuum brakes allowing the guard to travel in the front brake van. If the train was less than fully fitted, he would have to be at the back and ready to apply his hand brake. A total of 191 'Jubilee' 4 – 6 – 0s were built between 1934 and 1936. Four are preserved but, after withdrawal from Leeds (Holbeck) shed in early September 1967, *Achilles* was scrapped during May 1968. *(Colour-Rail)*

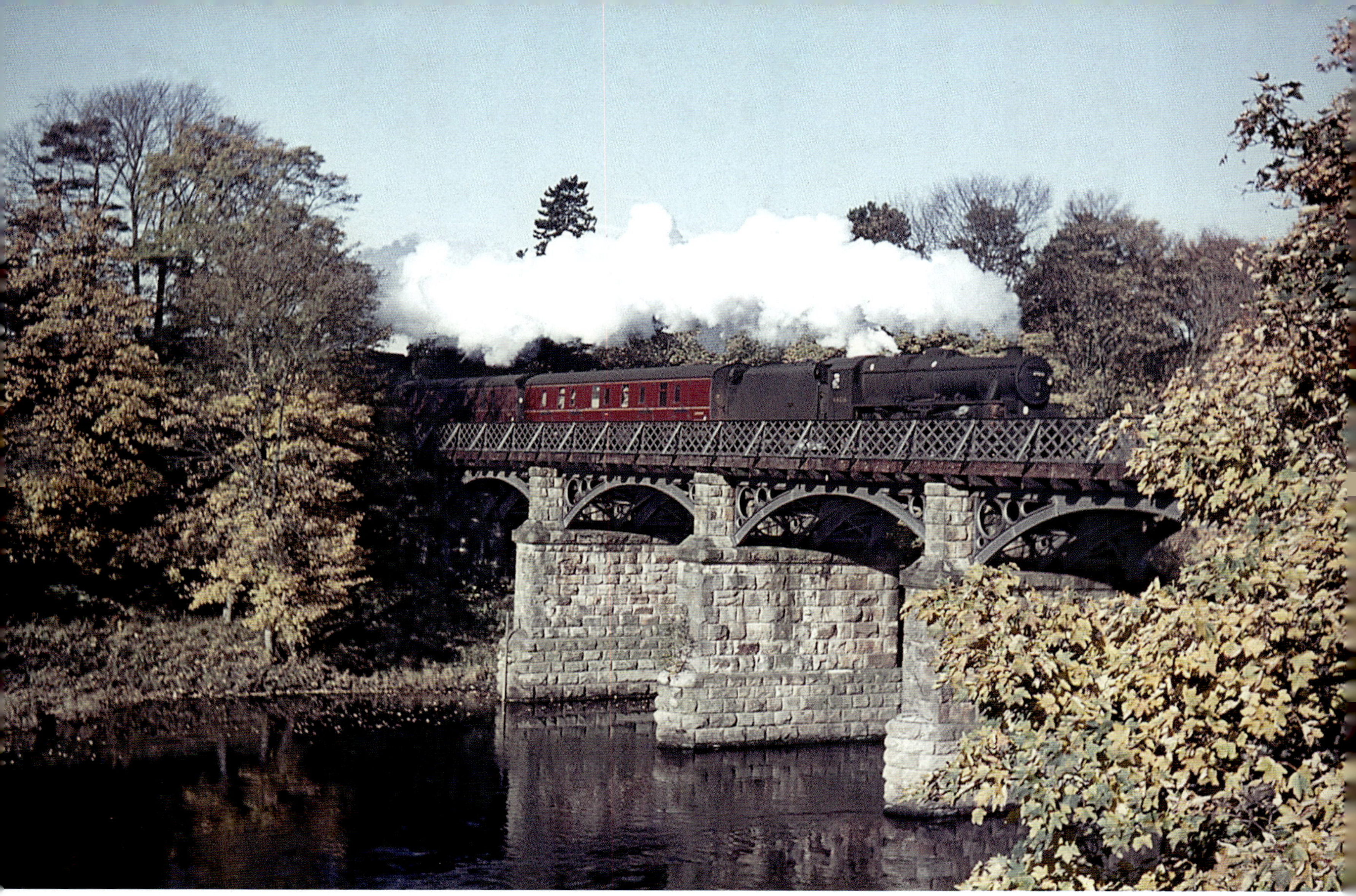

With the trees beginning to take on their autumn colours, Lostock Hall-based 'Black Five' No. 44816 crosses the East Viaduct at Crook O'Lune with a train from Morecambe to Leeds in 1964. Between Caton and Halton, the railway encountered a crook shaped loop in the River Lune which it had to cross twice. The East Viaduct has five arches. The West Viaduct is similar in appearance with six. Both can now be traversed on foot or bicycle. A total of 842 'Black Fives' were built between 1934 and 1951 and 18 have survived into preservation. *(P. L. Greenall, courtesy David Beeken)*

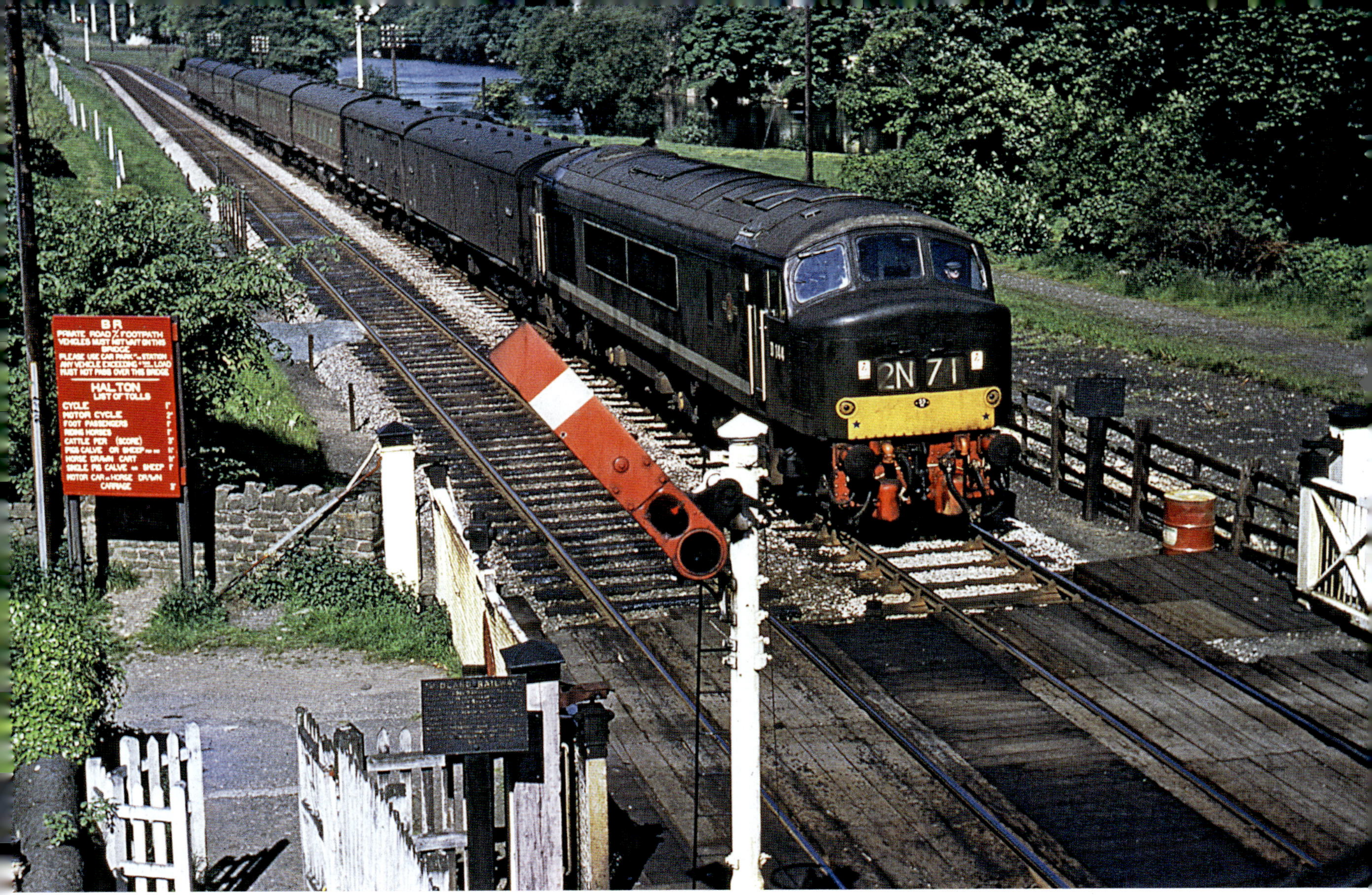

A new 'Peak' Type 4, No. D144, approaches Halton with a Morecambe to Leeds train in 1962. The notice gives the tolls for crossing the railway-owned bridge over the River Lune leading to Halton village. The toll was collected by the porter-signalman when he opened the level crossing gates to allow vehicles across the railway. The penny toll was probably not collected from pedestrians who could cross the railway by the station footbridge. But a lady with a pram would need the gates opening so would have to pay the toll. The present bridge was built in 1913 using materials recovered from the Greyhound Bridge at Lancaster. It is still in use. *(Colour-Rail)*

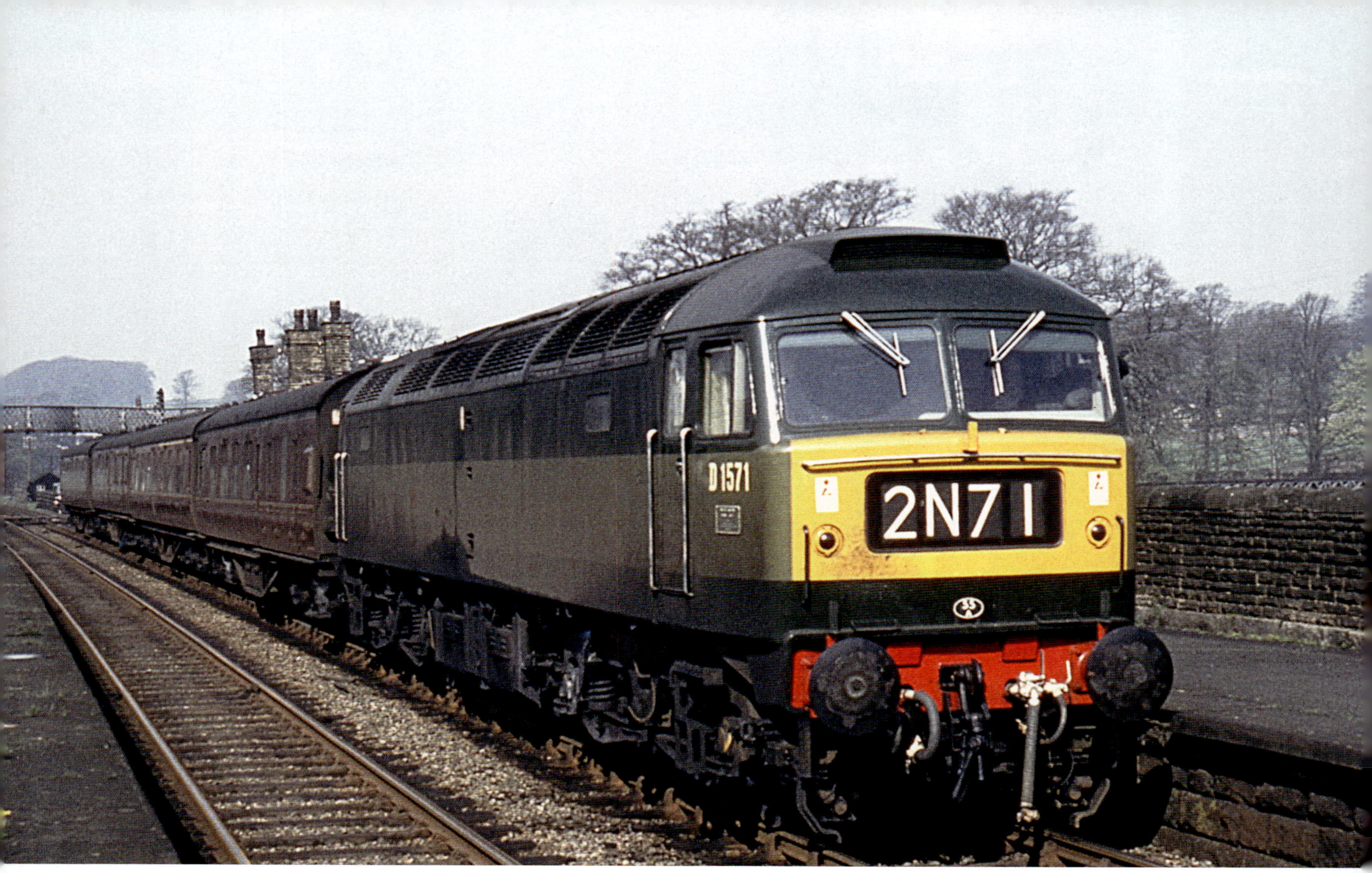

Morecambe to Leeds trains remained mostly steam-hauled but new diesels sometimes appeared on running-in turns, as seen here with a three weeks old Brush Type 4 No. D1571 pausing at Halton on 26 April 1964. It had been allocated to Leeds (Holbeck) shed earlier that month. Having been renumbered 47453 in March 1974, it survived until December 1992 after which it was scrapped. This class of main line diesel locomotive was the most numerous on BR with 512 built between 1962 and 1968, although there was never a full complement after two were written off with severe accident damage in 1965/66. Originally numbered D1500 – D1999 and D1100 – D1111, they were later designated Class 47. By 2018, there were still 116 in existence, 51 in main line service, 32 with preservation societies and 33 converted to Class 57 with General Motors engines. *(Colour-Rail)*

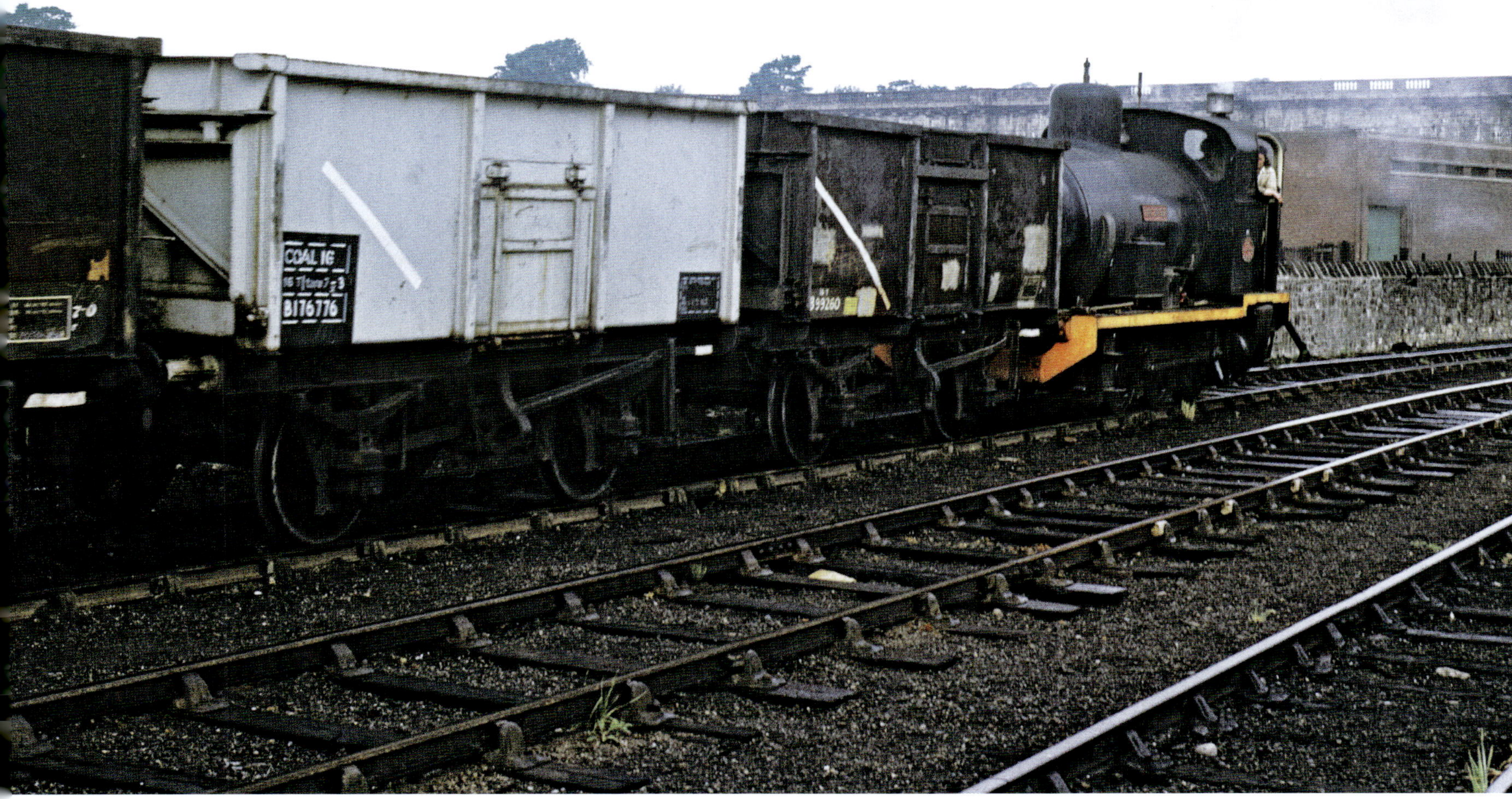

1¼ miles beyond Halton, the railway passed under the Lune Aqueduct using one of its five arches. The opening was wide enough for three tracks. The third one connected the coal dump on the east side with the power station and exchange sidings to the west. Opened in 1924, the power station received coal by rail until 1976. This kept a single track open from Lancaster Castle after closure of the through route. The power station sidings were worked by fireless 0 – 6 – 0 *Lancaster* which moved to Heysham power station in 1977. It is now at Carnforth, unrestored and out of sight. *(Les Tindall, courtesy Andrew Naylor)*

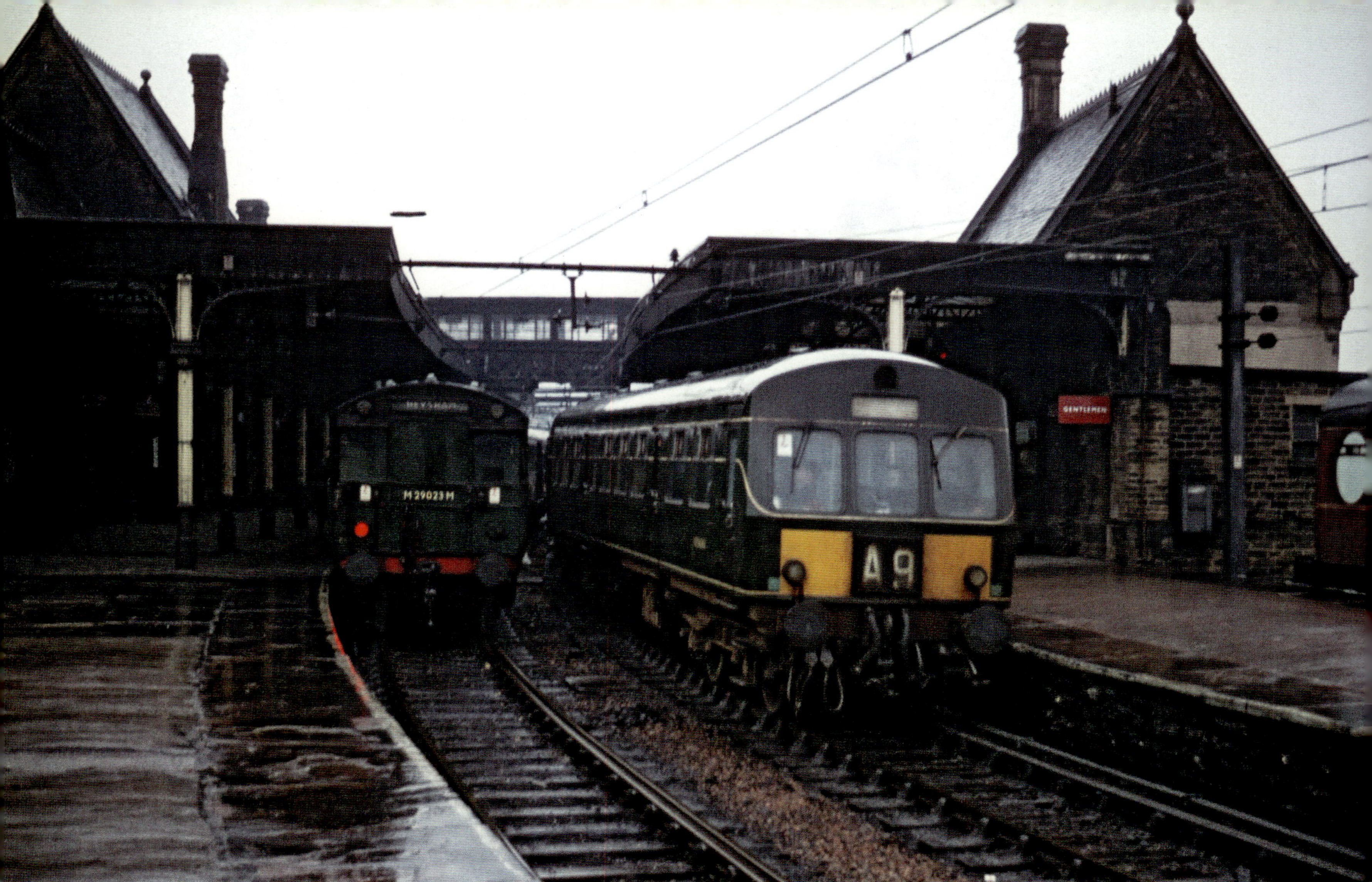

From March 1965, some Leeds - Morecambe services were operated by DMUs, freed up by service reductions in Airedale and Wharfedale. This Leeds bound Metro Cammell set has arrived at Lancaster Green Ayre in November that year. It is sitting alongside one of the pioneer electric trains, originally built for the LNWR by the Metropolitan Carriage, Wagon & Finance Company for use on the third-rail Willesden Junction to Earls Court route in London. In this view, driving trailer 29023 is now at the rear of the 3-coach set which has reversed direction en route from Lancaster Castle to Heysham. The electrics were shortly to be withdrawn and the line closed. *(D. J. Mitchell)*

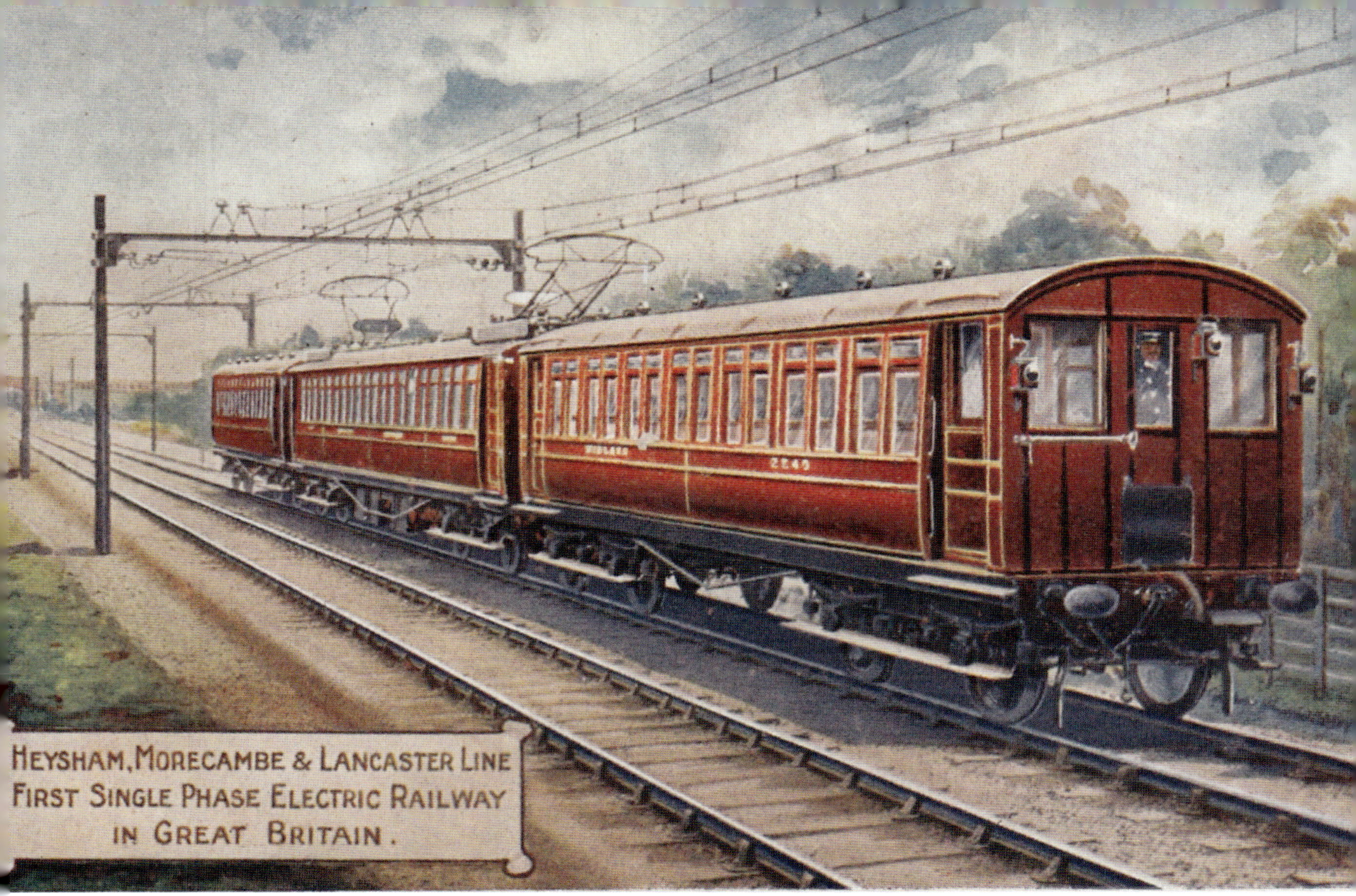

The ex-LNW sets were the second generation of pioneer electrics to have linked Lancaster, Morecambe and Heysham. In 1908, the Midland Railway electrified the route at 6,600 volts a.c. using power from its own plant at Heysham which supplied the dockyard equipment. Rolling stock comprised three power cars, LMS Nos 28610, 28611 and 28612. There were four purpose built driving trailers and two more converted from ordinary coaches. This publicity shot has the motor coach in the middle. Pick up is by bow collectors which were later replaced by pantographs. *(Midland Railway Study Centre)*

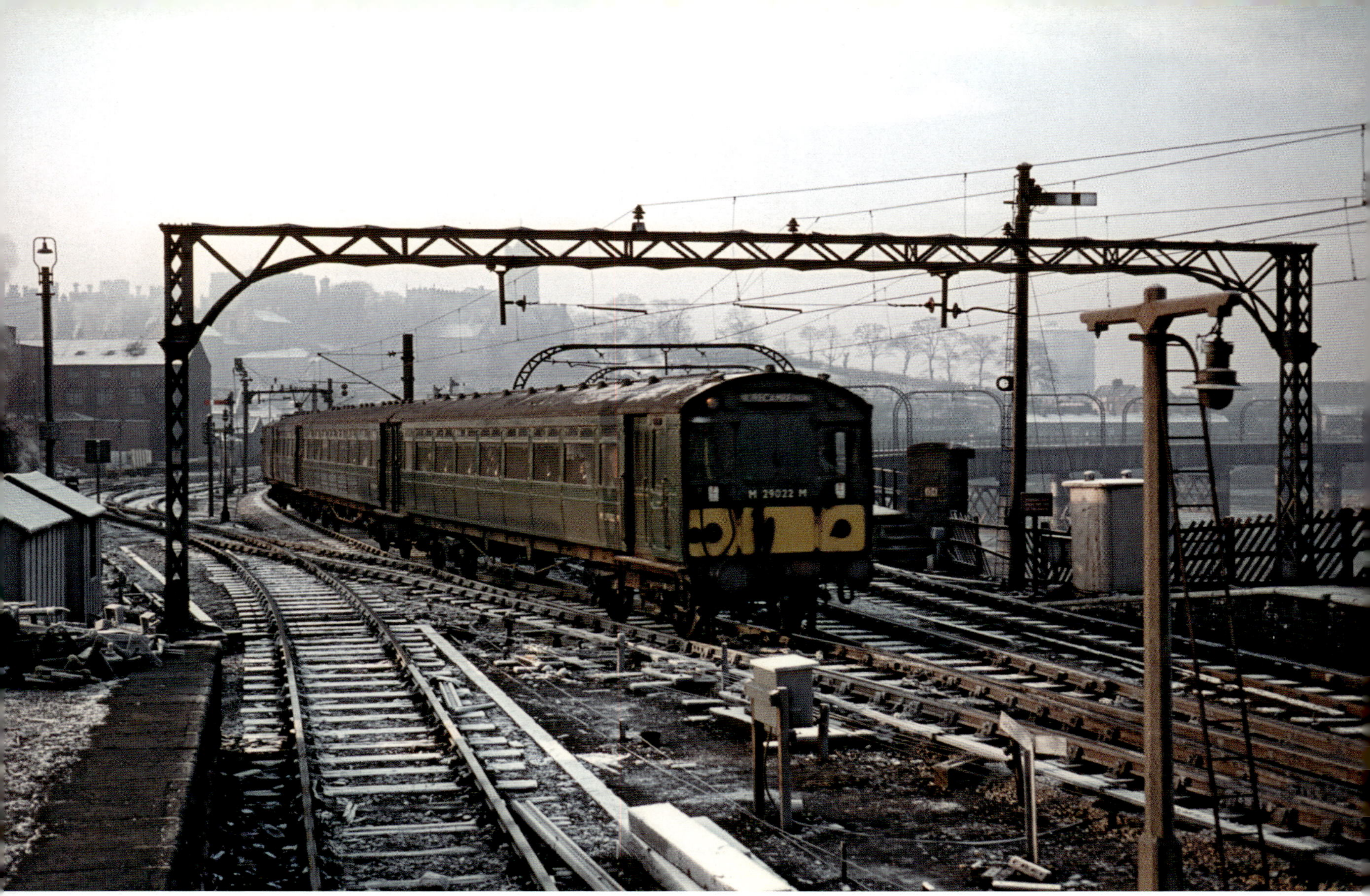

After withdrawal as life expired in February 1951, the venerable Midland electrics were initially replaced by a steam push – pull service. However, electric working was reintroduced on 17 August 1953 using trains which were almost as old as the Midland ones. Three sets, which had been in store since 1940, were converted and upgraded with English Electric equipment and pantographs for operating under wires. A fourth set with Metropolitan-Vickers equipment was added to the fleet in 1957. In this December 1965 view, driving trailer 29022 enters Lancaster Green Ayre where it will reverse for Morecambe. *(D. J. Mitchell)*

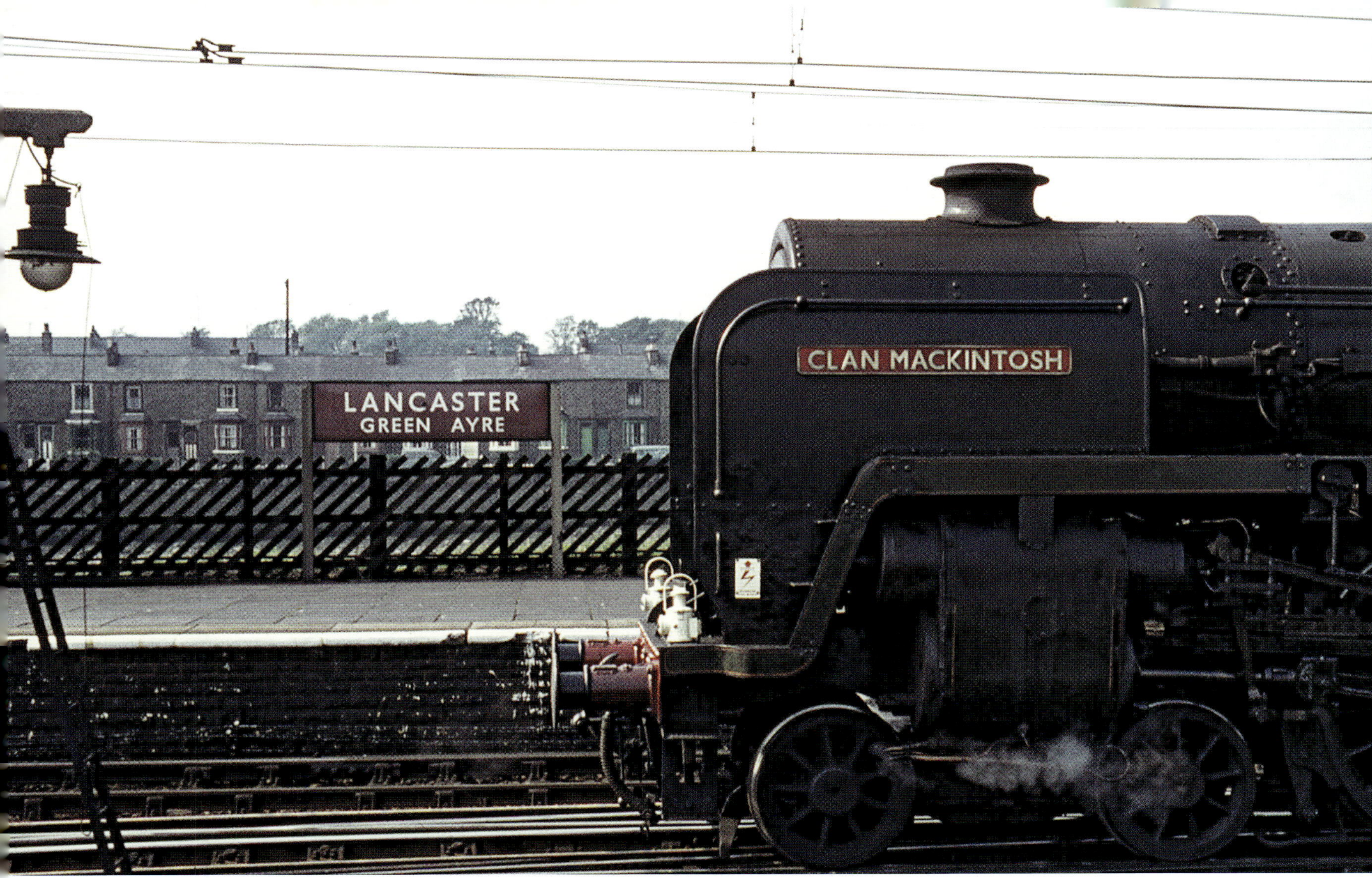

'Clan' Pacific No. 72007 *Clan Mackintosh* is seen at Lancaster Green Ayre while working a railtour special on 23 May 1964. Most stations were still gas lit, apart from those with no mains supply which relied on paraffin lamps. This was long after electric lighting had become standard almost everywhere else. Built in 1952 as one of a class of ten 'light Pacific' 4 – 6 – 2s, 72007 was based at Carlisle Kingmoor from where it was withdrawn in December 1965 after a wastefully short career. It was scrapped three months later. None of the Clans was preserved but there is a project to build one from scratch. If this achieves fruition, the locomotive will take the identity of 72010 *Hengist* which would have been the next member of the class, had the intended order for 15 more gone ahead. *(Martin Bairstow collection)*

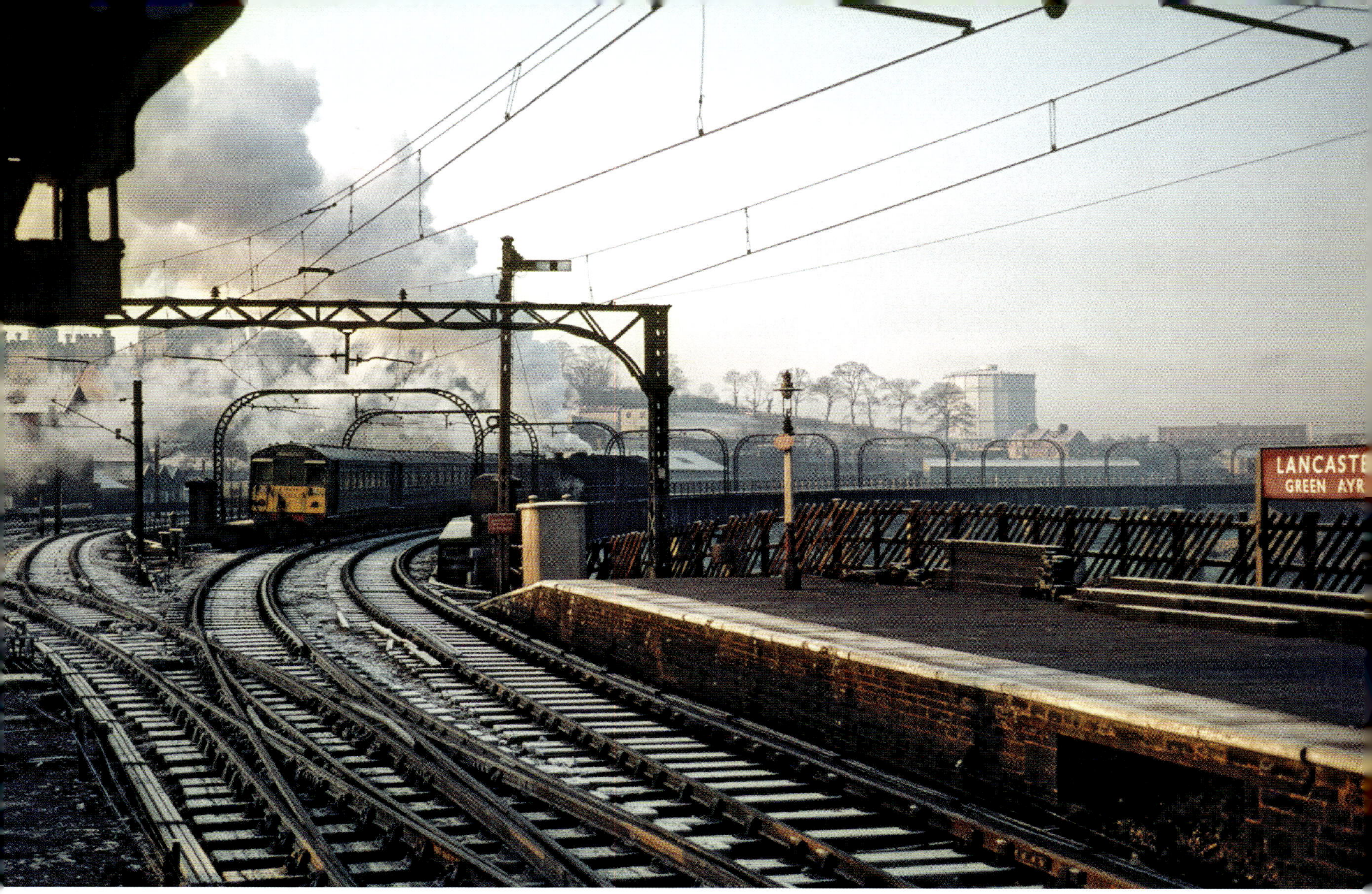

Immediately upon leaving Green Ayre, the line crossed the River Lune by the Greyhound Bridge. Originally of laminated timber, the bridge was rebuilt in wrought iron in 1864. It was replaced by the present nine-arch structure in 1911. Parts of its predecessor were then used to replace the toll bridge at Halton. 'Black Five' No. 44854 is hauling a failed electric passenger service towards Morecambe during the final days between Christmas 1965 and closure on New Year's Day 1966. The EMUs were vacuum braked so they could be steam hauled in passenger service, just as happened occasionally with failed Diesel Multiple Units. *(D. J. Mitchell)*

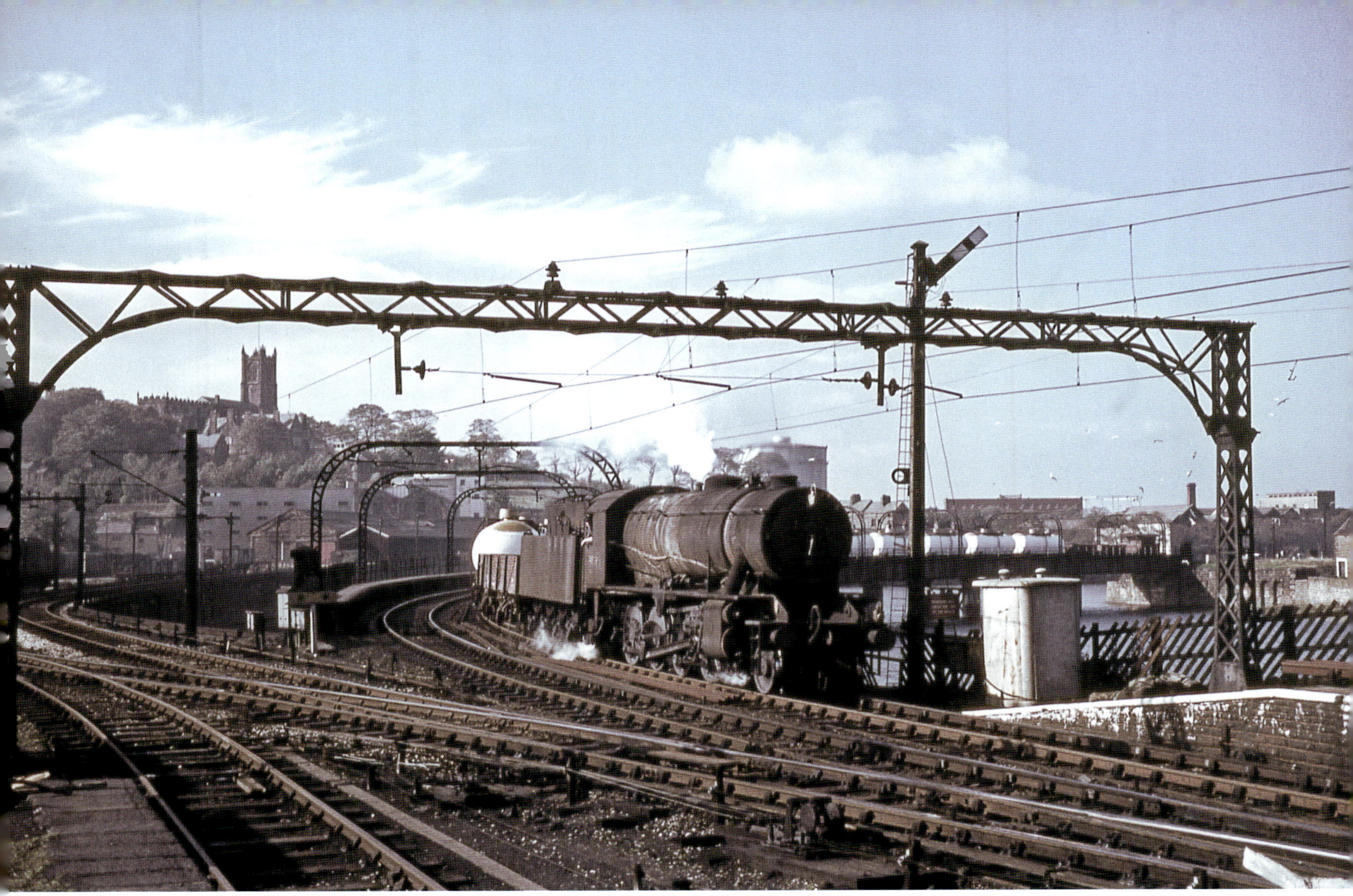

A WD 'Austerity' 2 – 8 – 0 brings the Heysham to Haverton Hill ammonia tanks train off the Greyhound Bridge and into Lancaster Green Ayre in 1965. A total of 935 of these locos were built between 1943 and 1945 for the War Department with 733 ending up as British Railways Nos. 90000 to 90732. None of these are preserved. Many of the remaining 202 were sold to the Netherlands, from where two were re-sold to Sweden. One of these was eventually repatriated and restored on the Keighley & Worth Valley Railway, becoming No. 90733. *(D. J. Mitchell)*

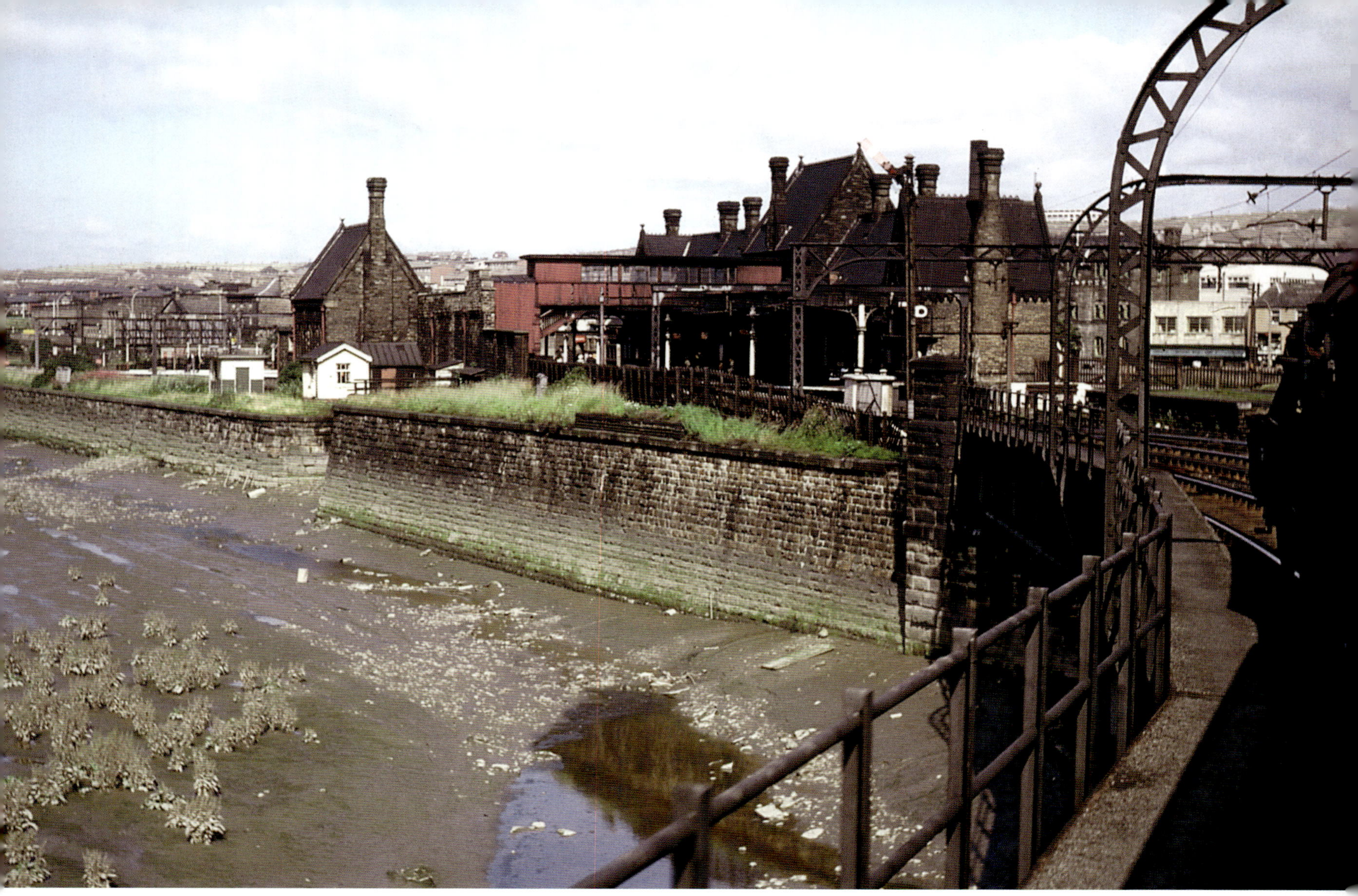

'Black Five' No. 44667 leads its Morecambe to Leeds train off the Greyhound Bridge and into Lancaster Green Ayre on 26 July 1965. Had BR management considered passenger traffic when they eliminated duplicate routes, they would surely have kept the Midland from Wennington to Lancaster Castle and the LNWR thence to Morecambe. The road lobby could still have had the Greyhound Bridge but Leeds – Morecambe trains would now be doing worthwhile business at Caton, Halton and Green Ayre in less time than they take to navigate the detour via Carnforth. *(Roger Hepworth)*

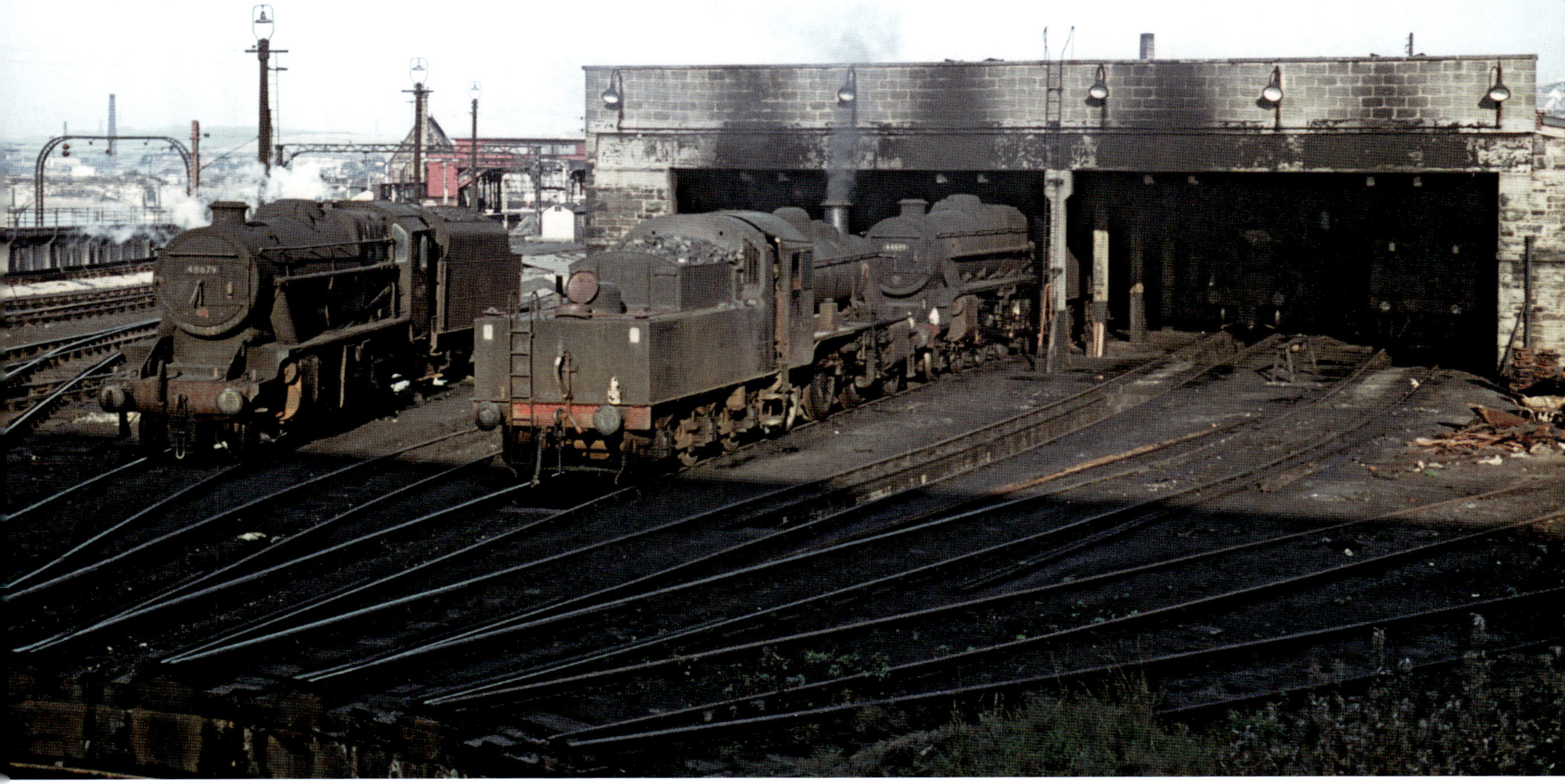

Lancaster Green Ayre engine shed in October 1965 plays host to Stanier 8F No. 48679, 'Black Five' No. 44889 and an Ivatt Class 2, No. 46422. The shed was on a cramped site now occupied by Sainsbury's just to the south of the Lancaster Castle branch. It closed in April 1966 when most of its allocation was transferred to Carnforth, one of the three sheds destined to remain to the end of BR steam in August 1968. By 1965, there were still 19 locos allocated to Green Ayre, including four 8Fs for use on heavy freight out of Heysham. *(D. J. Mitchell)*

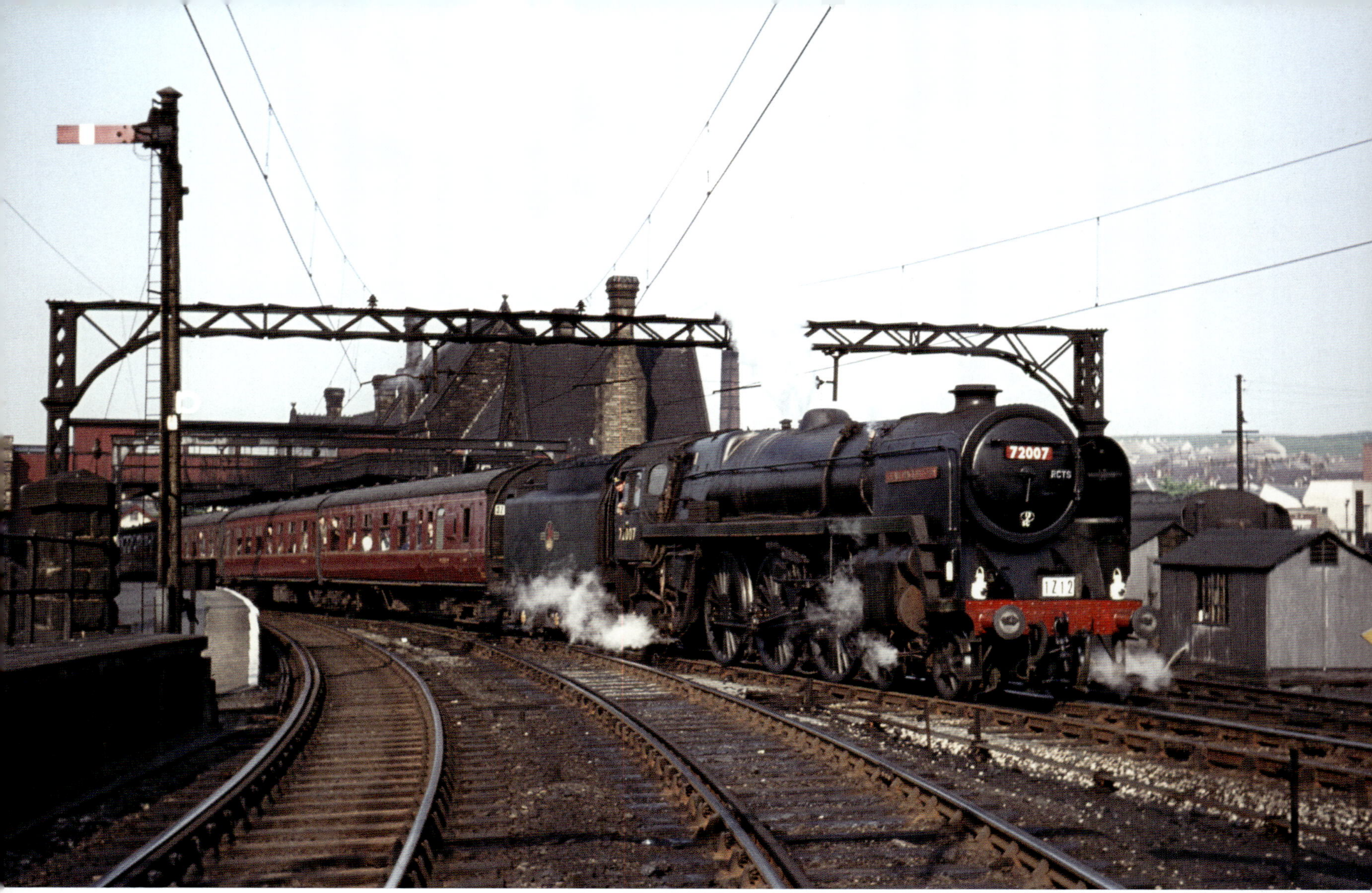

'Clan' Pacific No. 72007 *Clan Mackintosh* restarts the 'Ribble-Lune' railtour from Green Ayre station on 23 May 1964. It is taking the single line to Lancaster Castle whence it will continue to Lancaster No. 1 box and then propel back to the goods station at the original terminus of the Preston & Lancaster Junction Railway. The tour had started with a run over the West Lancashire Railway between Preston and Southport which was soon to close. It had then done a circuit via Blackburn, Hellifield and Wennington before taking the Midland line to Heysham. 72007 worked throughout, except when 46441 hauled the six coaches from Heysham to Morecambe Promenade. *(Howard Malham)*

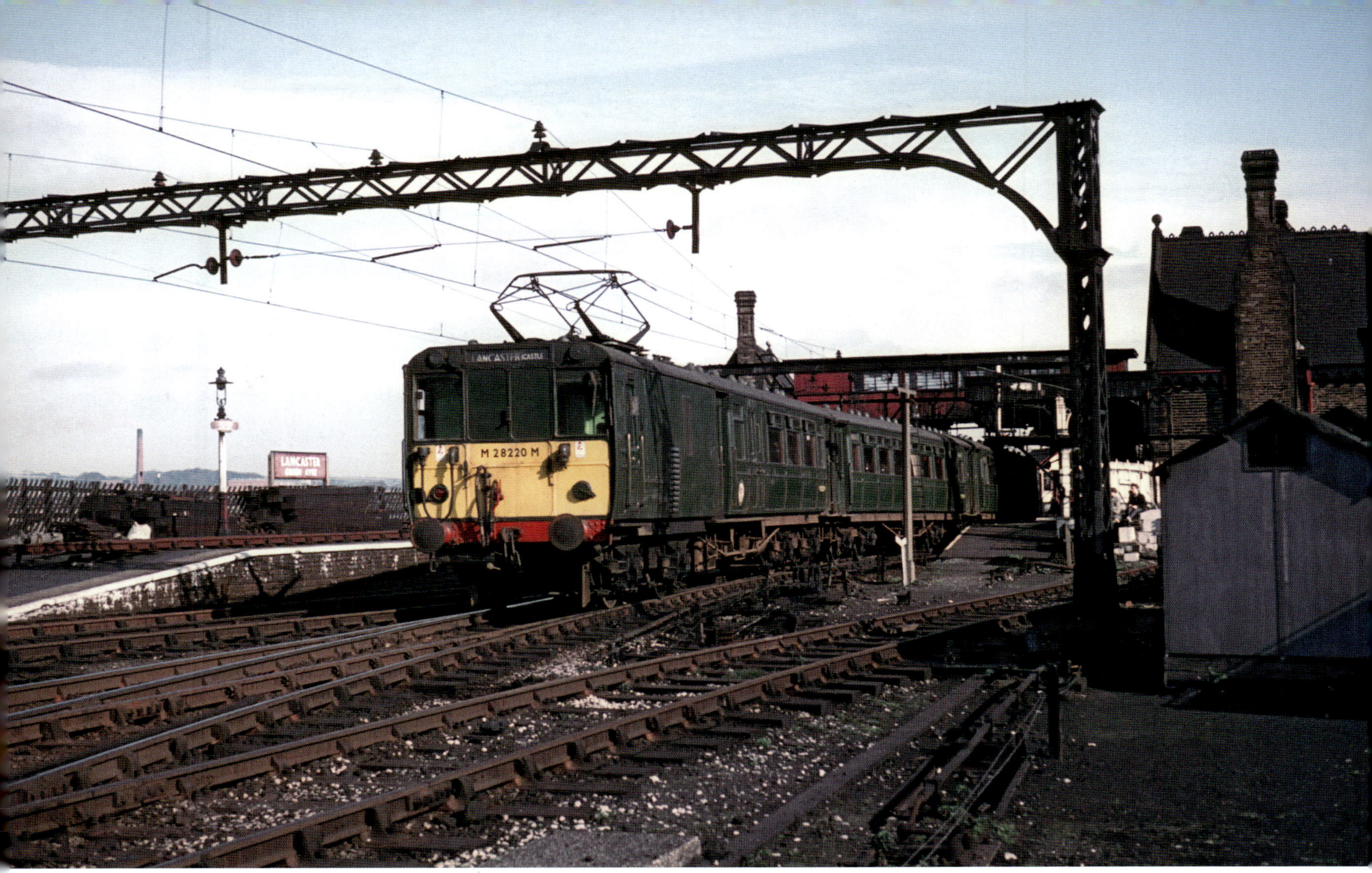

Driving car 28220 arrives at Green Ayre from Morecambe where it will reverse to complete its journey to Lancaster Castle. This vehicle was fitted with the first Germanium semiconductor rectifiers on BR. These represented one of the first applications of electronics on railway traction in this country. Under the Railways (Standardisation of Electrification) Order 1932, all future electrification schemes were to be at 1,500v d.c. overhead, apart from extensions to existing third rail networks. Little was done thanks to the Second World War and, by the early 1950s, BR had begun to consider whether high voltage a.c. might have greater merit. So in August 1953, they re-introduced electric working between Lancaster, Morecambe and Heysham. The voltage was kept at 6,600, with the supply taken from the national grid at industrial frequency. *(D. J. Mitchell)*

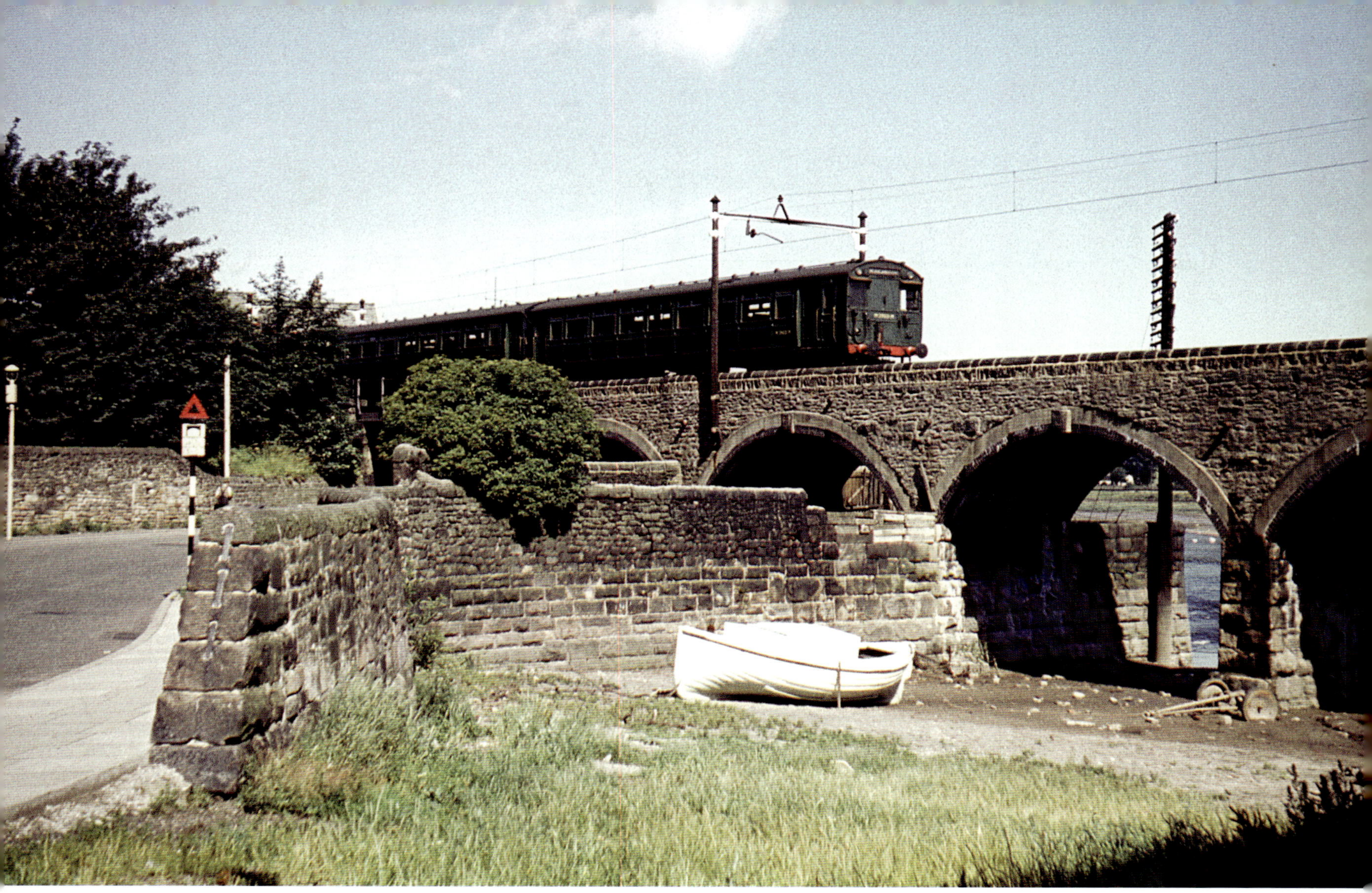

From Green Ayre, a single track branch ascended to join the West Coast Main Line at Lancaster Castle. This short connection was opened in December 1849 to provide a link between the Midland's station and the Lancaster & Carlisle Railway's facility. Driving trailer 29022 is at the rear of Set No. 20 in this 1960 view. It doesn't carry any plastic 'Danger Overhead Live Wires' plates which were introduced after the first section of the West Coast Main Line electrification had opened between Crewe and Manchester in September of that year. Until then, electrification schemes had been considered purely local affairs which would be familiar to any staff needing to climb on vehicles. *(Peter Sunderland)*

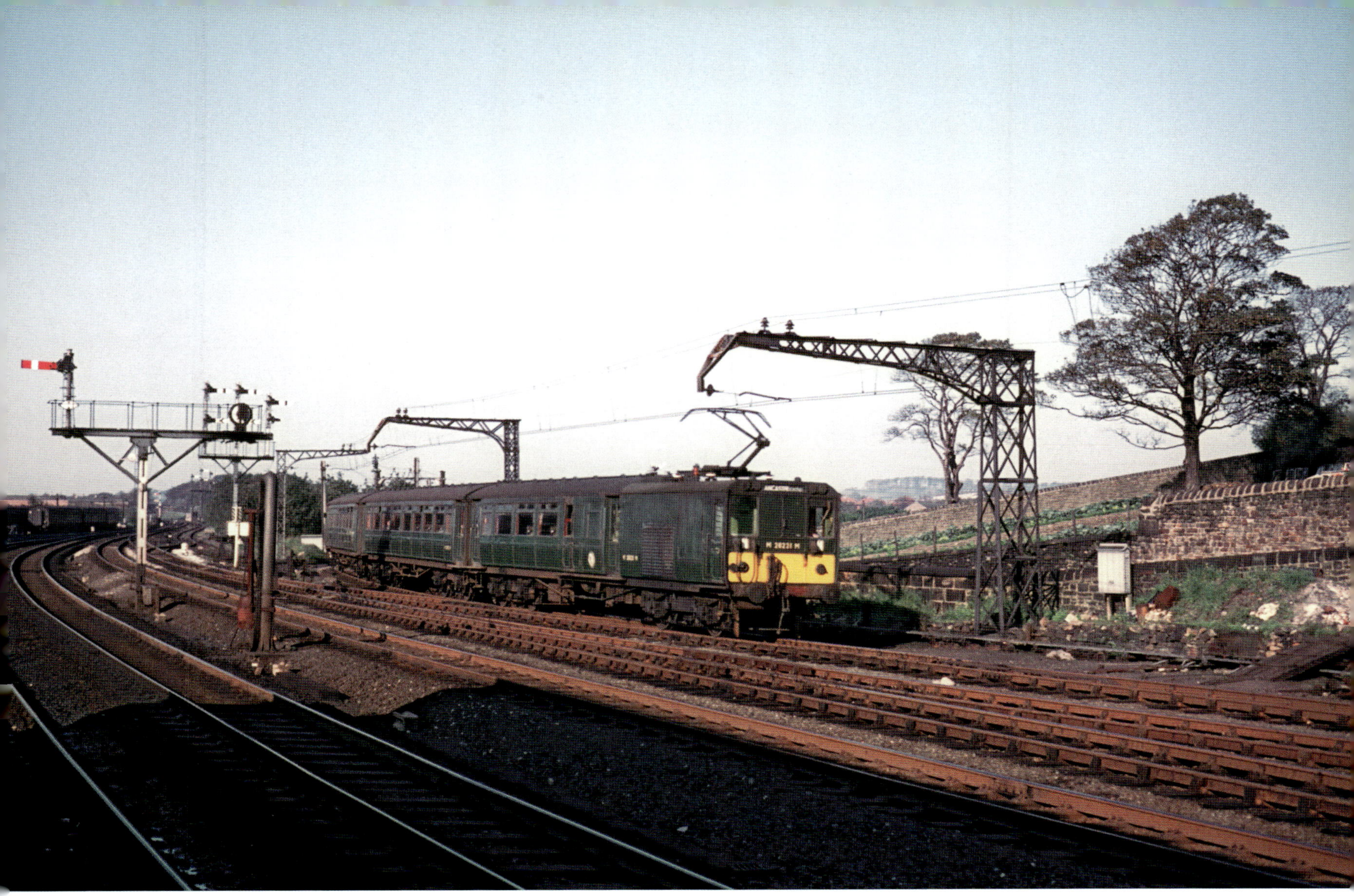

Set 21, led by driving car 28221, with a French-designed single-arm pantograph, comes off the branch from Green Ayre opposite Lancaster No. 4 box. The signalman doesn't have to cross all the tracks to collect a token because the single track section was controlled by direction levers. The electric trains comprised motor coach, centre car and driving trailer. They were designated by BR as Class AM1 which would have become Class 301, had they lasted long enough. They didn't have set numbers but were known unofficially as 19, 20, 21 and 22 - the last two digits of the power cars. *(D. J. Mitchell)*

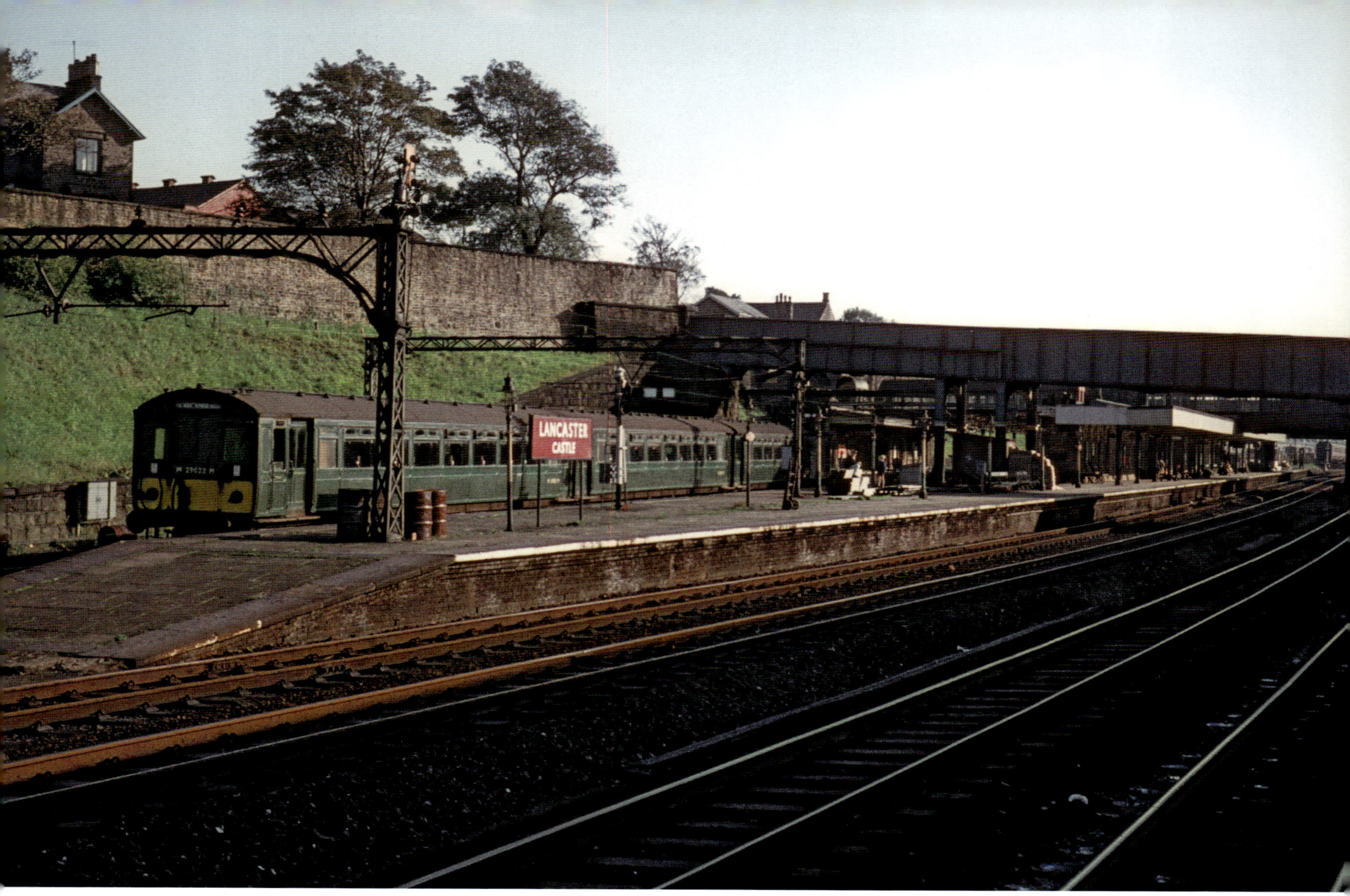

Set No. 20 arrives in Platform 5 at Lancaster Castle in October 1965. The station dates from 1846 and was the headquarters of the Lancaster & Carlisle Railway. Their substantial building is still in place, out of the photo to the right, adjoining the main northbound Platform 3. Between this and the southbound island Platforms 4 and 5 there are two through lines for freight and non-stop passenger trains. This arrangement dates from 1902. Previously, there were just the two main lines between the up and down platforms with goods loops by-passing the station on the east side. *(D. J. Mitchell)*

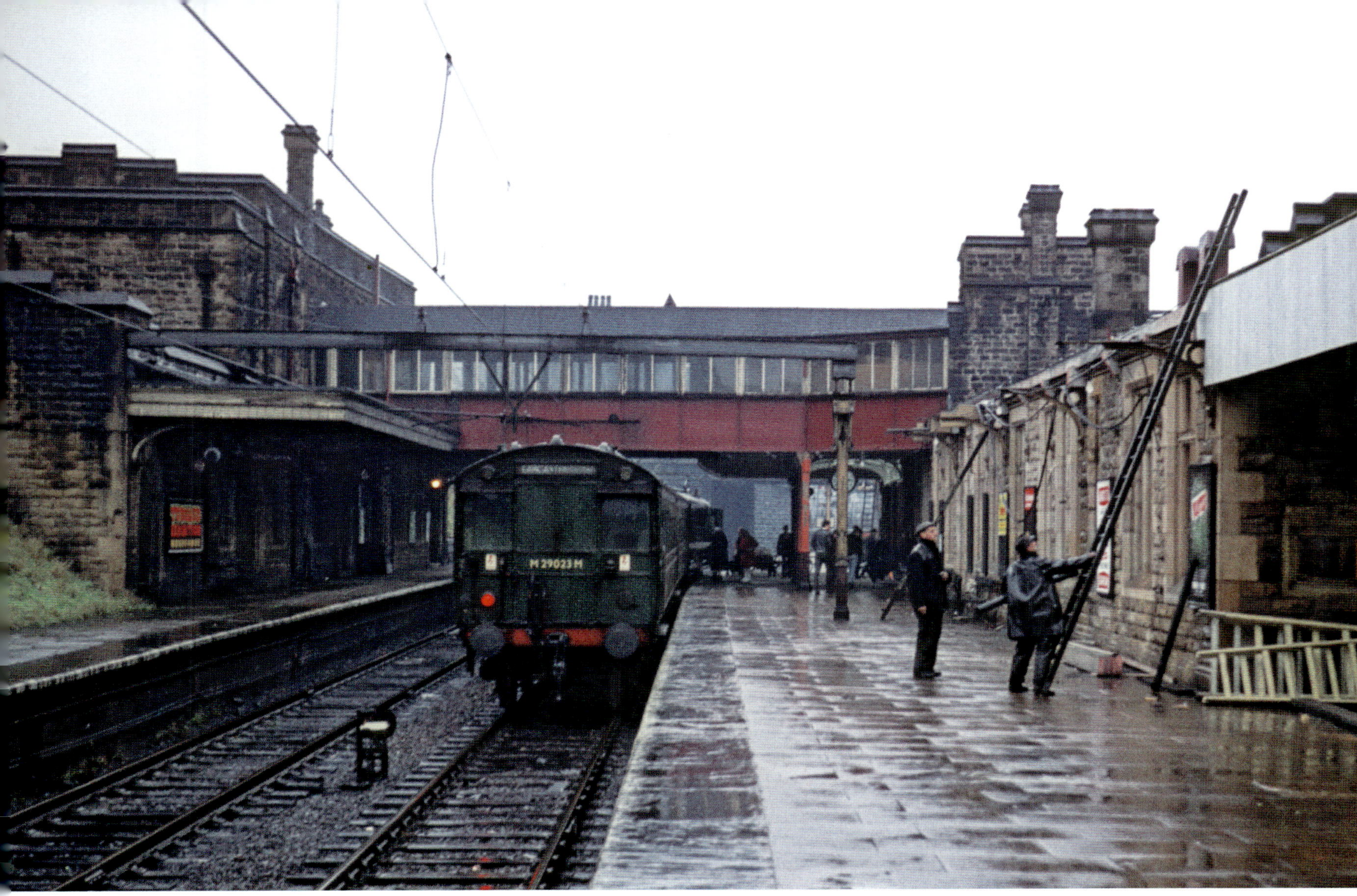

Driving trailer No. 29023, of Set 21, is seen in Platform 5 at Lancaster Castle on a rainy day during November 1965. The canopy has already been cut back, although the section beyond the footbridge is still in place in 2019. The building top left, which dates from the 1902 remodelling, houses the ticket office and is the main entrance from the city. When the Platform 5 and 6 lines were electrified in 1908, the LNWR required a facility to switch the power off in an emergency. This resided in No. 4 signal box. Before 1902, Midland trains had used a bay at the north end of the southbound platform. *(D. J. Mitchell)*

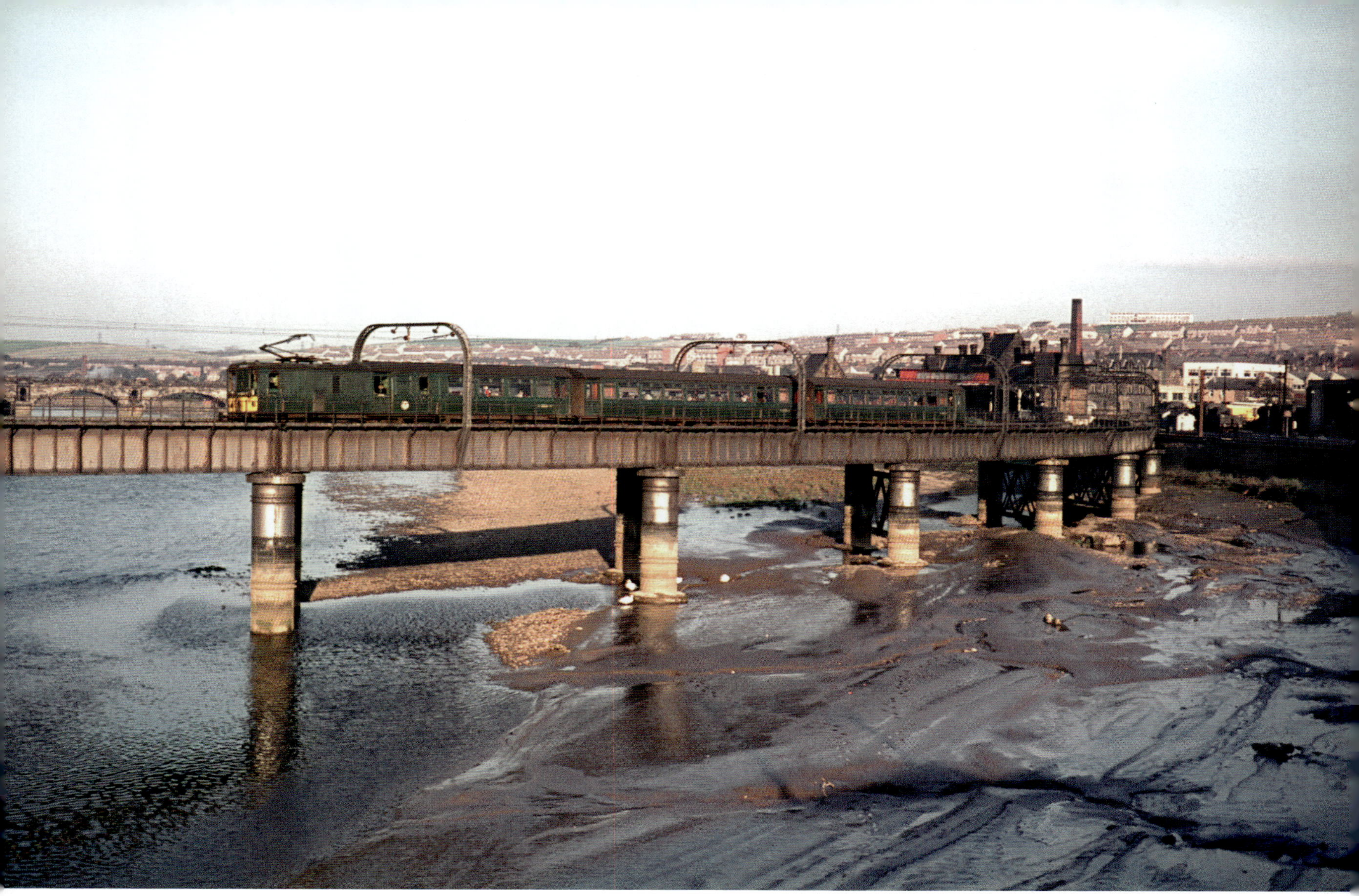

28221 again – this time crossing the Greyhound Bridge on its way to Morecambe in October 1965. The four power cars had a number of technical variations to reflect the experimental nature of the enterprise. As mentioned earlier, 28221 had a single arm pantograph, the first such application on British Railways. The other three had diamond pantographs in common with the locomotives and multiple units on the small number of other overhead electrified lines in operation at that time. *(D. J. Mitchell)*

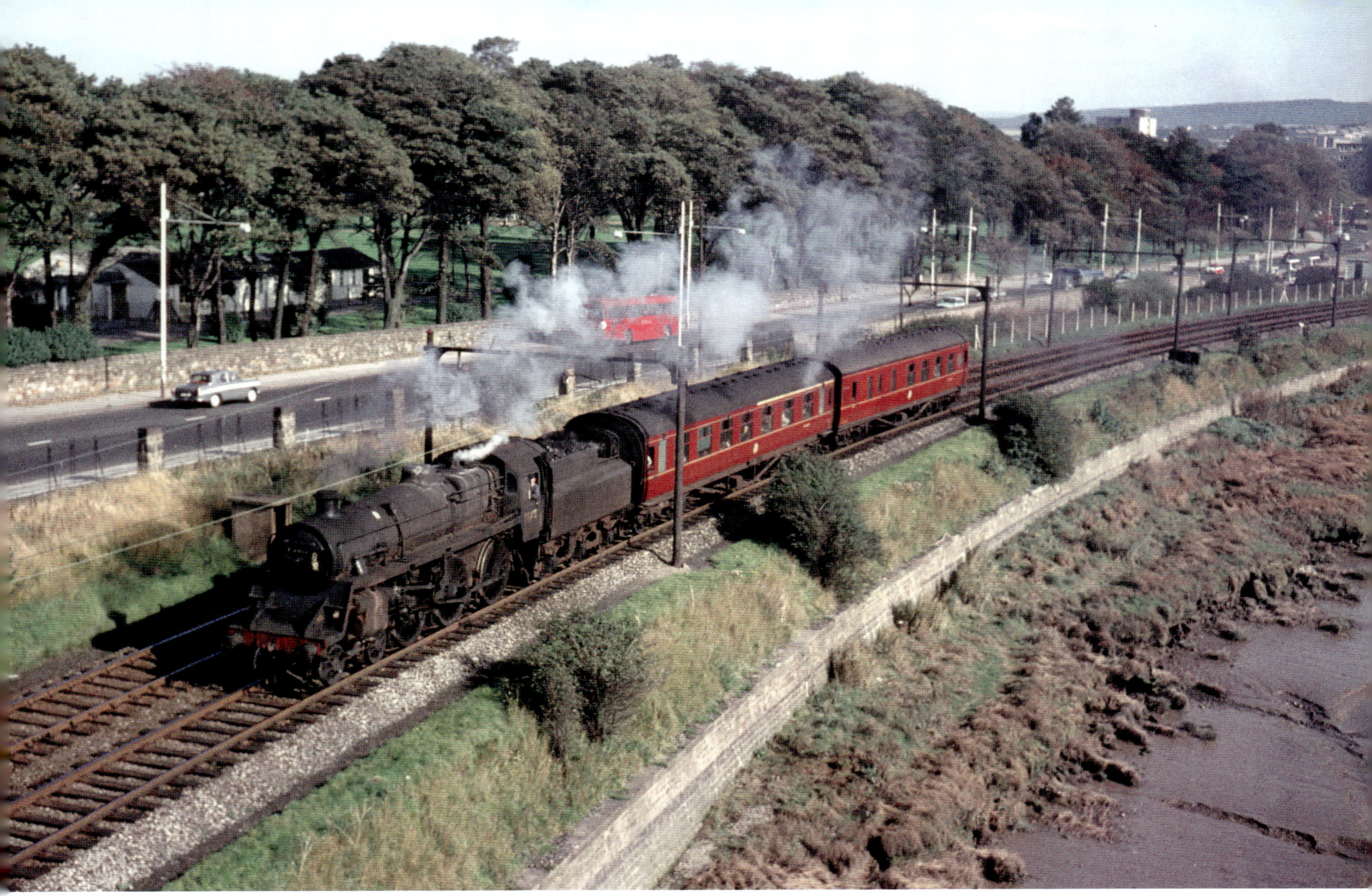

'Standard' Class 4 No. 75019 has crossed the Lune by the Greyhound Bridge and is about to go under Carlisle Bridge in August 1965. This is probably the 1.54 p.m. from Leeds, the main part of which went to Carnforth. The two Morecambe coaches are a CK and BSK in order to make up a complete train with First and Second Class, van space and a brake. BR built 999 'Standard' locos in 12 classes between 1951 and 1960, combining features from the four predecessor companies but, in practice, mainly the LMS. The overhead wires are supported by the original Midland telegraph poles of Norwegian fir. *(D. J. Mitchell)*

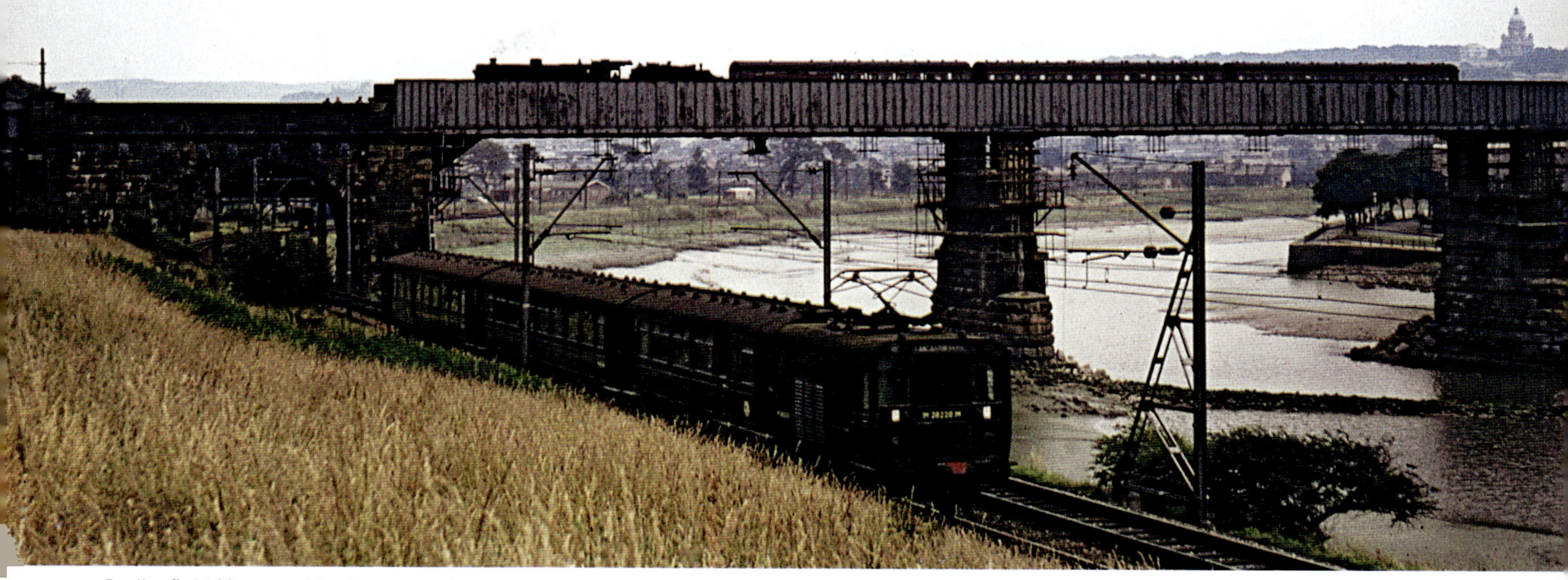

For the first 109 years of the Lancaster Green Ayre to Morecambe line, there was no intermediate station. This was rectified on 8 June 1957 when a station opened at Scale Hall to serve a growing suburb of Lancaster which been expanded with new post war housing developments. Here we see 28220 accelerating away from Scale Hall and about to pass under the Carlisle Bridge. A three-coach train passes over, bound possibly for Barrow or Windermere. The stone piers date from the opening of the Lancaster & Carlisle Railway in 1846 but the original spans were of laminated timber. These were replaced in 1866 by the wrought iron spans, seen here, which blocked the view of trains below the waist line. Scaffolding is beginning to appear for the reconstruction which took place over several months during 1962-63. *(Peter Sunderland)*

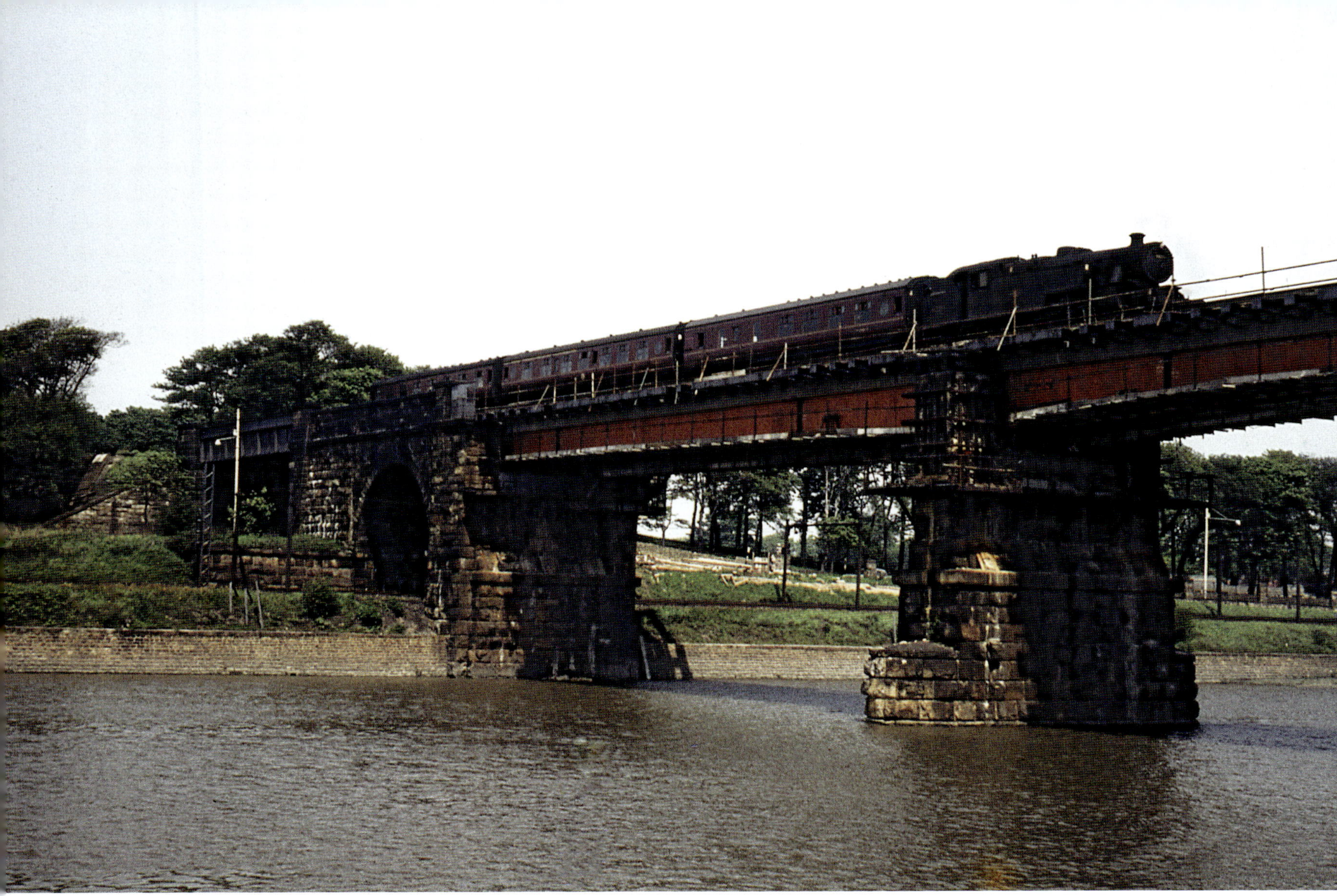

A Fairburn tank engine heads for Lancaster Castle over the newly rebuilt Carlisle Bridge in May 1963. Gone are the girders which obscured the lower halves of trains. The electrified Morecambe line goes underneath. The reconstruction had been achieved without interruption to rail traffic, except on Sundays when trains were diverted between Lancaster Castle and Hest Bank. These ran with a loco on each end between Green Ayre and Morecambe Promenade to ease the reversals at those two stations. *(Peter Sunderland)*

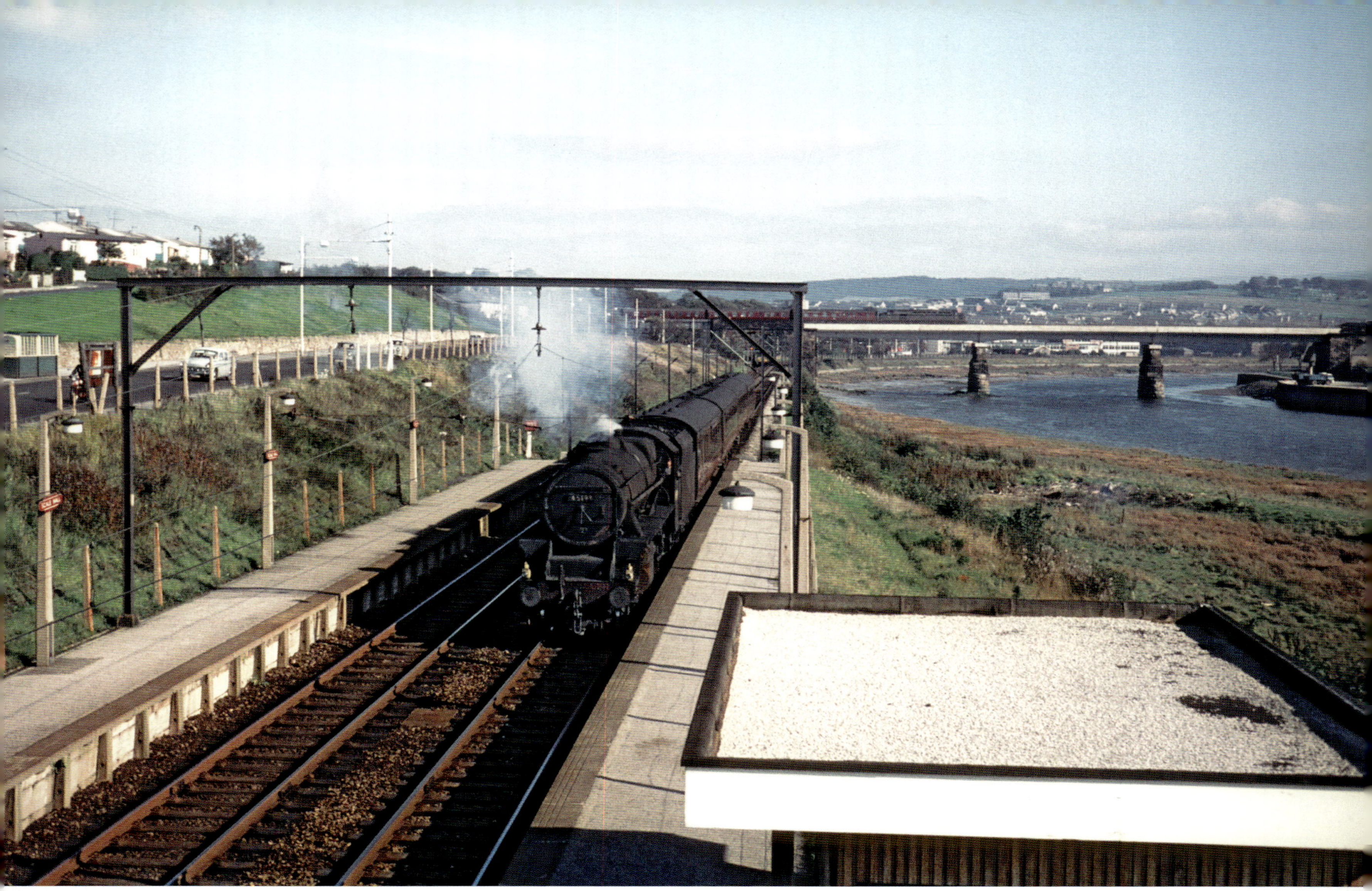

Scale Hall station had long concrete platforms and a footbridge but was normally served only by the electric trains. These were sometimes operated as six-coach double sets in particularly busy periods so the platform length at Scale Hall had presumably been designed with that in mind. The longer distance expresses didn't stop. Having been opened in June 1957, the station lasted only 8½ years, being closed when the electric services were axed at the beginning of January 1966. Here, 'Black Five' No. 45193 is passing through in October 1965, heading for Morecambe. In the background, a southbound express, hauled by an English Electric Type 4 diesel, is crossing the Carlisle Bridge. *(D. J. Mitchell)*

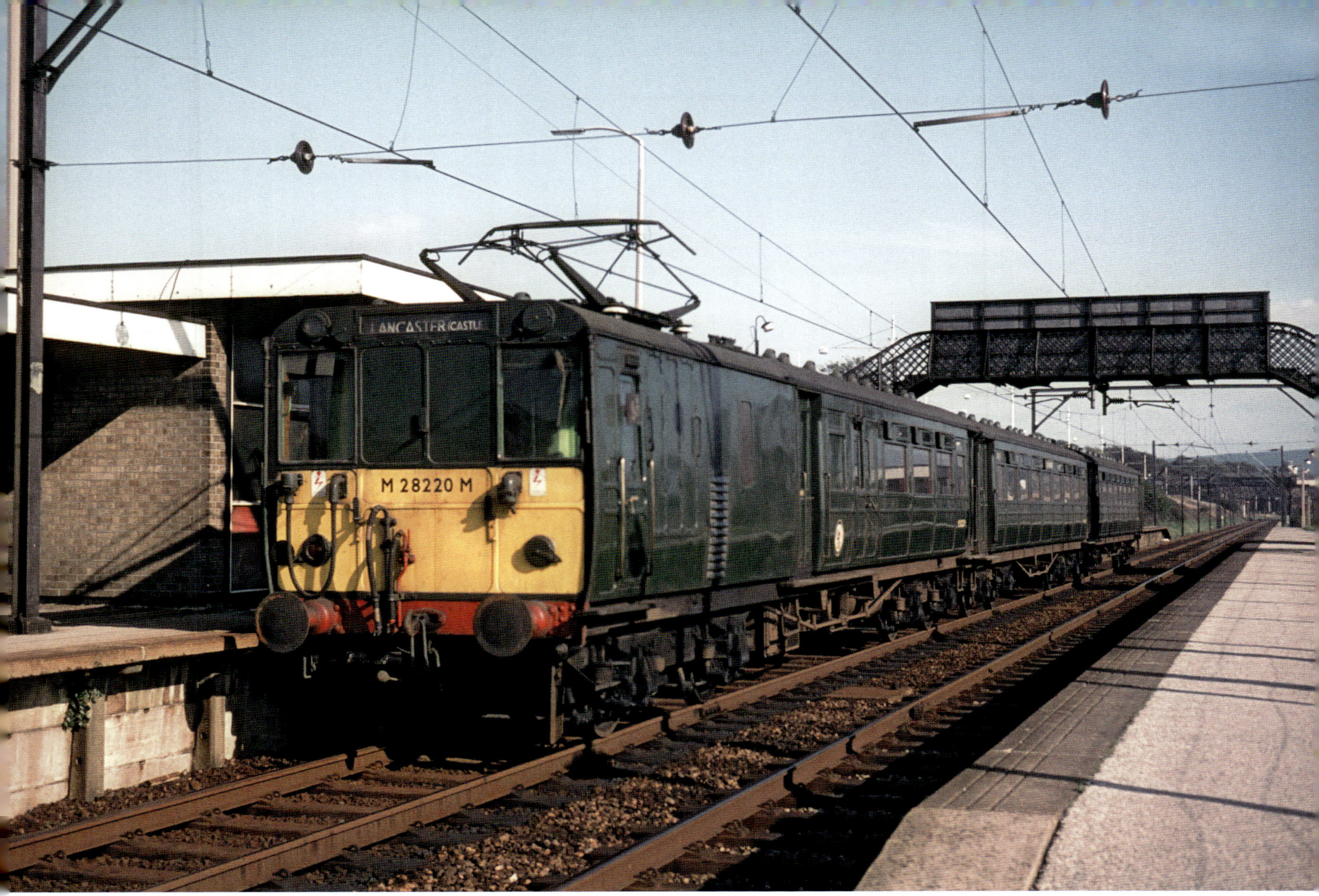

Another view of Set 20, with 28220 at the rear, as it calls at Scale Hall on its way from Morecambe to Lancaster Castle in October 1965. The M prefix denotes allocaticn to the London Midland Region whilst the M suffix indicates that the vehicle was LMS - owned before nationalisation in 1948. 'Danger Overhead Live Wires' plastic plates and, later, stickers were affixed to all rolling stock by this time. *(D. J. Mitchell)*

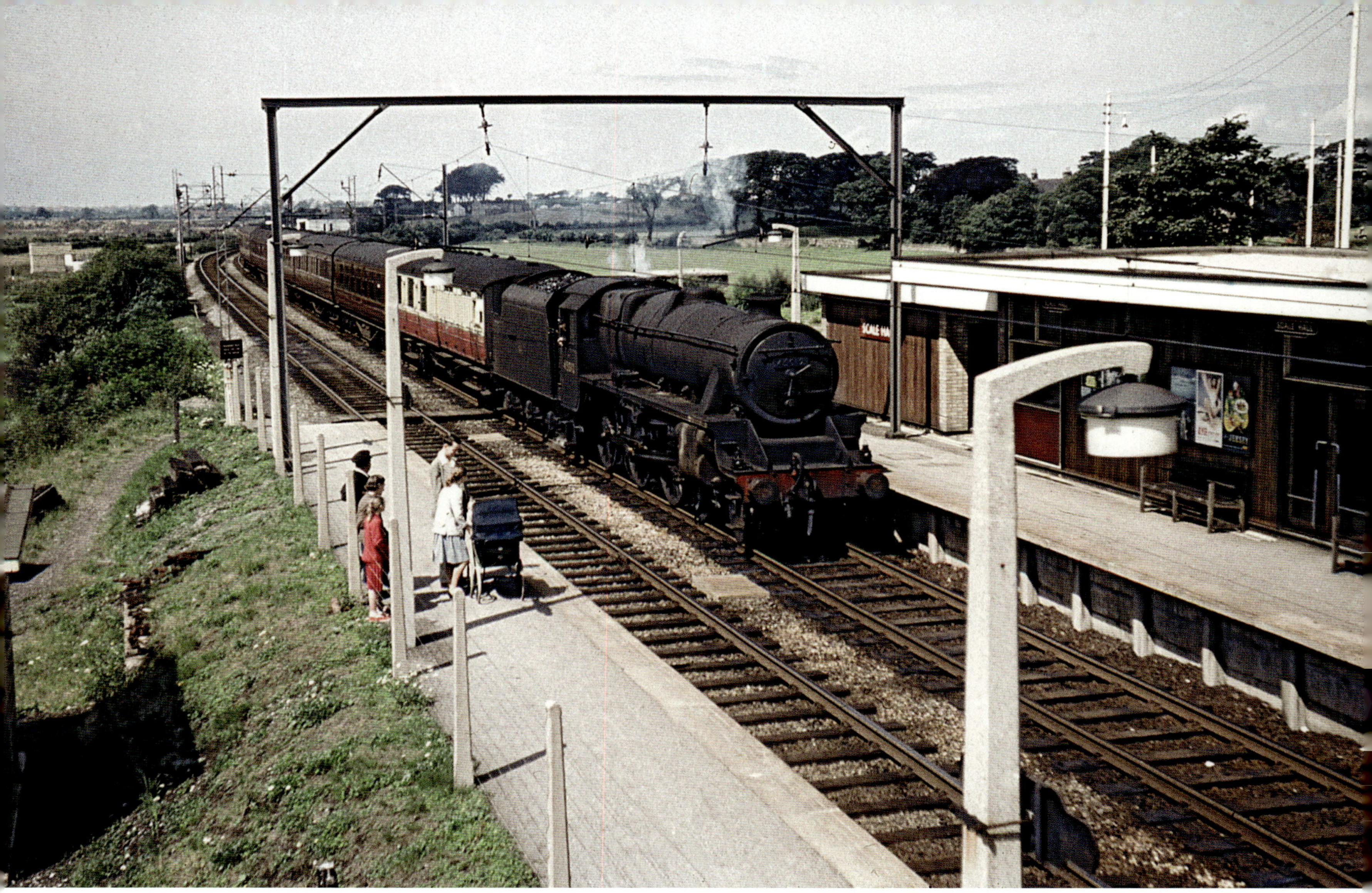

Scale Hall station was served by electric trains which ran half hourly in each direction. On Mondays to Saturdays they left Morecambe at 7.28 a.m. and then every 30 minutes from 8.10 a.m. until 11.10 p.m., all through to Lancaster Castle. A Sunday service ran only from late April to mid-October with departures from Morecambe every half hour from 12.10 to 11.10 p.m. From mid-June to the first Sunday in September, they started two hours earlier and ran every 15 minutes. The through journey took 12 minutes, including the reversal at Green Ayre. 'Black Five' No. 45012 is seen here passing Scale Hall with a Morecambe to Leeds train in 1960. *(Peter Sunderland)*

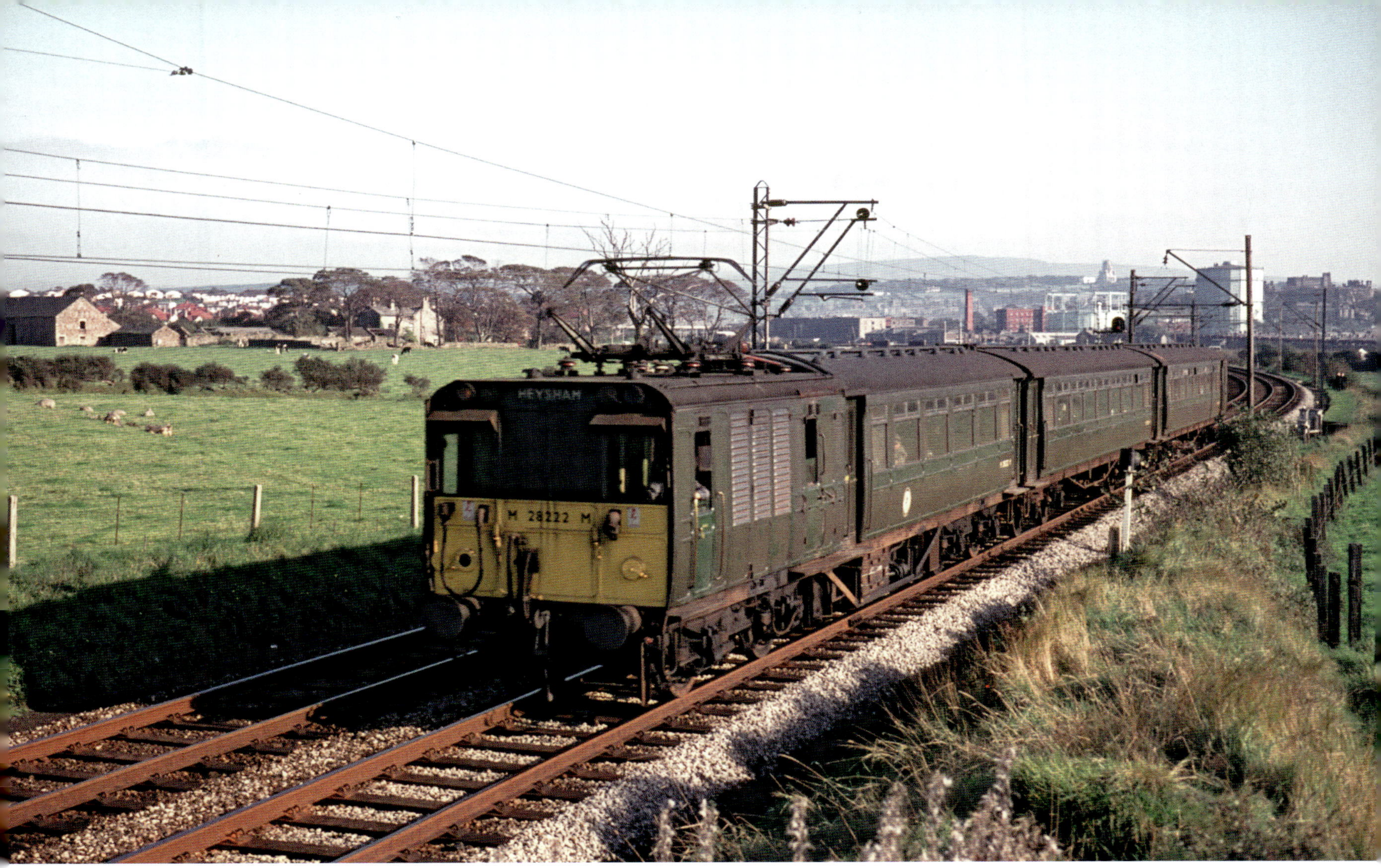

This is Set 22, the fourth and last of the ex-LNWR units to be converted for use on Lancaster-Morecambe and Heysham services. It arrived in 1957 and, unlike the others, had a standard Metropolitan-Vickers pantograph, like those in use on the Manchester-Woodhead-Sheffield-Wath 1,500v d.c. electrics. It also had a Metro-Vick transformer and was fitted experimentally with Westinghouse ignitron mercury arc rectifiers which caused a few problems in cold weather. Driving car 28222 is seen here in October 1965 approaching Ovangle Road Bridge on the ¾ mile stretch west of Carlisle Bridge where the overhead was renewed for the 1953 re-electrification. This was done at the expense of the contractor hoping to benefit from future projects. Elsewhere, the Midland wiring remained in place. *(D. J. Mitchell)*

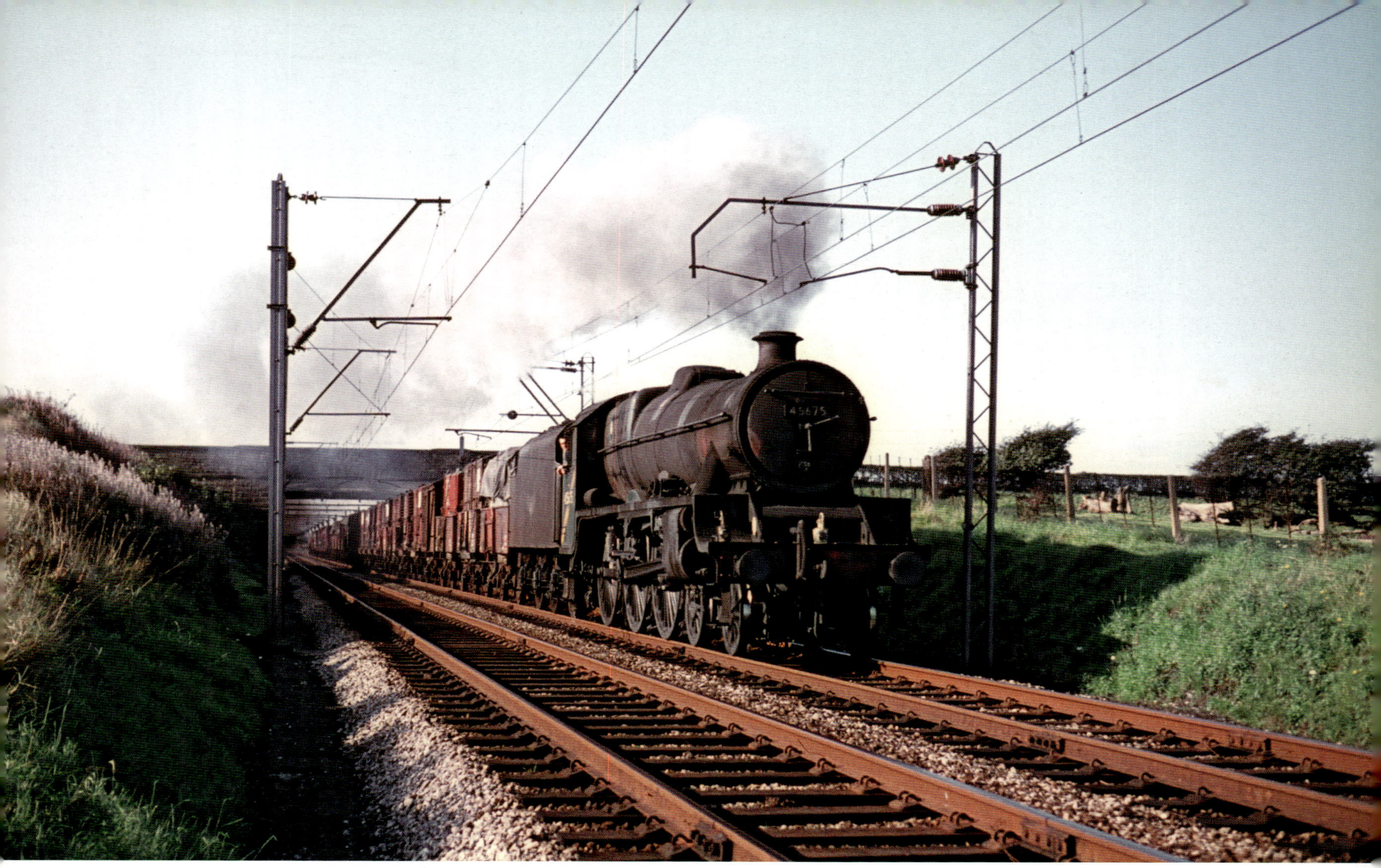

Leeds (Holbeck) 'Jubilee' No. 45675 *Hardy* passes under Ovangle Road Bridge with an express freight from Heysham to Stourton, near Leeds, in October 1965. The two headlamps on the centre and right hand brackets (left as we see it) confirm that the train is fully fitted. All the wagons have automatic vacuum brakes under the control of the driver. If there was any logic in diverting via Carnforth after 1966, it must have been for this type of traffic. As suggested on page 22, the best route for passenger trains after closure of the electrics would have been via Bare Lane, Lancaster Castle, Green Ayre and Halton. But heavy freight would have had difficulty with the reversal at Castle and the steep single track thence to Green Ayre. So they diverted via Carnforth to the detriment of passengers but for the benefit of freight which had all gone by 1986. *(D. J. Mitchell)*

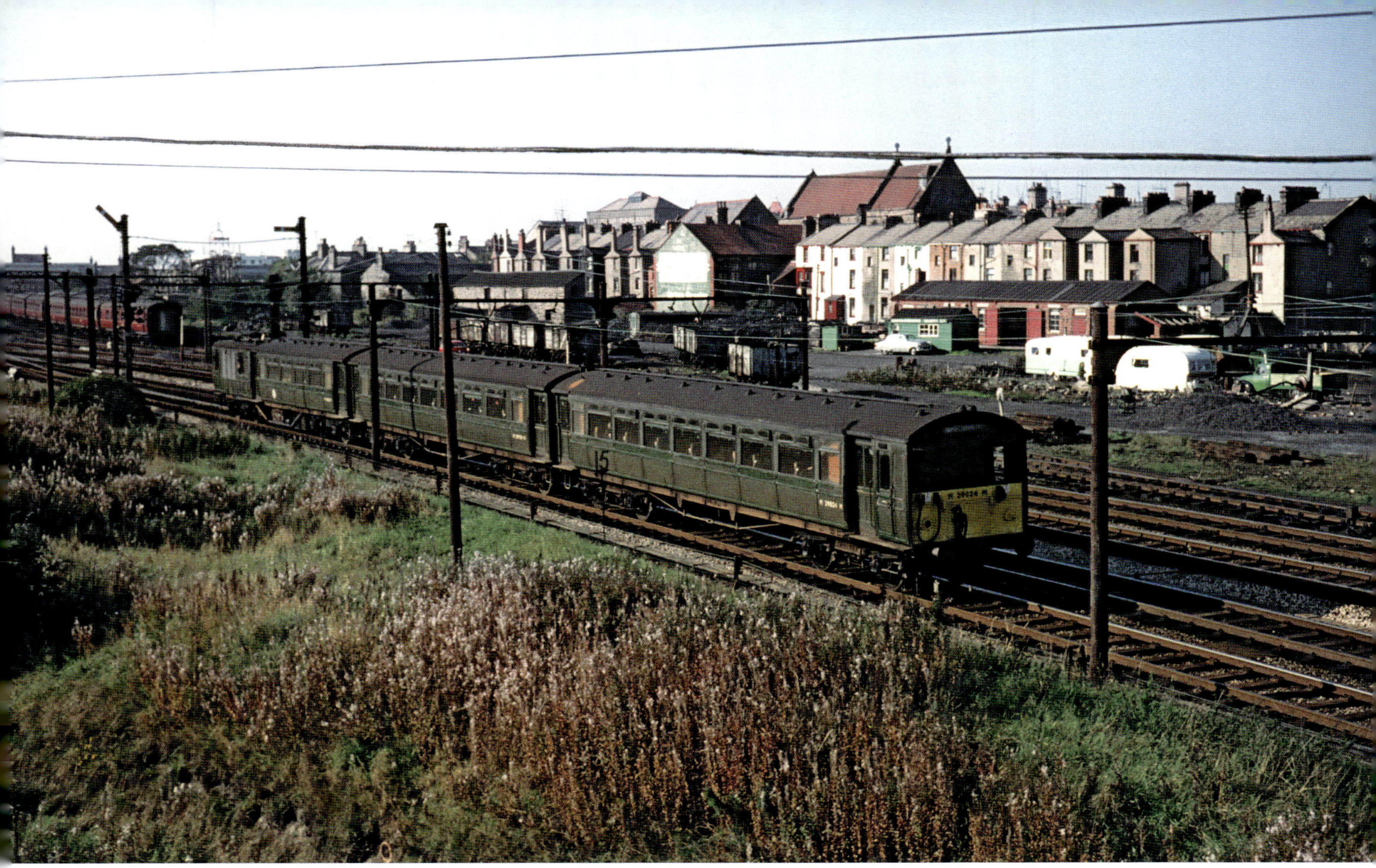

29024, of Set 22, approaching Morecambe Promenade from Heysham in October 1965. The LNWR had planned a number of London area electrification schemes. Willesden Junction to Earls Court was completed in May 1914 but the First World War delayed further progress. It also prevented the use of Siemens equipment on other than the first four trains. Later ones obtained electrical parts from Oerlikon in neutral Switzerland. When the West London line was bomb damaged in October 1940, the four Siemens trains were put in store to await resumption of the Willesden Junction to Earls Court service which never happened. Therefore, they were available when BR needed trains for its self-contained experimental system on the North West coast. This gave the vintage quartet an unexpected new lease of life. *(D.J. Mitchell)*

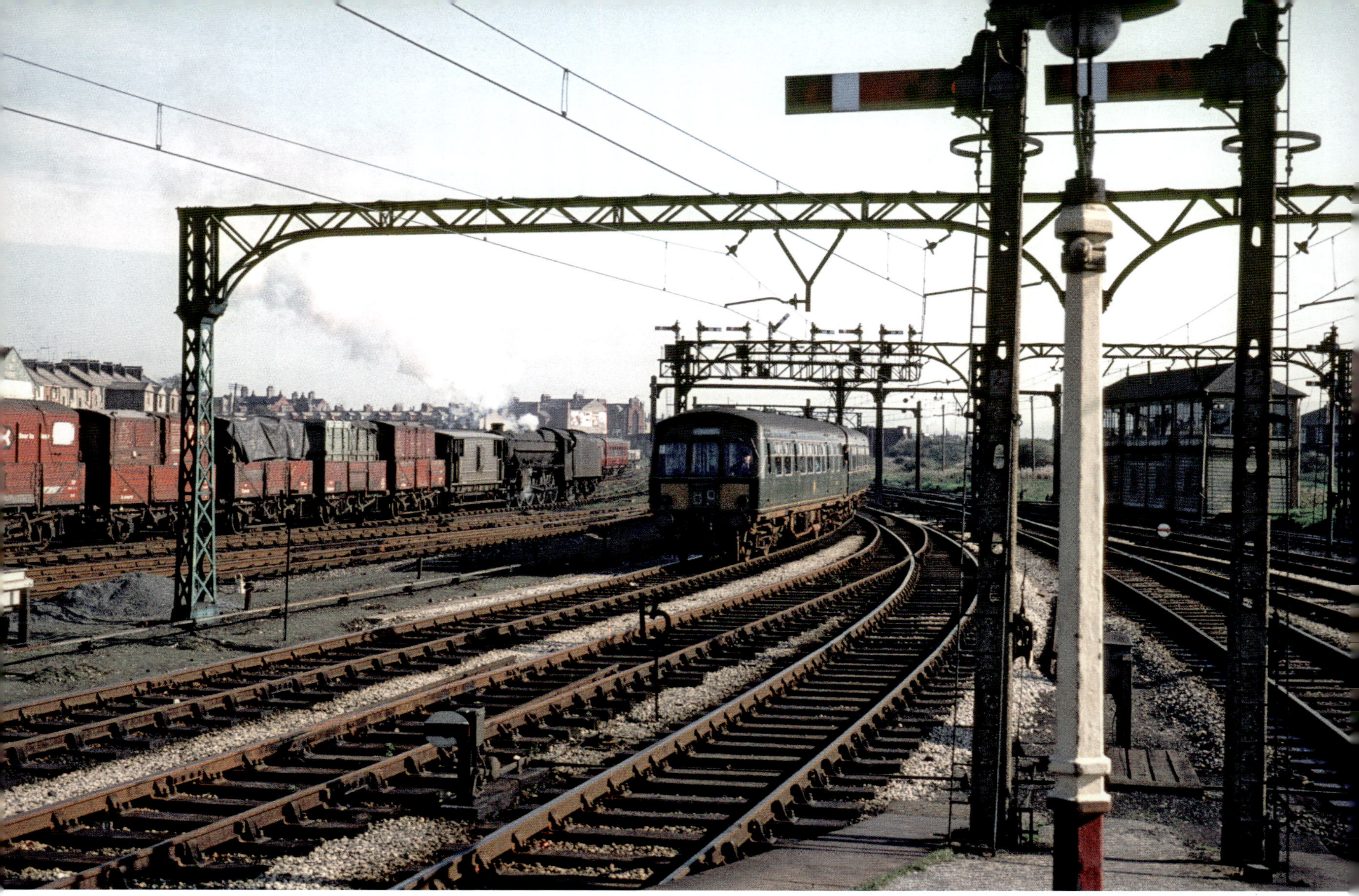

A Metro Cammell DMU enters Morecambe Promenade in October 1965, probably on the 10.48 from Leeds which will have detached a rear two coach set for Carnforth at Wennington. The 92-lever signal box was commissioned along with Morecambe Promenade Station in 1907 and both closed in 1994. A 'Black Five' can be seen shunting wagons in the goods yard. Their bauxite brown livery confirms that they are vacuum fitted or, at least, piped. A piped vehicle does not itself have power operated brakes but it preserves the continuity of the vacuum. *(D. J. Mitchell)*

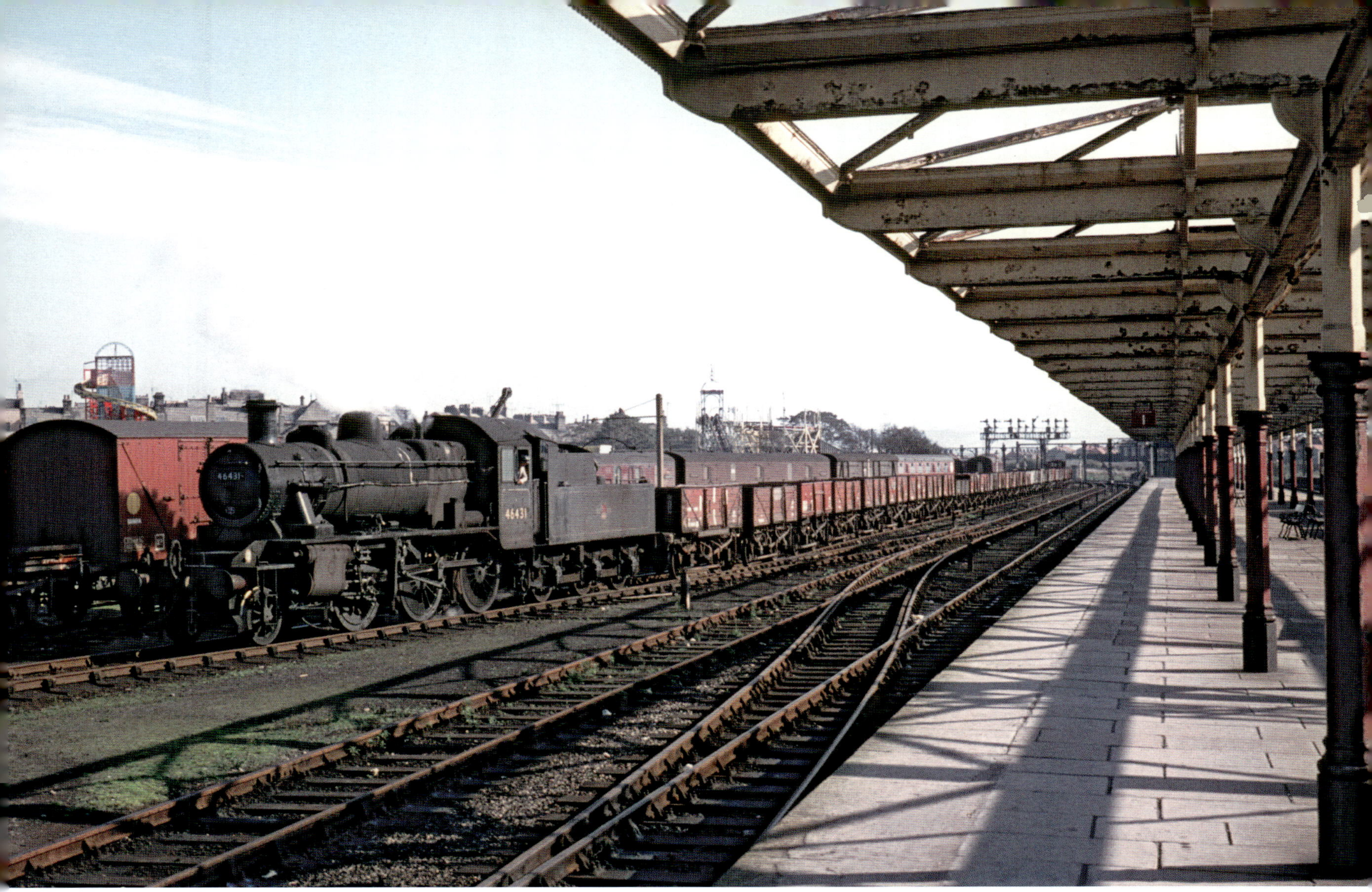

Ivatt Class 2 'Mogul' No. 46431 arrives at Morecambe Promenade with a train of empty wagons. The first nine in brown livery are vacuum fitted but the tenth is grey and, therefore, unfitted. On a partially fitted train, the wagons nearest the engine have automatic brakes under the control of the driver but the rest of the train is un-braked, apart from the guard's hand brake at the very end. The front portion was known as the fitted head. Continuous automatic brakes have been mandatory on passenger trains since 1889 but there were so many goods wagons in the pre-Beeching age that it was impractical to equip them all. *(D. J. Mitchell)*

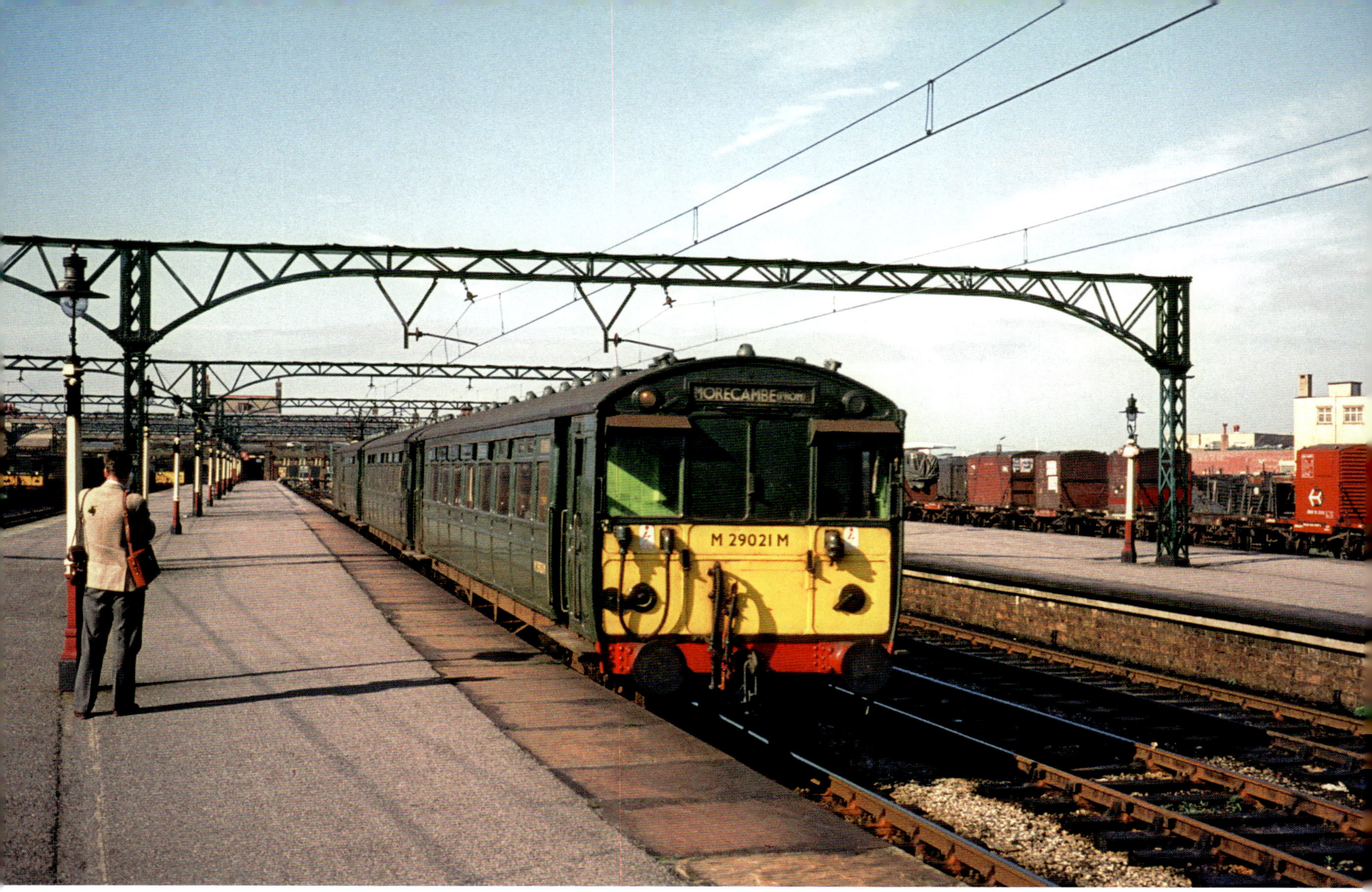

Another view of 29021, this time leaving Morecambe for Heysham in October 1965, although the driver hasn't changed the destination blind. The electric trains were then 51 years old, though they had not run between 1940 and 1952 when they started testing on the Lancaster – Morecambe – Heysham sections. They had been third-rail d.c. powered in their earlier lives. The centre trailers included a First Class section for London commuters but they were Third Class only after transfer to Lancashire, with seating similar to contemporary diesel multiple units. The small containers in the goods yard have curved tops which prevents stacking. These pre-dated the larger standard stackable containers which became widespread after 1968. *(D. J. Mitchell)*

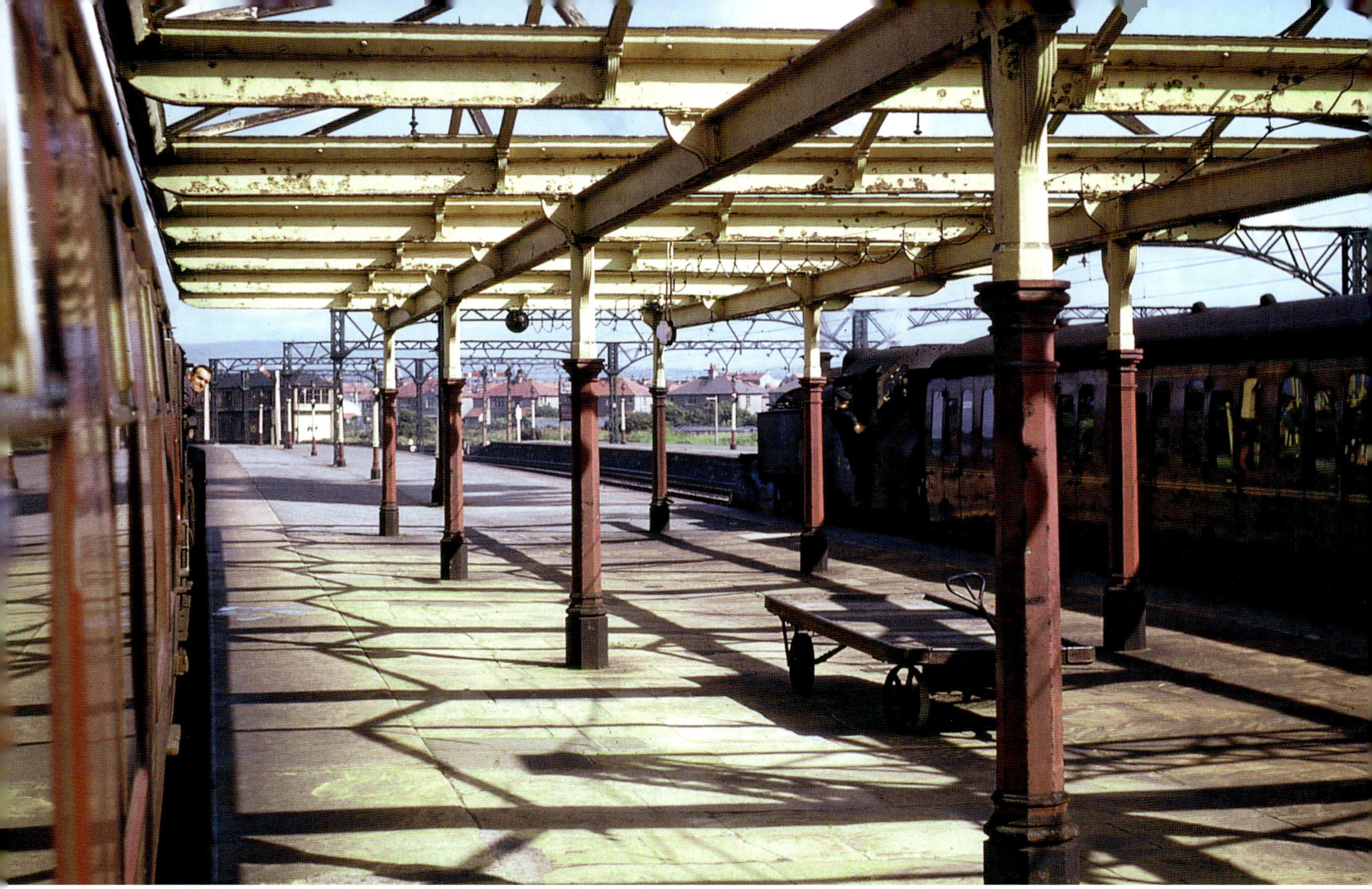

An Ivatt 2- 6 – 2T, possibly on a local to Lancaster Castle via Bare Lane, in Platform 2 at Promenade station during July 1965. Up to 1958 - and in summer until 1962 - this service had run from the LNWR terminus a short distance away at Euston Road. In 1950, there had been 17 trains each way, less than half the number on the electric route. By the early 1960s, it was down to eight a day from Morecambe and only five from Lancaster. These were mostly timed into Lancaster in the morning and back around tea time, creating a lot of empty stock workings. The main purpose must have been to cater for commuters from Bare Lane. *(Roger Hepworth)*

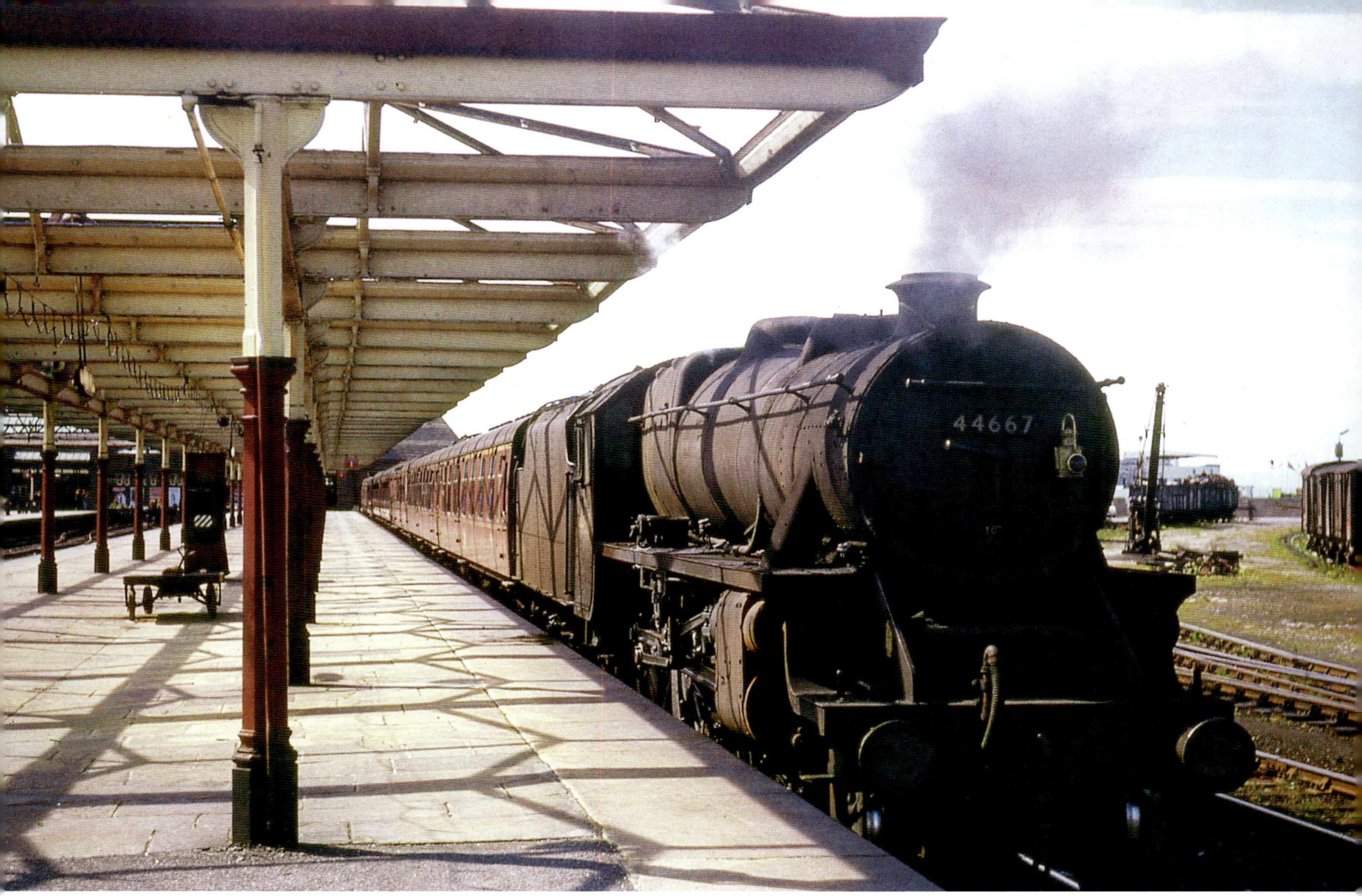

Lancaster Green Ayre's 'Black Five' No. 44667 awaits departure from Morecambe Promenade with the 4.20 p.m. to Leeds on 26 July 1965. This was the last summer that trains would take the direct former Midland route via Green Ayre and Halton. From 3 January 1966, they were re-routed via Carnforth, thereby missing out Lancaster, the most important place en route. Passengers for Lancaster were offered the inconvenience of a change at Carnforth but in 1970 the main line platforms there were closed, greatly reducing the number of possible connections. *(Roger Hepworth)*

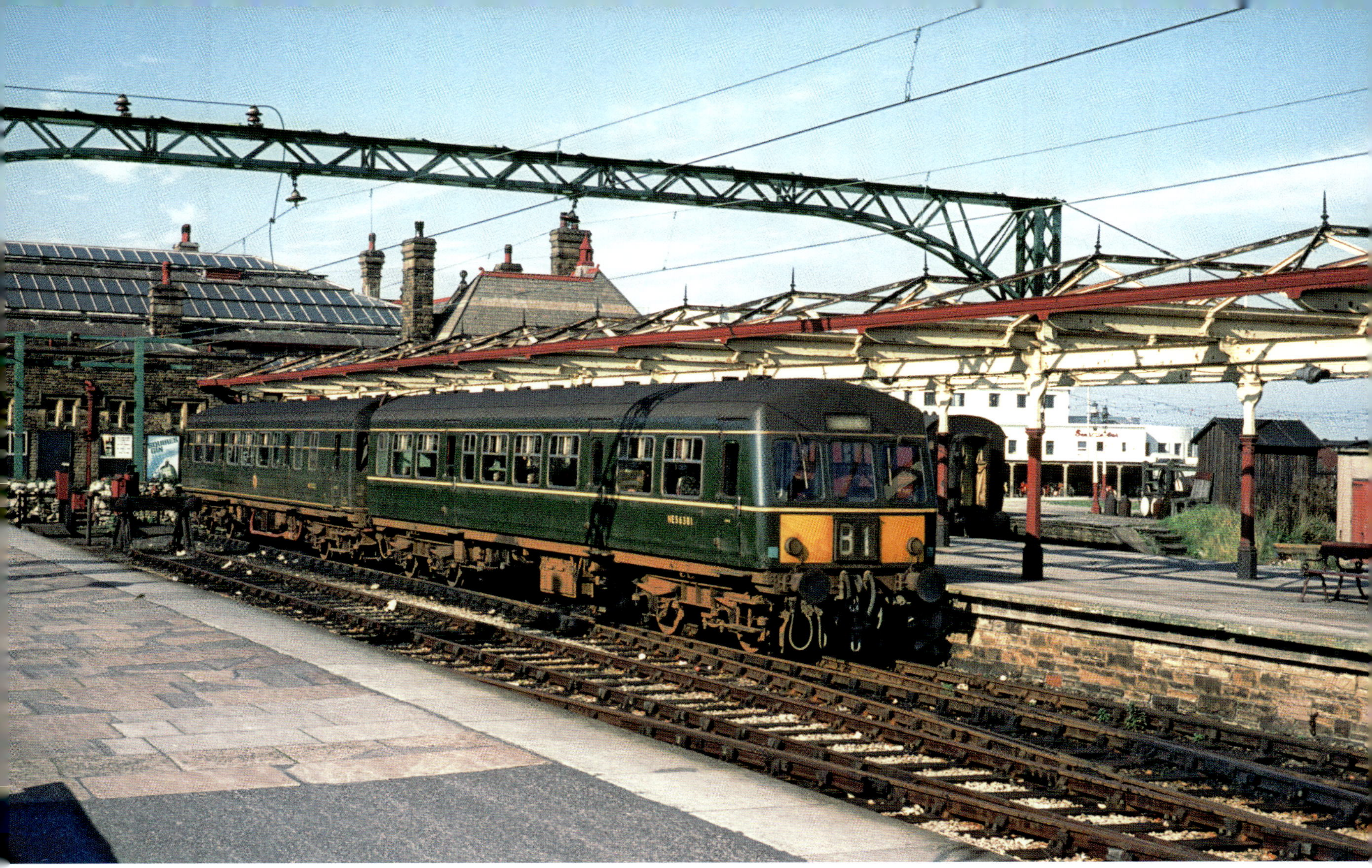

Driving trailer No. 56381 leads a two-car Metro Cammell DMU at Morecambe Promenade in October 1965, waiting to depart for Leeds. What later become Class 101 appeared in various two, three and four-car formations. A power car and trailer set was not much good on gradients but should have been adequate on this route. It would have been joined at Wennington by something similar, or even more powerful, coming from Carnforth. A total of 760 Metro Cammell DMU vehicles were built between 1956 and 1960 and a few remained in main line service until the early 2000s. Some still operate in service on heritage lines. To the right of the train can be seen the Midland Hotel, opened by the LMS in 1933. Sold out of railway ownership in 1952, it closed in 1998 but was superbly refurbished and reopened ten years later. *(D. J. Mitchell)*

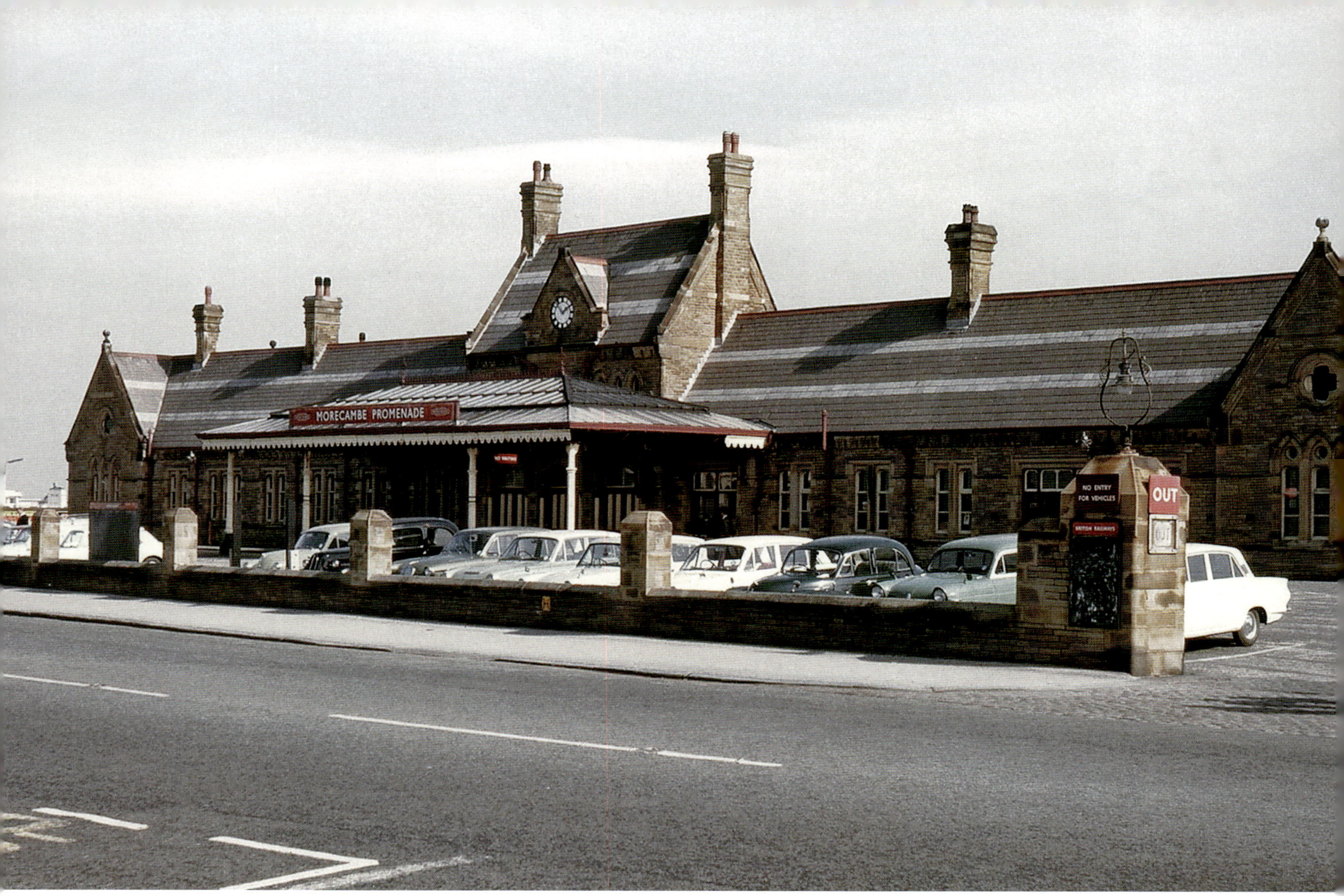

Morecambe Promenade viewed from the sea front in March 1965. The station opened in 1907 to replace the smaller one depicted on Page 1. Until 1926, a horse tramway passed in front, the last on the British mainland. The Promenade suffix was applied from June 1924. Previously it had just been known as the Midland Station. Following the 1923 Grouping, the LMS articulated a number of station names. Morecambe (LNWR) became Morecambe Euston Road whilst Bradford (Midland) became Bradford Forster Square as part of the same programme. *(Peter Sunderland)*

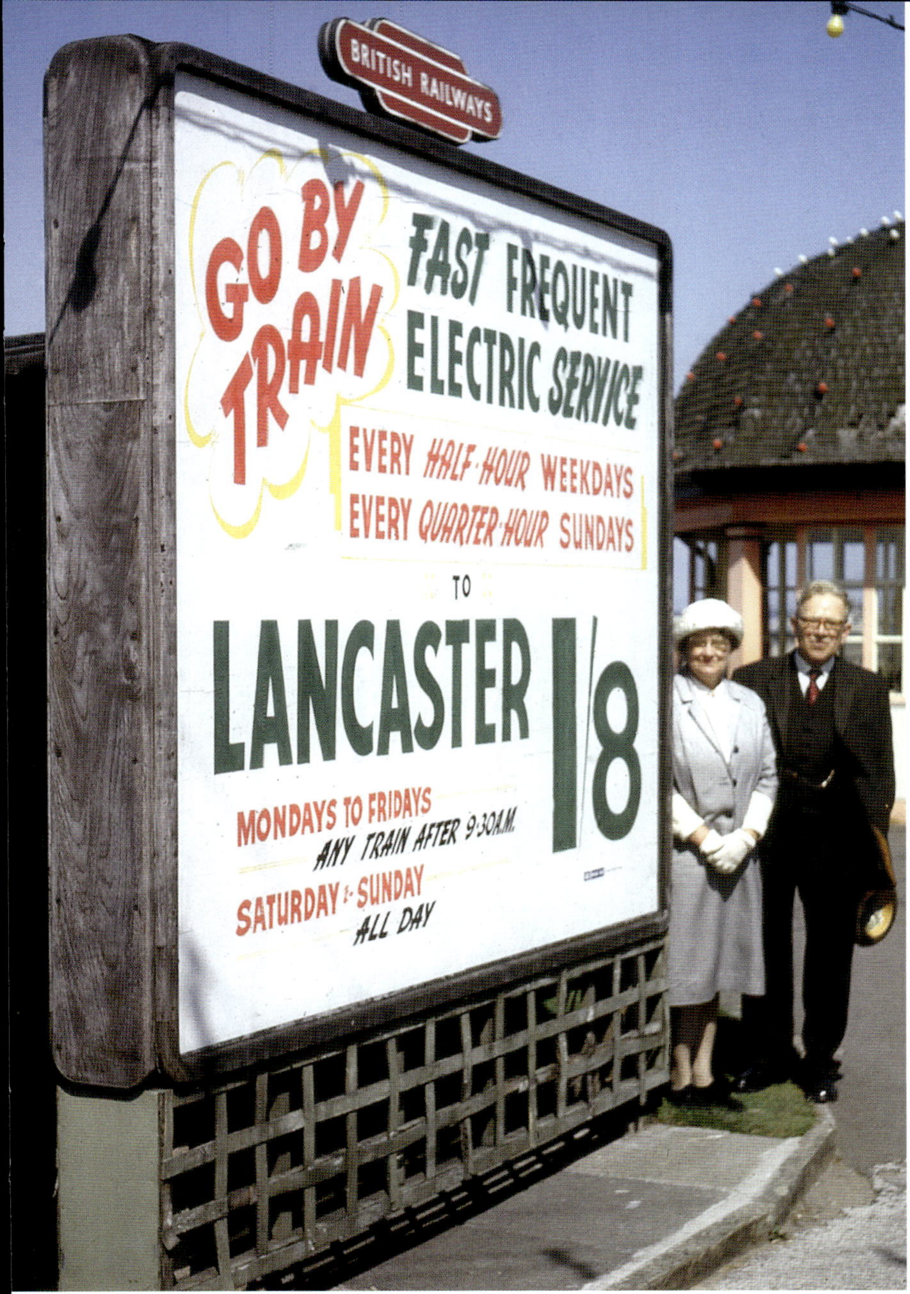

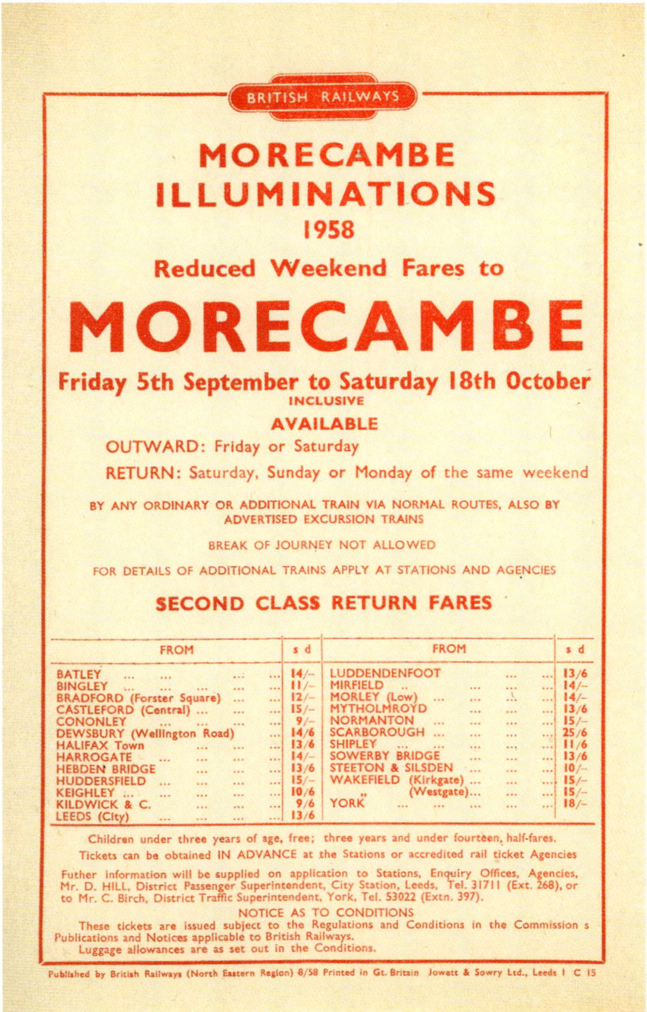

BRITISH RAILWAYS

MORECAMBE ILLUMINATIONS 1958

Reduced Weekend Fares to

MORECAMBE

Friday 5th September to Saturday 18th October

INCLUSIVE

AVAILABLE

OUTWARD: Friday or Saturday

RETURN: Saturday, Sunday or Monday of the same weekend

BY ANY ORDINARY OR ADDITIONAL TRAIN VIA NORMAL ROUTES, ALSO BY ADVERTISED EXCURSION TRAINS

BREAK OF JOURNEY NOT ALLOWED

FOR DETAILS OF ADDITIONAL TRAINS APPLY AT STATIONS AND AGENCIES

SECOND CLASS RETURN FARES

FROM	s d	FROM	s d
BATLEY	14/–	LUDDENDENFOOT	13/6
BINGLEY	11/–	MIRFIELD	14/–
BRADFORD (Forster Square)	12/–	MORLEY (Low)	14/–
CASTLEFORD (Central)	15/–	MYTHOLMROYD	13/6
CONONLEY	9/–	NORMANTON	15/–
DEWSBURY (Wellington Road) ...	14/6	SCARBOROUGH	25/6
HALIFAX Town	13/6	SHIPLEY	11/6
HARROGATE	14/–	SOWERBY BRIDGE	13/6
HEBDEN BRIDGE	13/6	STEETON & SILSDEN	10/–
HUDDERSFIELD	15/–	WAKEFIELD (Kirkgate)	15/–
KEIGHLEY	10/6	„ (Westgate)...	15/–
KILDWICK & C.	9/6	YORK	18/–
LEEDS (City)	13/6		

Children under three years of age, free; three years and under fourteen, half-fares.

Tickets can be obtained IN ADVANCE at the Stations or accredited rail ticket Agencies

Futher information will be supplied on application to Stations, Enquiry Offices, Agencies, Mr. D. HILL, District Passenger Superintendent, City Station, Leeds, Tel. 31711 (Ext. 268), or to Mr. C. Birch, District Traffic Superintendent, York, Tel. 53022 (Extn. 397).

NOTICE AS TO CONDITIONS

These tickets are issued subject to the Regulations and Conditions in the Commission s Publications and Notices applicable to British Railways.

Luggage allowances are as set out in the Conditions.

Published by British Railways (North Eastern Region) 8/58 Printed in Gt. Britain Jowett & Sowry Ltd., Leeds 1 C 15

A sea front poster promoting the electric service to Lancaster in July 1965. This was ironic as, by this time, BR were well on the way to convincing the Transport Users Consultative Committee and the Minister of Transport that the service was unnecessary and that no hardship would result from its withdrawal. In those days both ladies and gentlemen wore hats. Our photographer's parents made no exception, even on a day trip to Morecambe! *(Roger Hepworth, Handbill: Alan Whitaker collection)*

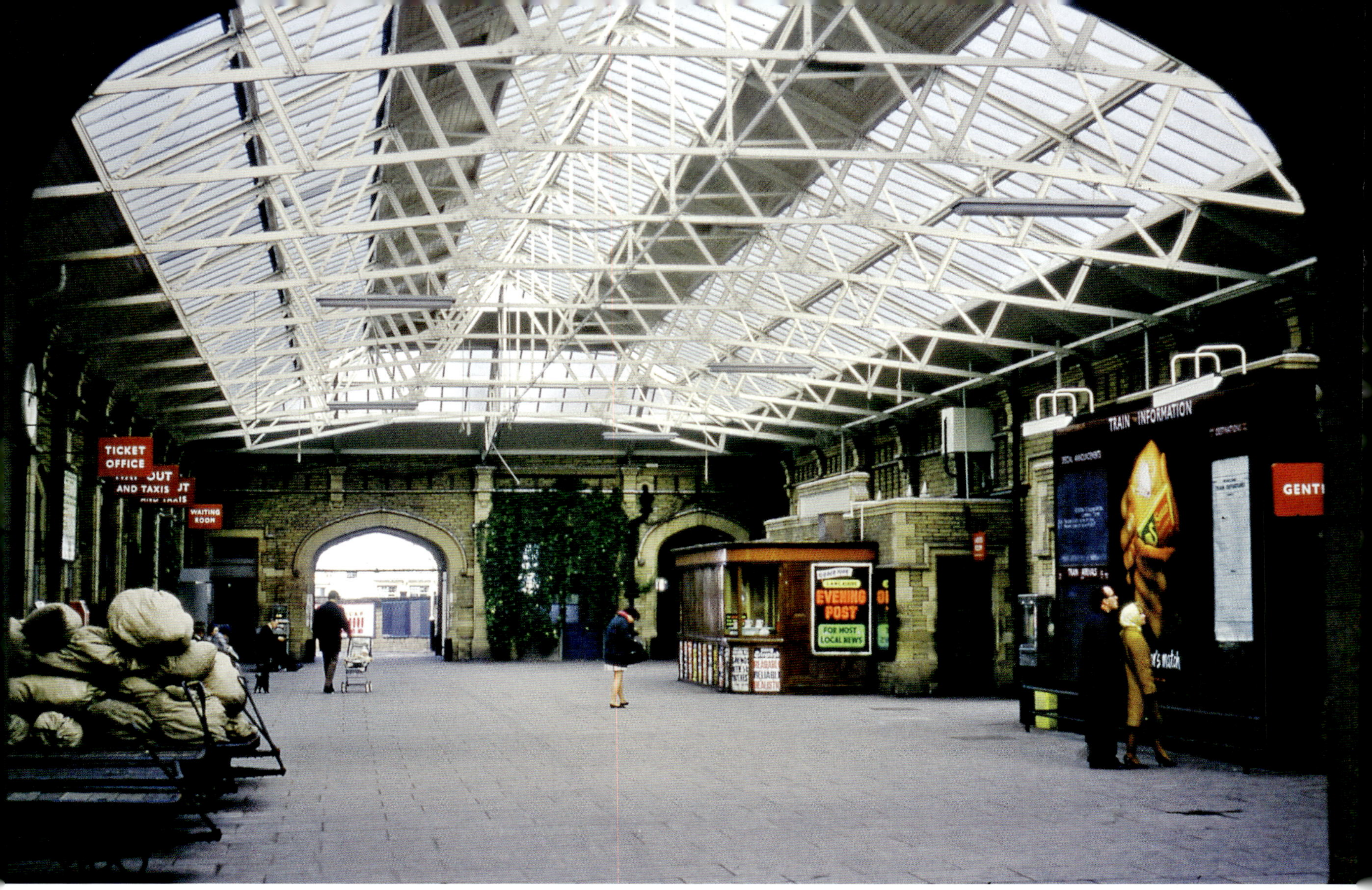

A view of the concourse at Morecambe Promenade in 1969. The Ladies` lavatory, with its large water tank, stands behind the bookstall which appears no longer to be W H Smith. The rather grand Gents` is behind the camera. These facilities were vital for passengers about to embark, or just arrived, on non-corridor excursion trains. The mail bags recall an age when passenger trains carried mail and parcels. The platforms are to the right, the sea front and Midland Hotel to the left. The station buildings now house a pub, a restaurant and a live entertainment and music venue known as 'The Platform.' *(Roger Hepworth)*

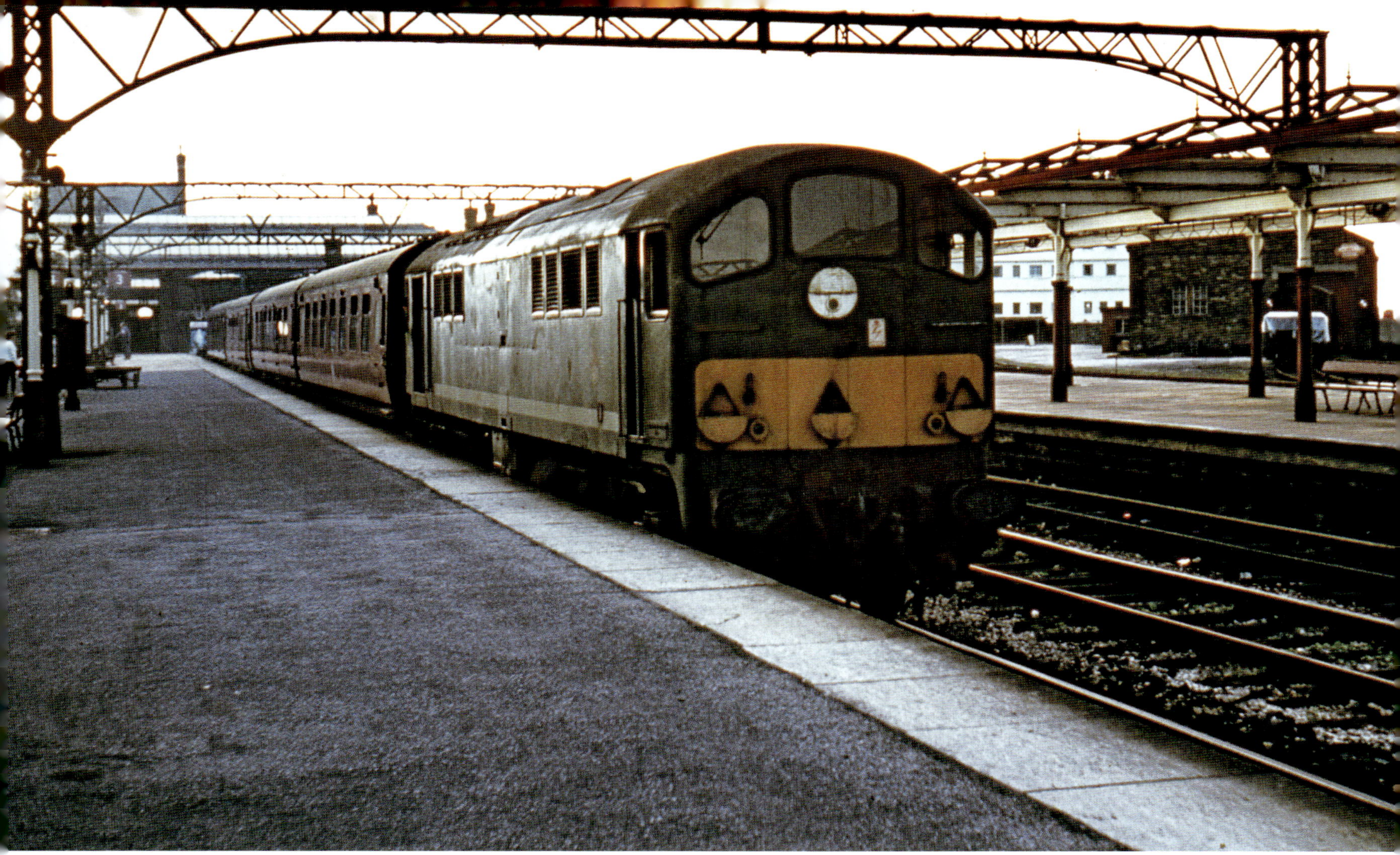

Metro-Vick Co-Bo diesel No. D5718 awaits departure with a passenger train from Morecambe Promenade in August 1966. The wires are already down, eight months after closure of the electrified system. Twenty Co-Bos were built in 1958/59 and were introduced on the Midland Main Line. However, teething troubles and repeated failures led to the whole class being taken out of service and modified by their manufacturers. Upon reinstatement in 1962, they were all allocated to at Barrow in Furness and became a familiar sight in the Morecambe area on passenger, parcels, freight and empty stock workings. Their unique wheel arrangement of a two-axled bogie at one end and a three-axled bogie at the other was to spread the weight. Although they had become more reliable in their latter days, they were regarded as non-standard and the last 12 examples were withdrawn in September 1968 - except for D5705 which spent several years with the BR Research Department before eventually being acquired for preservation. It is a long term restoration project on the East Lancashire Railway at Bury. *(Colour-Rail)*

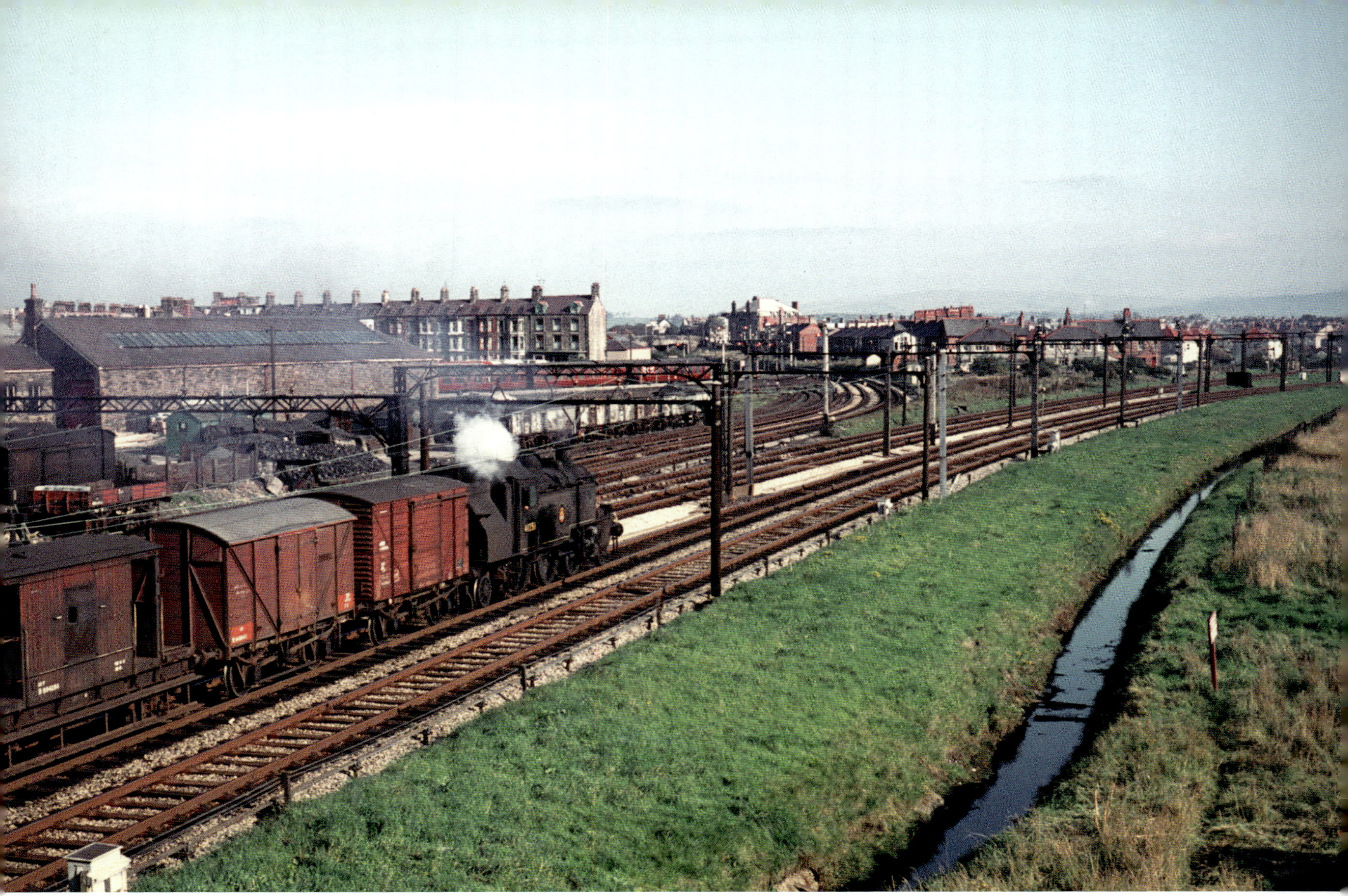

Ivatt 2 – 6 – 2T No. 41251 leaves Morecambe with a short fitted freight for Heysham in October 1965. The second electrified pair of tracks are for Lancaster Green Ayre. The line curving left is towards Bare Lane. The goods facilities and warehouse belong to Morecambe Euston Road Station which was still in use as carriage sidings following its closure in September 1962. Temporary storage of empty stock at the station had first begun after it was closed to all but summer traffic at the end of the 1958 season. A train of empty carriages is visible through the electrification gantry. *(D. J. Mitchell)*

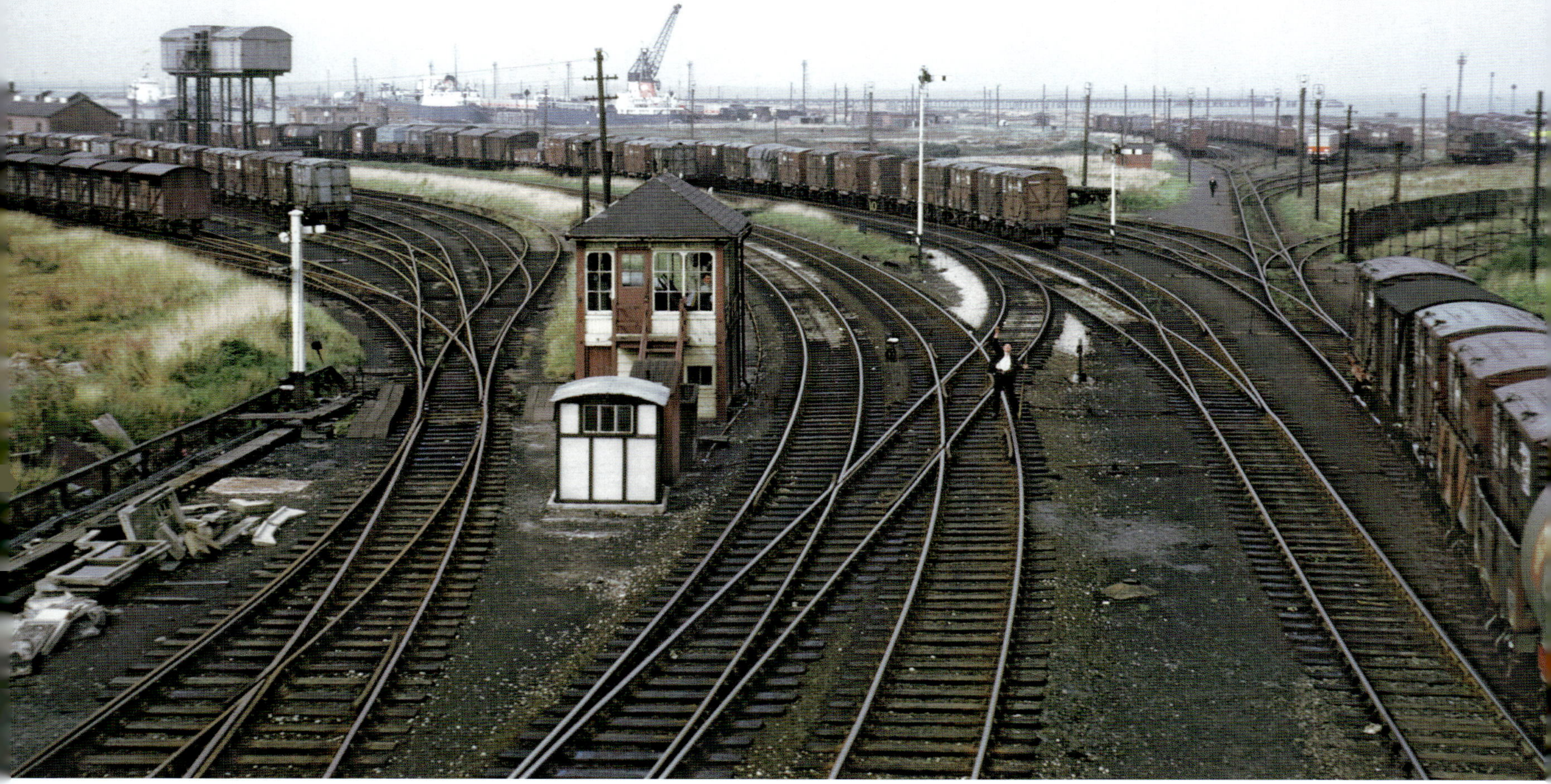

Heysham Harbour Junction looking towards the port in 1968. Immediately to the right of the signal box are the passenger lines curving towards the station on the South Quay. To the left of the box are the sidings which used to serve the cattle dock. Those straight ahead reach towards the North Quay. The layout was rationalised in 1970 when a new station and car ferry berth opened. A new flat roofed signal box replaced the two Midland boxes at the Junction and Station but railway activity soon declined and, today, the whole area is covered by an enormous lorry park. The photo on page 107 shows the scene part way through that transition. *(Alan Bullimore, courtesy Andrew Gardiner)*

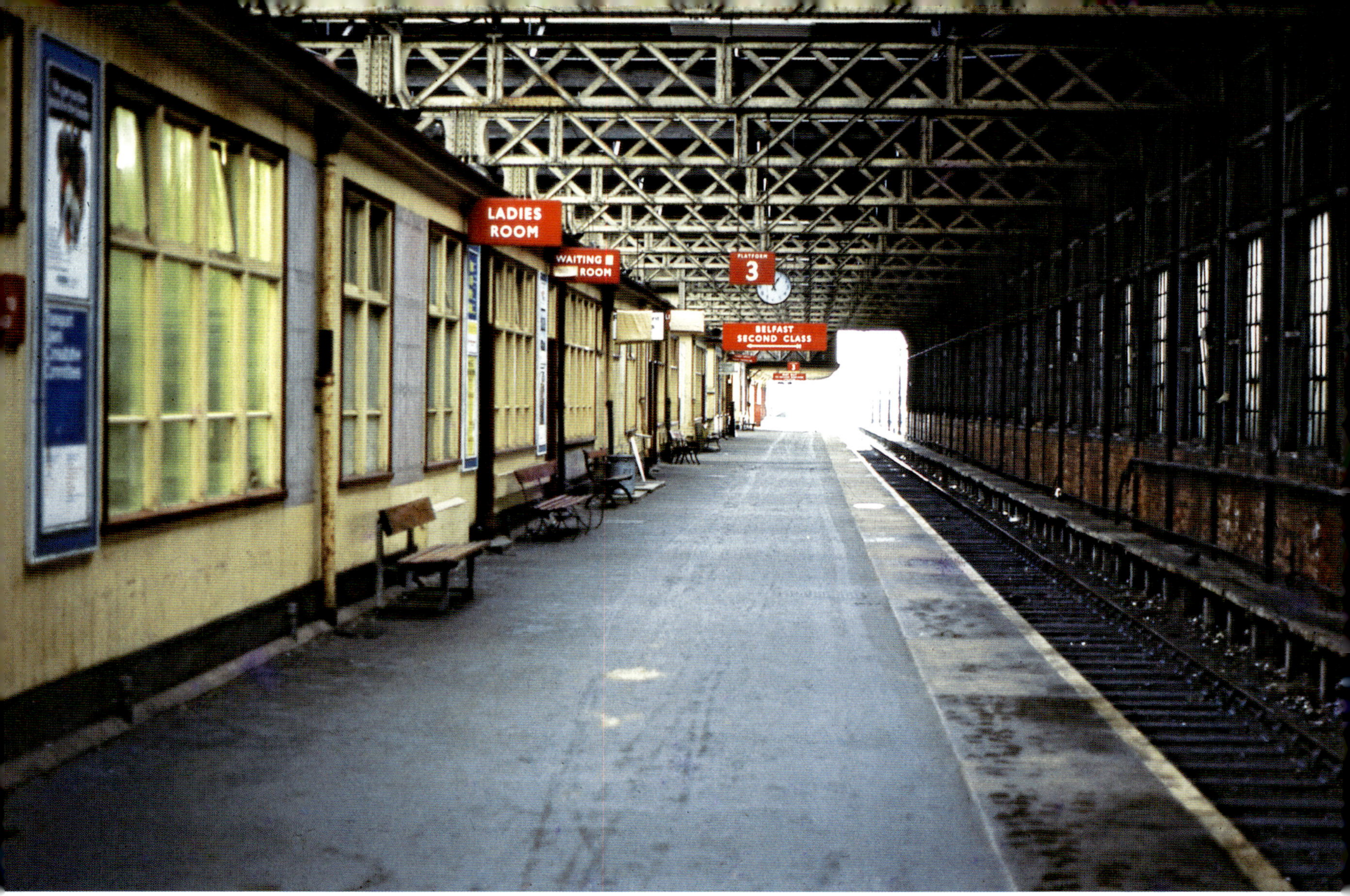

Heysham was an island platform under an overall roof which gave way to canopies at the Morecambe end. The station was separated from the quayside by transit sheds and dock lines. These were traversed by two footbridges, one for First and one for Second Class passengers heading for Belfast. The platform buildings included waiting and refreshment facilities. This view was taken looking along the length of Platform 3 towards Morecambe in 1969. *(Peter Sunderland)*

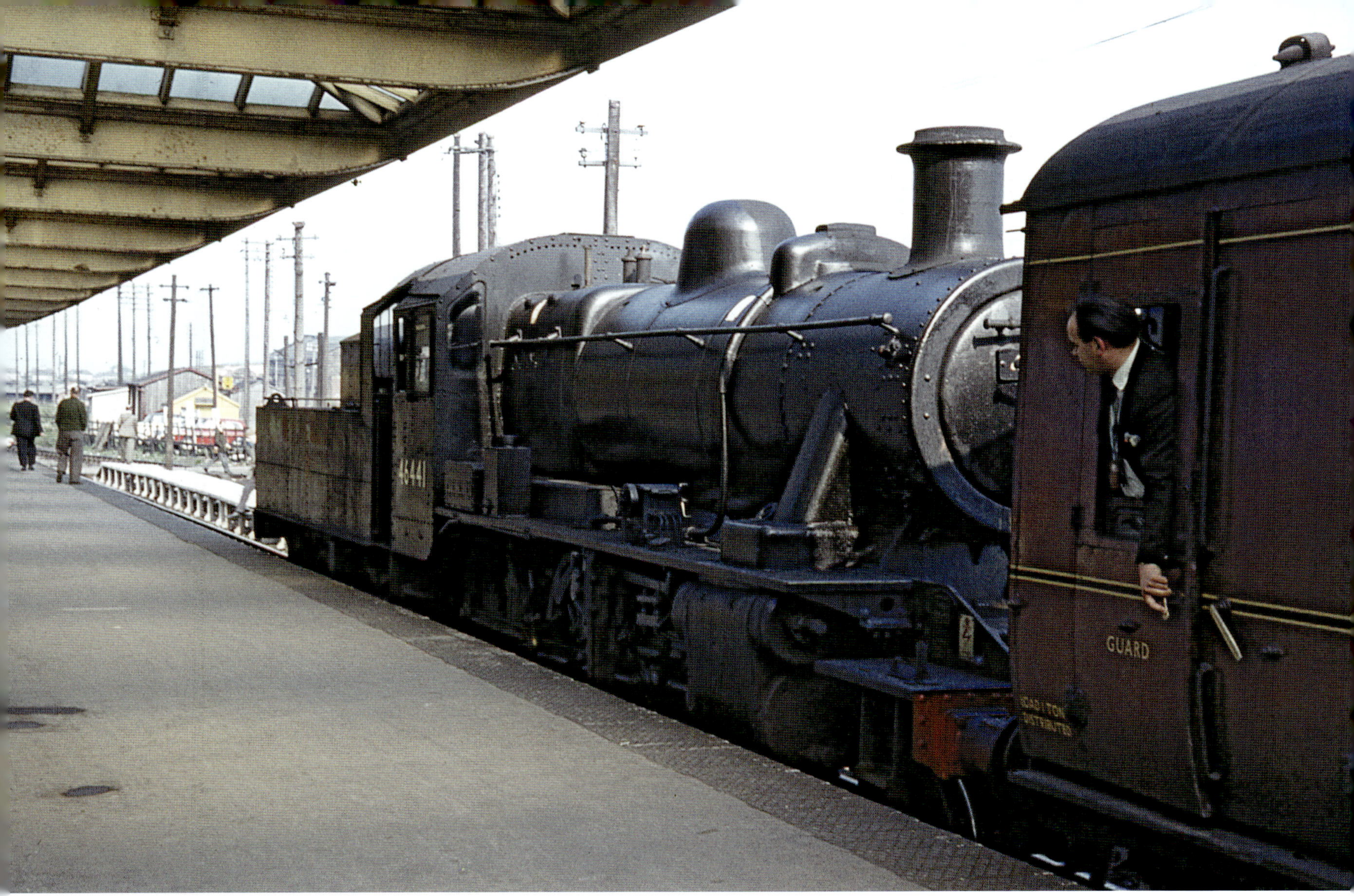

Southport shed's Ivatt 'Mogul' No. 46441 is seen at the canopied end of Platform 3 waiting to depart for Morecambe with the 'Ribble-Lune' railtour on 23 May 1964. Built in 1950, 46441 ended its career as a Carnforth loco and was bought privately for preservation upon withdrawal in 1967. It has not steamed since 2002 but was moved in 2018 to the Lakeside & Haverthwaite Railway where it is being overhauled. A total of 128 Ivatt Class 2s were built between 1946 and 1953 and the last were withdrawn in 1967. Seven have been preserved. *(Martin Bairstow collection)*

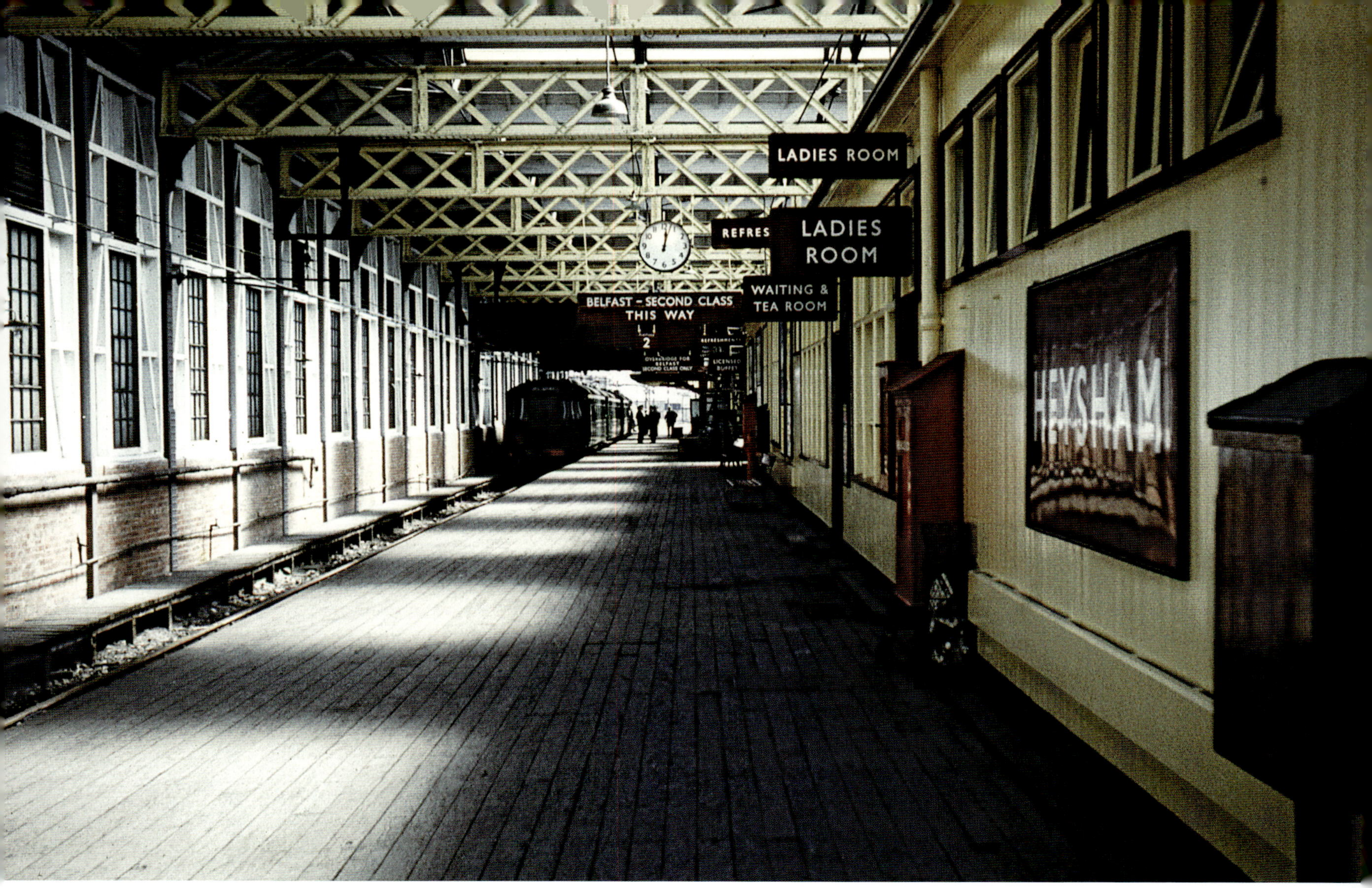

The view along Platform 2 at Heysham in 1960 with an EMU at the Morecambe end. Second Class passengers for Belfast were invited to proceed along the platform to a point near the electric train where they would ascend steps up to the footbridge. First Class patrons were offered a similar opportunity in the opposite direction (behind the camera). The Midland had tried to encourage local tourist traffic by opening the Heysham Tower Hotel in 1896. Forty years later, the LMS tried a different approach with no fewer than 36 camping coaches at Heysham. Both enterprises were killed off by their respective world wars. *(Peter Sunderland)*

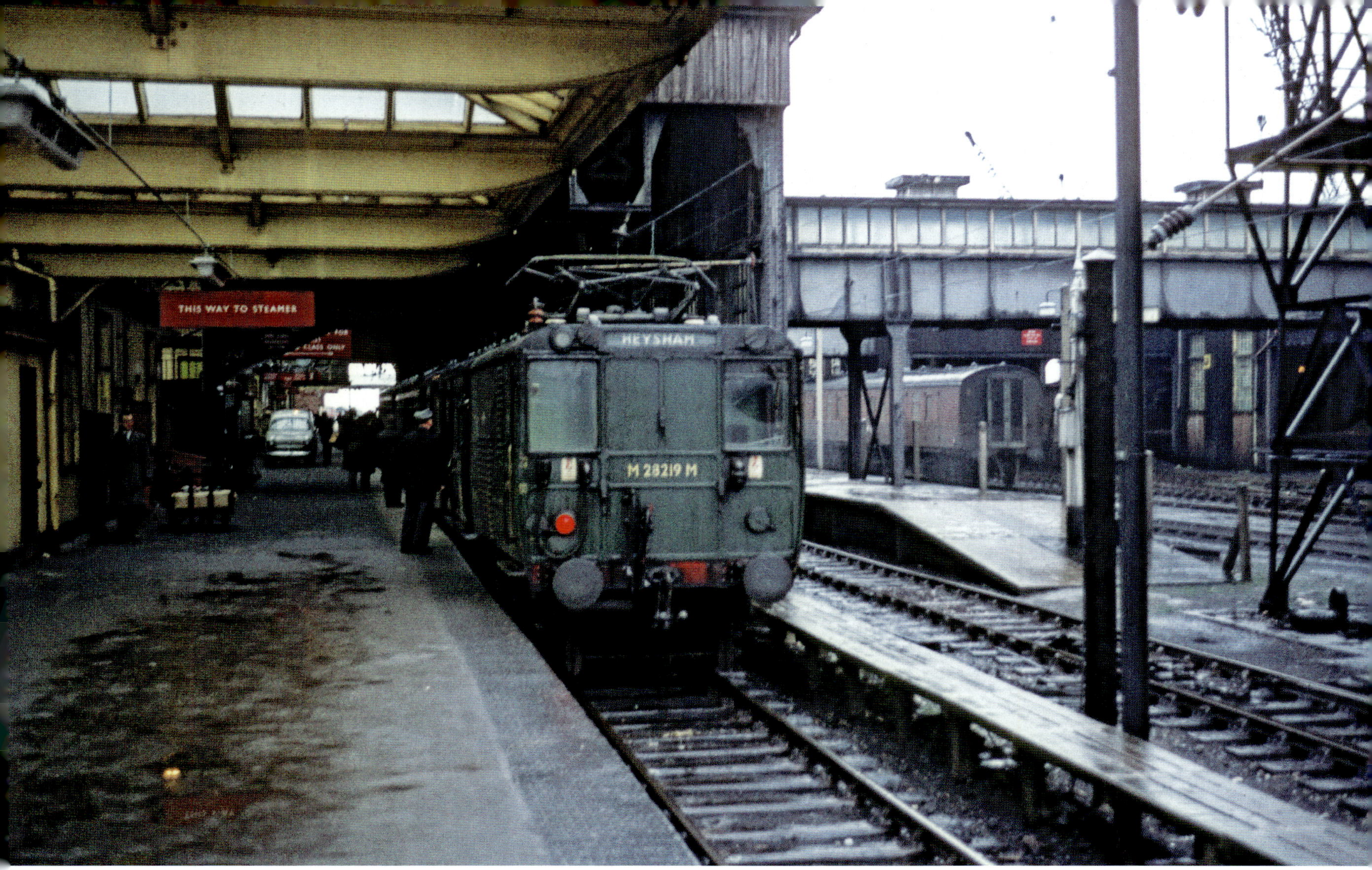

Driving car No. 28219 has arrived from Morecambe in November 1965 at the position on Platform 2 where the overall roof gave way to canopies. The more exposed Platform 1 is on the right. This, the goods lines and the transit sheds were crossed by the two footbridges. Local passengers could exit by a level crossing at the Morecambe end of the island platform but their numbers would be few as the station was some way beyond Heysham village. The electric trains were less frequent at Heysham than between Morecambe and Lancaster. During their time operating the system, the AM1s were the oldest complete train sets on the entire BR network. Each received an annual overhaul at the Meols Cop depot at Southport with day to day maintenance being carried out by a small team of engineers based at Morecambe. *(D. J. Mitchell)*

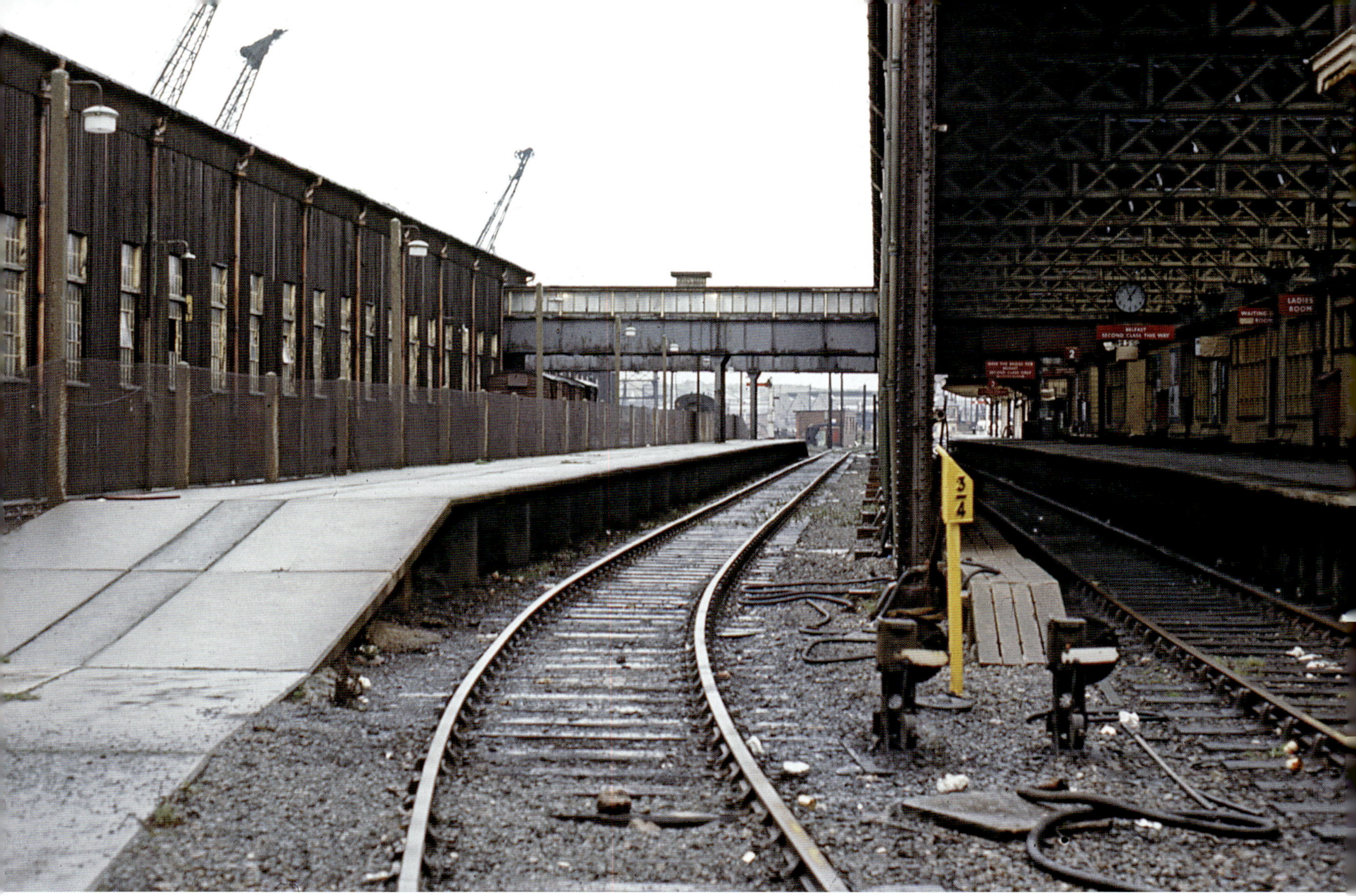

The view towards Morecambe along Heysham station's exposed Platform 1, with Platform 2 the inner face of the island under the roof. Milepost 266¾ gives the distance from London St. Pancras. When the Midland Railway was re-measured in 1907, lines with facing junctions were counted by the shortest route from St. Pancras. Those with trailing junctions were measured from a zero post at the junction. The 1967 closures left Heysham in the latter category. BR re-measured the line with new mileposts from zero just outside Morecambe to 4 at the 1970 Heysham Station. *(Peter Sunderland)*

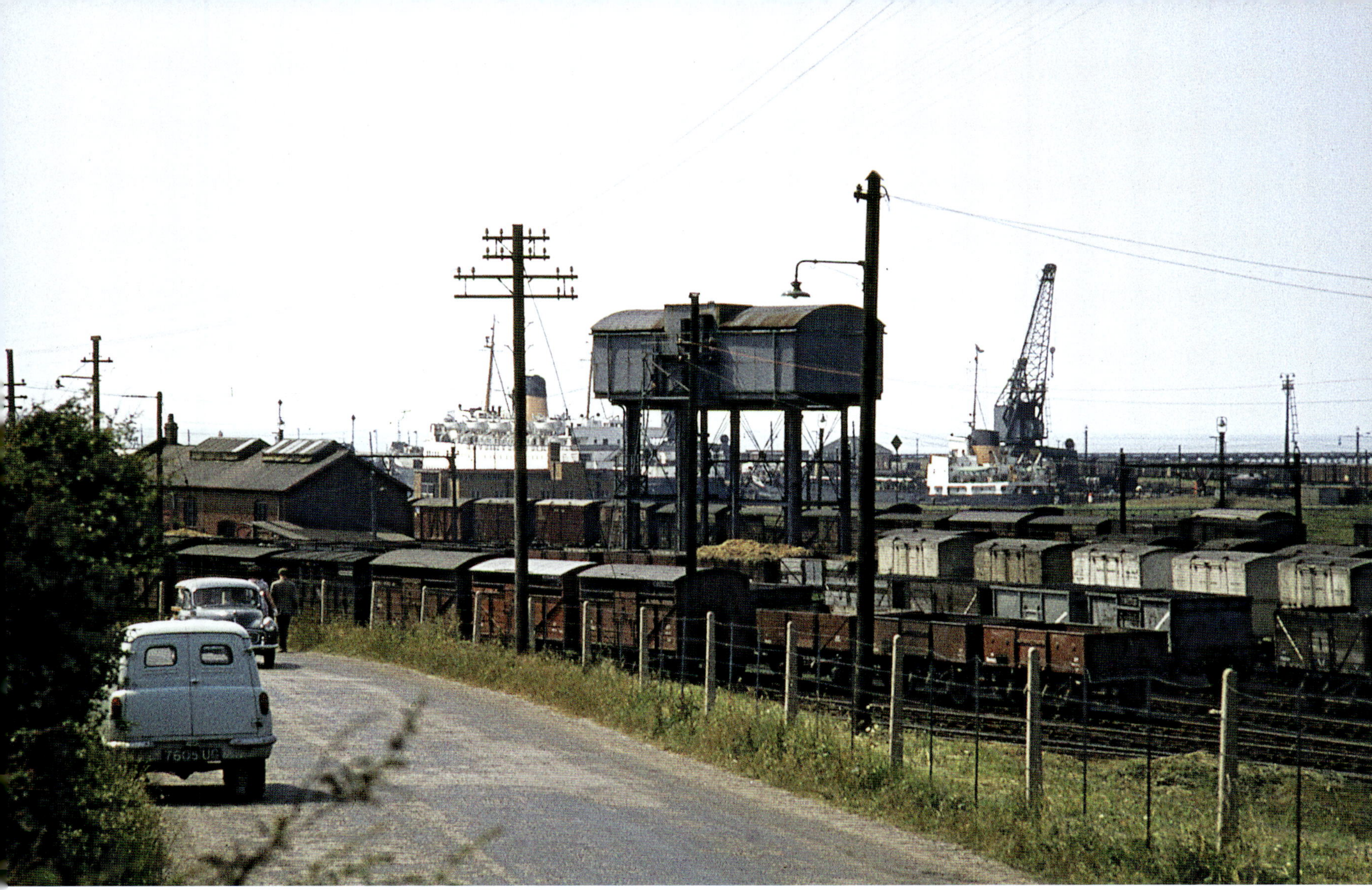

Cattle trucks feature prominently among a variety of goods wagons at Heysham in 1962. Up to that time, most beef exports from Ireland were 'on the hoof.' Facilities at Heysham included a subway direct from the South Quay to the cattle dock and grazing paddocks for animals recovering from the sea journey whilst awaiting their onward rail connections. But the Irish food processing industry was developing rapidly and the export of live animals went into sharp decline. The Burns & Laird steamer from Londonderry to Heysham finished in 1963 and the BR vessels soon gave up bringing cattle from Belfast. *(Peter Sunderland)*

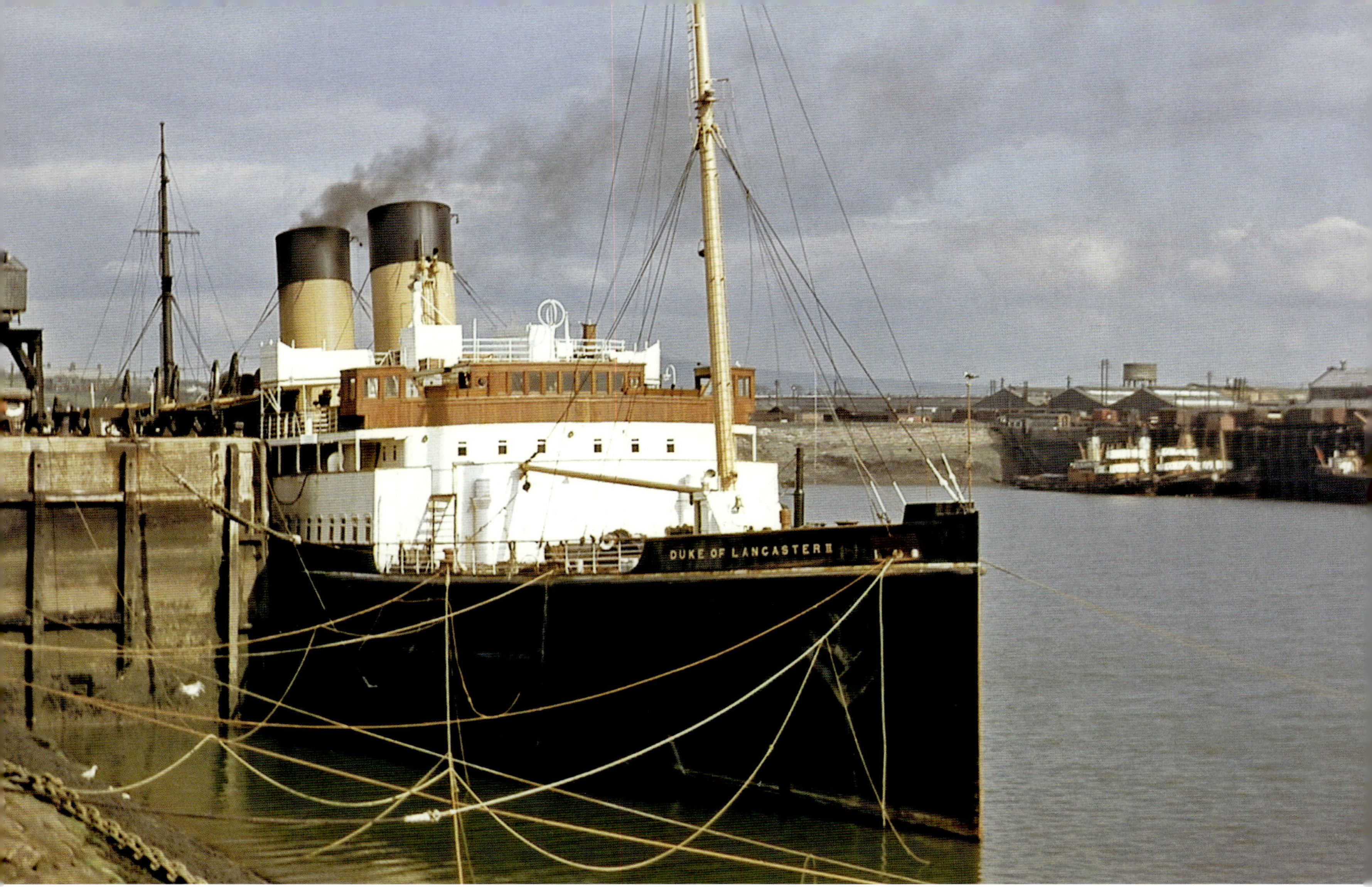

The 1928 *Duke of Lancaster* at Heysham towards the end of its life in 1956. The LMS had rationalised its Belfast routes in 1928, ending sailings from Fleetwood and increasing capacity via Heysham. Three new turbine steamers were built by Wm. Denny of Dumbarton. As a concession to Fleetwood, they were named in the style of the former London & North Western and Lancashire & Yorkshire Railways joint fleet. The 1904 Midland vessels had been *Antrim, Donegal* and *Londonderry*. Only *Londonderry* was a turbine steamer. The other two were conventional steamships as the Midland was being cautious with the new technology. *(Peter Sunderland)*

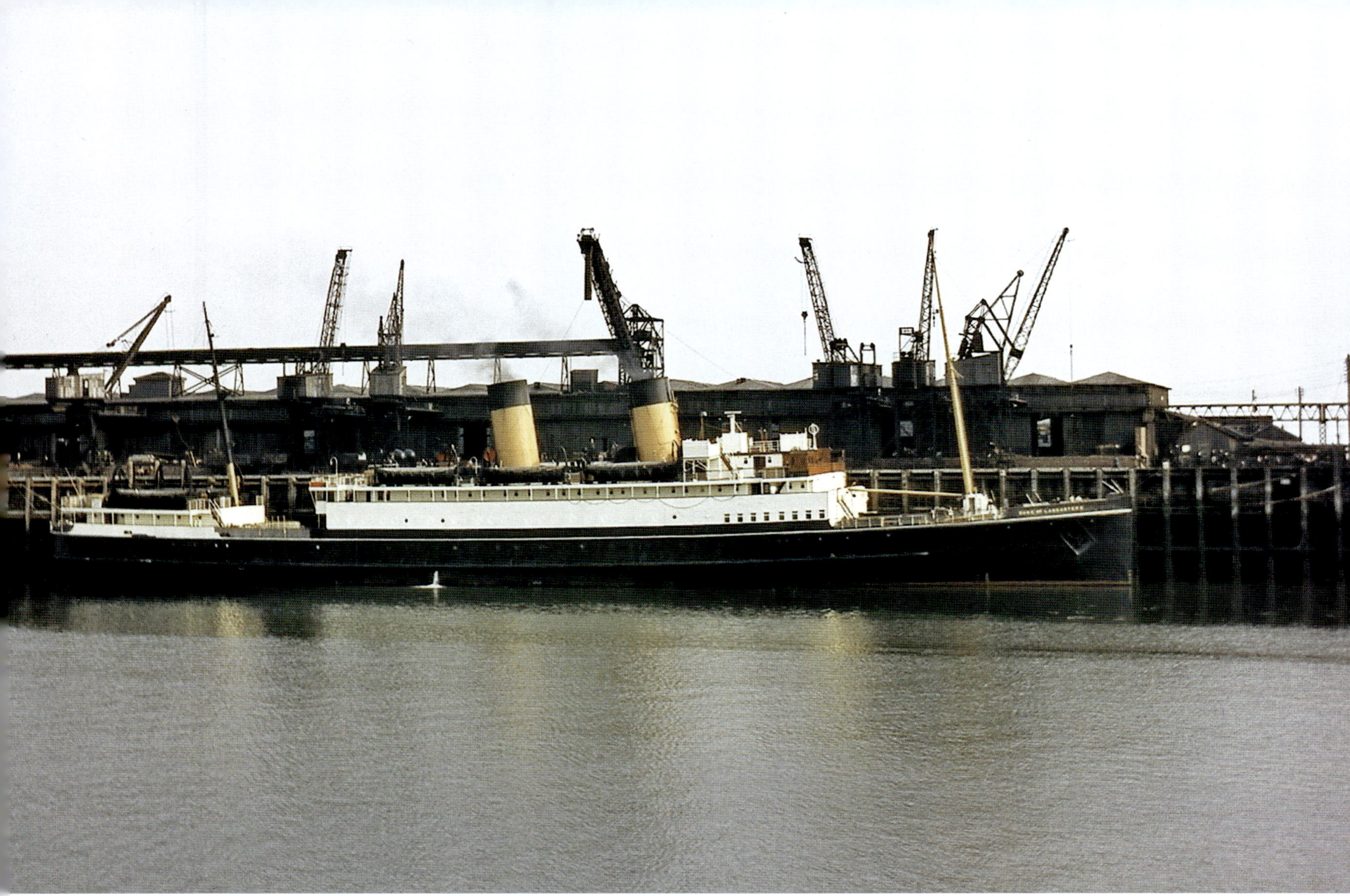

The old *Duke of Lancaster* berthed alongside Heysham Station in 1956. Under the 1928 changes, Heysham had gained direct 'boat trains' from London Euston and Manchester Victoria which had to reverse at Morecambe Promenade. In 1956, the three 'Dukes' were replaced by larger vessels with the same names. The turbine era had begun for passenger ships in 1901 with *King Edward* operating between Greenock and Campbeltown. The principle of forcing high pressure steam through turbines to drive the propellers quickly found favour on longer routes. *(Peter Sunderland)*

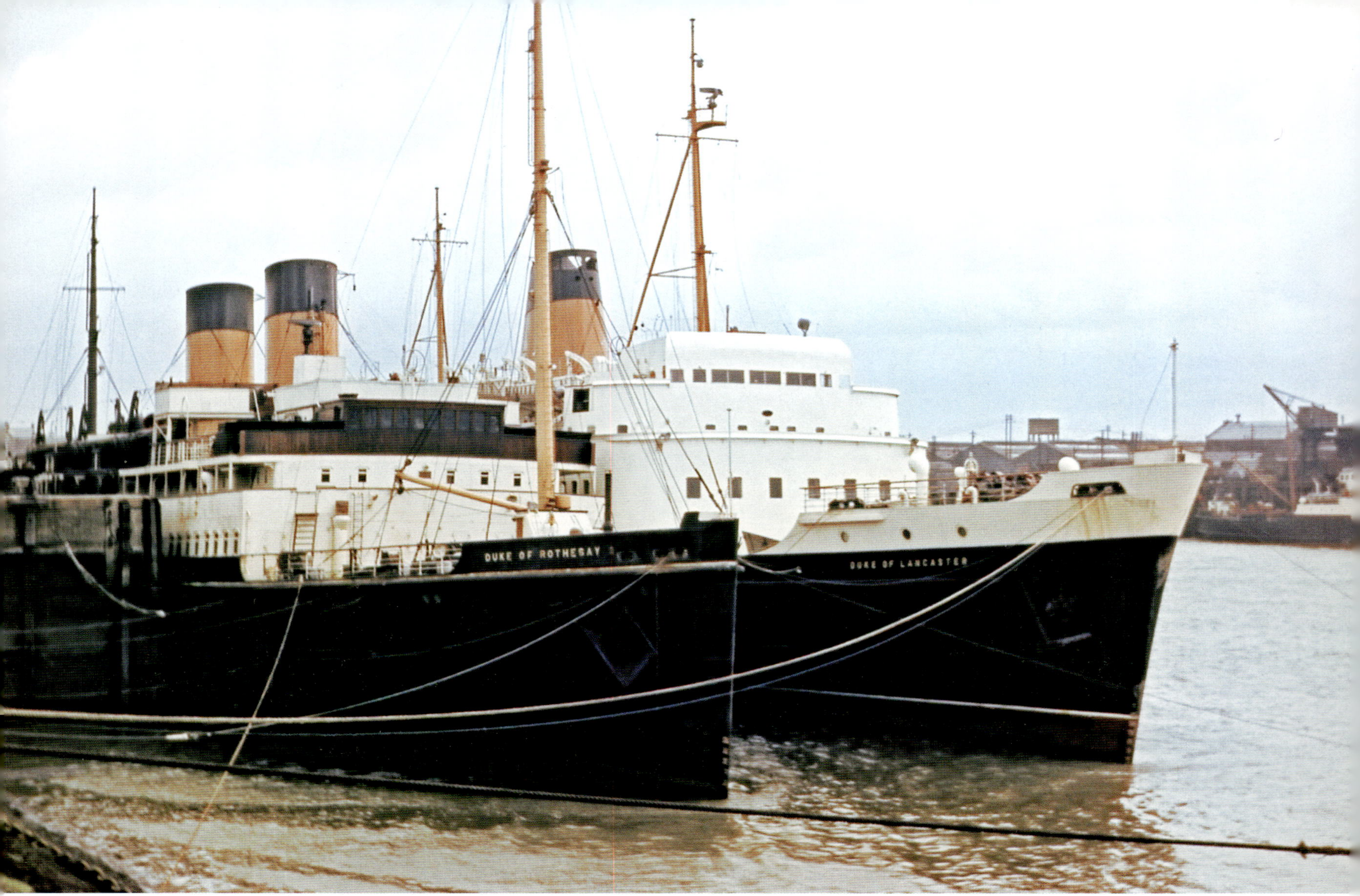

The new *Duke of Lancaster* is moored alongside the old *Duke of Rothesay* on the North Quay in 1956. Both are turbine steamers. BR remained loyal to this technology for a further generation. By contrast, the Belfast Steamship Company had been using diesels on its main route since 1929. Each morning, the overnight turbine steamer from Heysham would tie up at Belfast Donegall Quay between the Belfast Company's motor vessel from Liverpool and Burns & Laird's diesel from Glasgow. *(Peter Sunderland)*

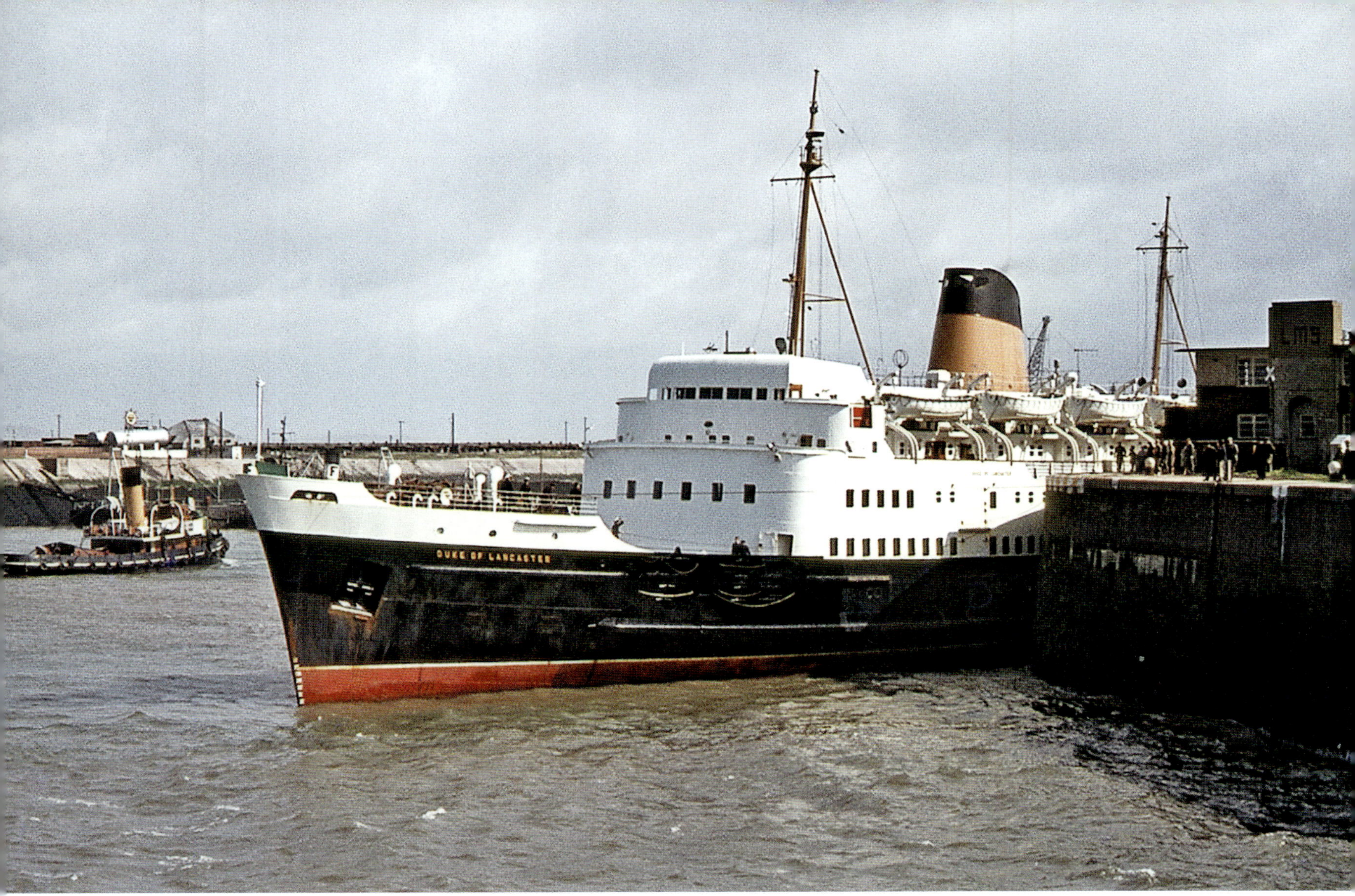

Duke of Lancaster is seen here requiring tug assistance to change berths in 1962. The ships carried cargo as well as passengers and sometimes needed to cross over to the North Quay during their day long layover in Heysham. The tug *Ramsden* had been built for the LMS in 1934. It was named after one of the Barrow docks, which was itself named after the General Manager of the Furness Railway. The service normally required only two ships. The third covered for winter overhaul and relief sailings at busy times but was also available for cruises. These took *Duke of Lancaster* to Scotland and Spain. *(Peter Sunderland)*

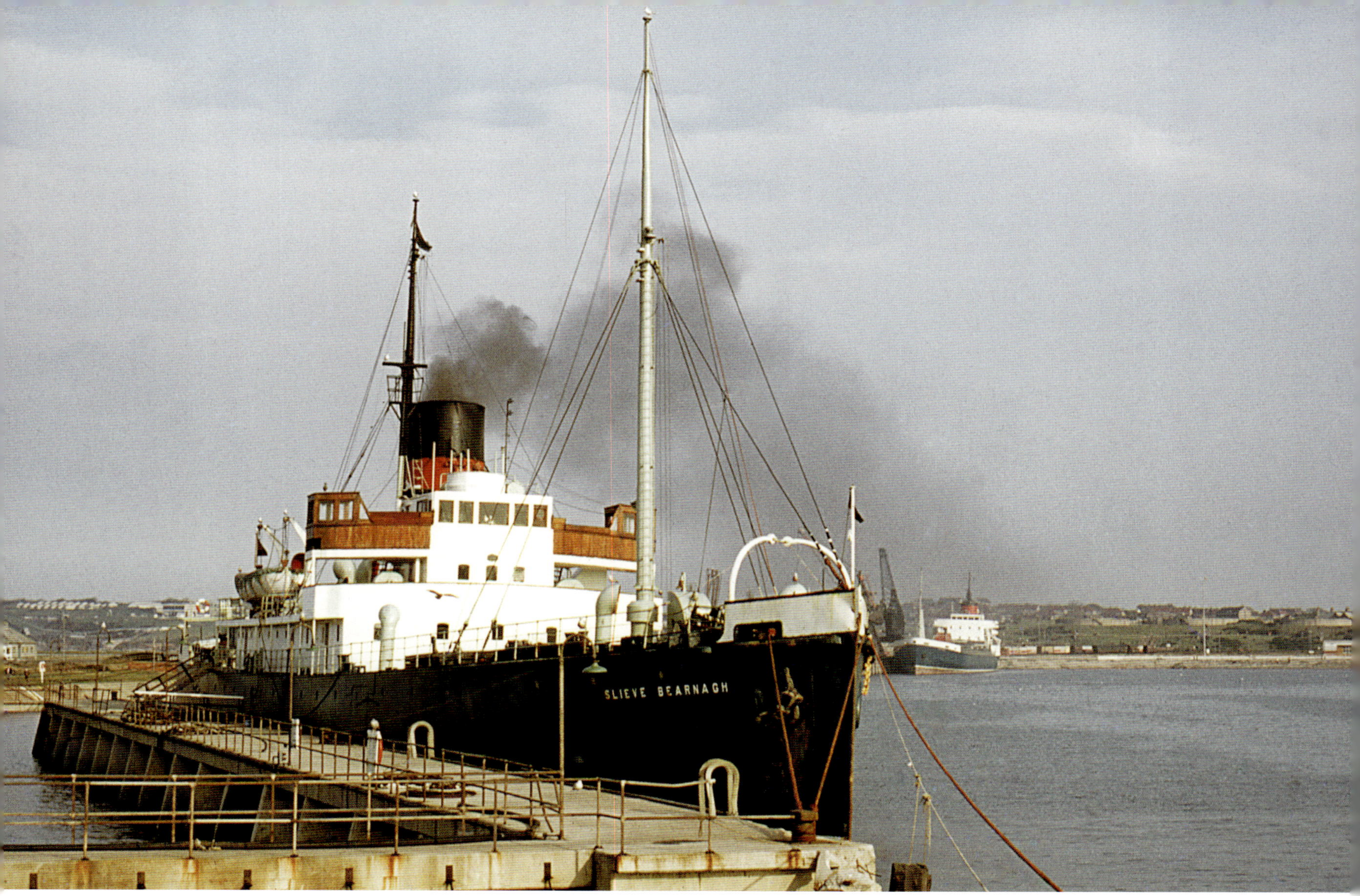

Slieve Bearnagh moored on the North Quay in October 1971 just before withdrawal. The vessel was a turbine steamer built in 1936 to carry cattle and cargo between Belfast and Heysham. In later years, it carried some cars, with their owners sailing on the passenger steamers before these became car ferries. *Slieve Bearnagh* was registered in Lancaster but named in a Holyhead series. It was converted from coal to oil firing in 1961. Slieve Bearnagh is a 2,425 summit in the Mourne Mountains of County Down. *(Peter Sunderland)*

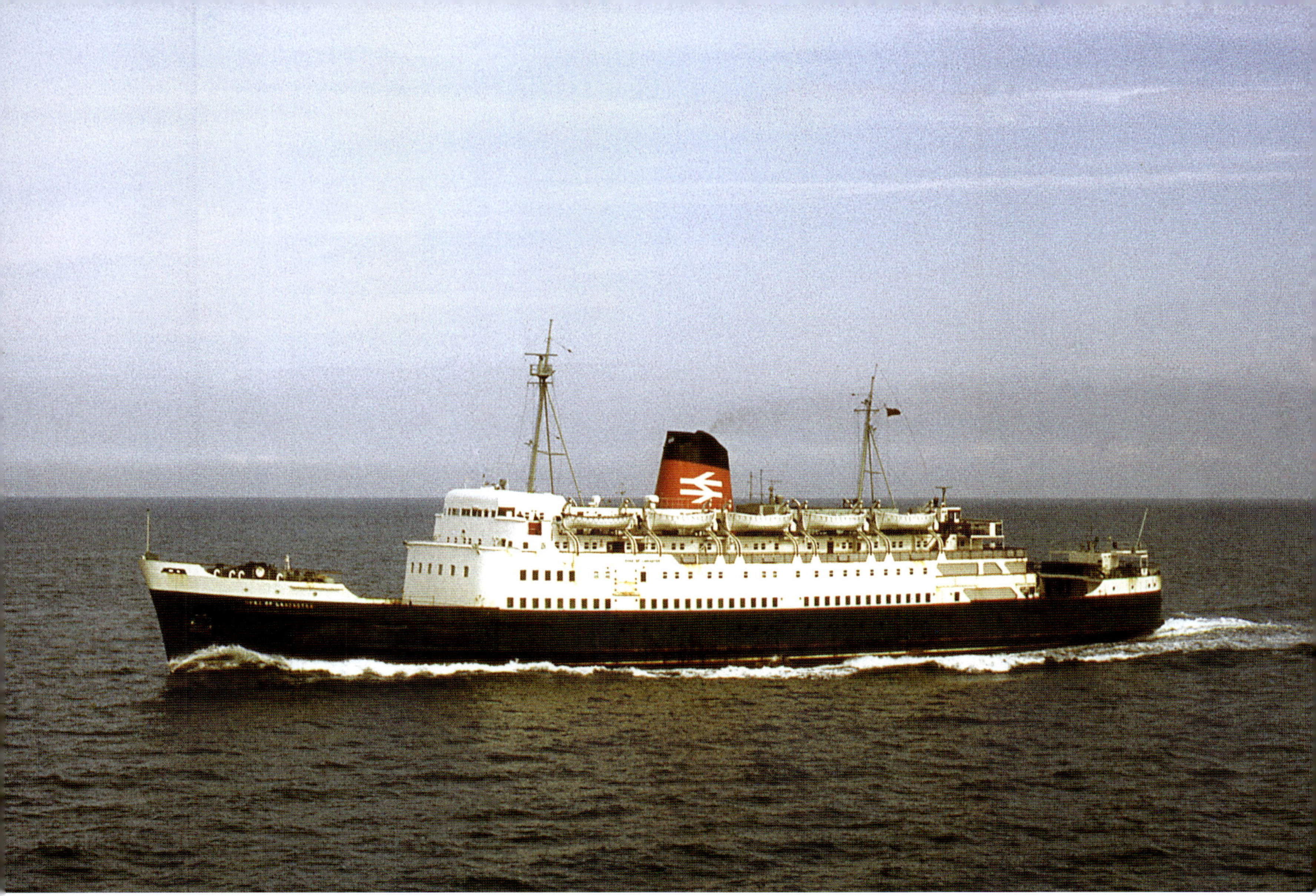

Viewed from the deck of the inbound *Duke of Argyll* near the north tip of the Isle of Man, *Duke of Lancaster* is half way through its voyage to Belfast in September 1967. Heysham to Belfast was essentially an overnight service with the ships usually spending all day in port. Day time crossings were limited to peak summer dates. The BR double arrow was always 'wrong way round' on the port side. *(Peter Sunderland)*

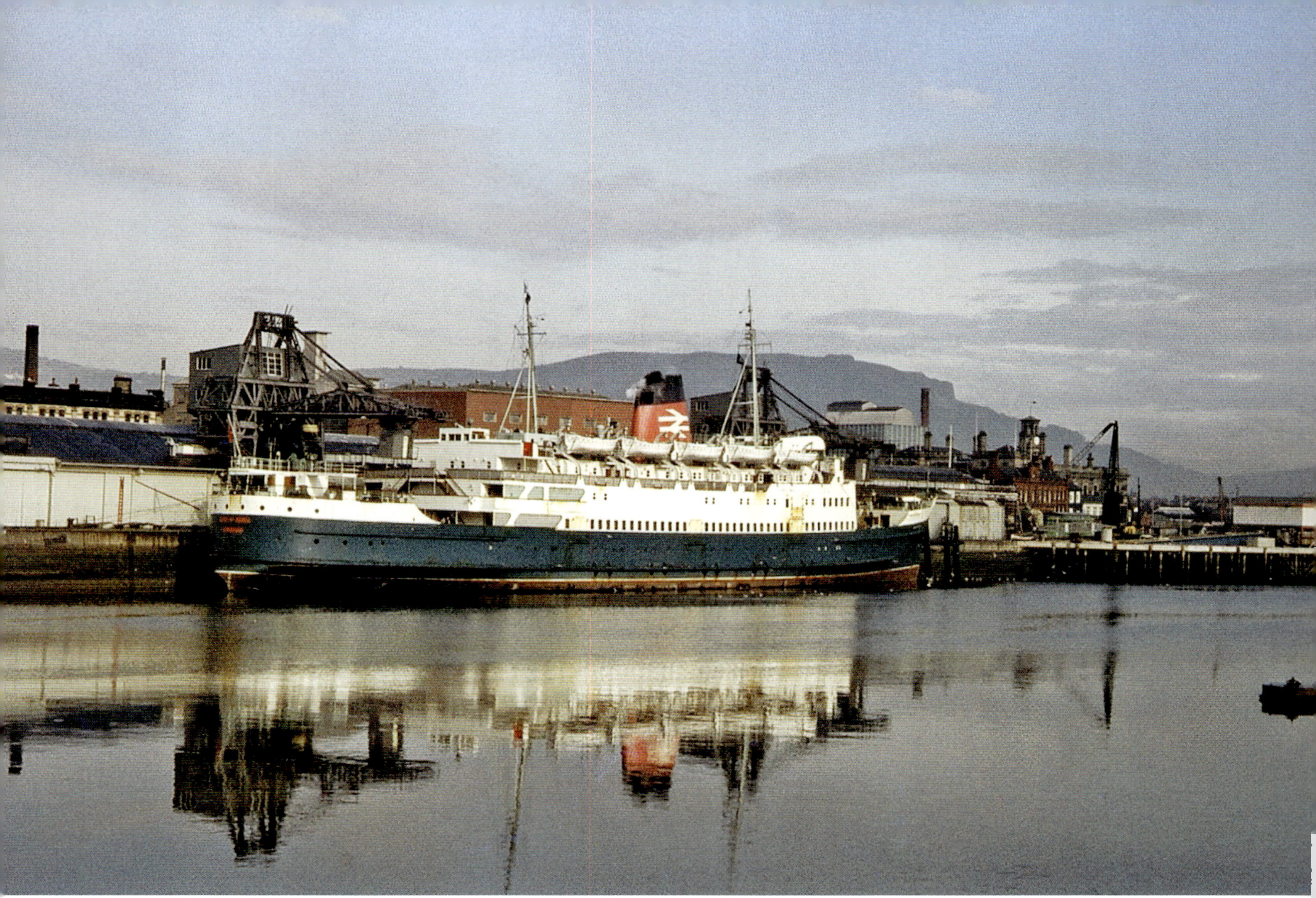

Duke of Argyll is berthed at Belfast Donegall Quay in September 1967 facing out to sea. It will have arrived stern first having turned in the Lough before entering the channel. The new blue and white livery had started to appear during 1964 and was to last until privatisation twenty years later. The double arrow is the normal way round on the starboard side. *(Peter Sunderland)*

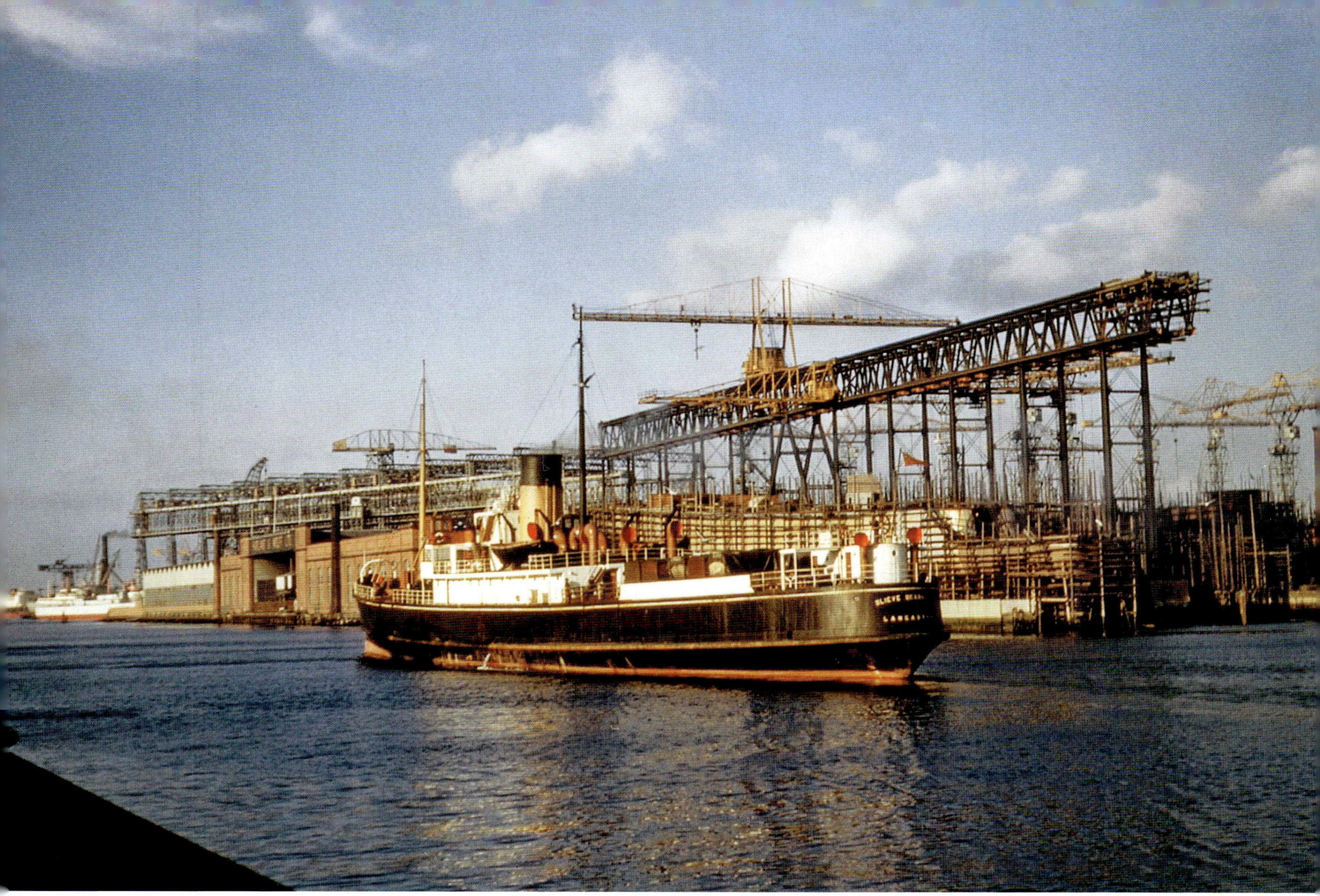

Slieve Bearnagh passing the birthplace of some of its contemporaries at Harland & Wolff as it steams stern first towards Belfast Donegall Quay. The 1956 *Duke of Lancaster* and *Duke of Argyll* both came from Harland & Wolff. *Duke of Rothesay*, like *Slieve Bearnagh*, was built by Wm. Denny of Dumbarton who had also built the three 1928 'Dukes.' *(Peter Sunderland)*

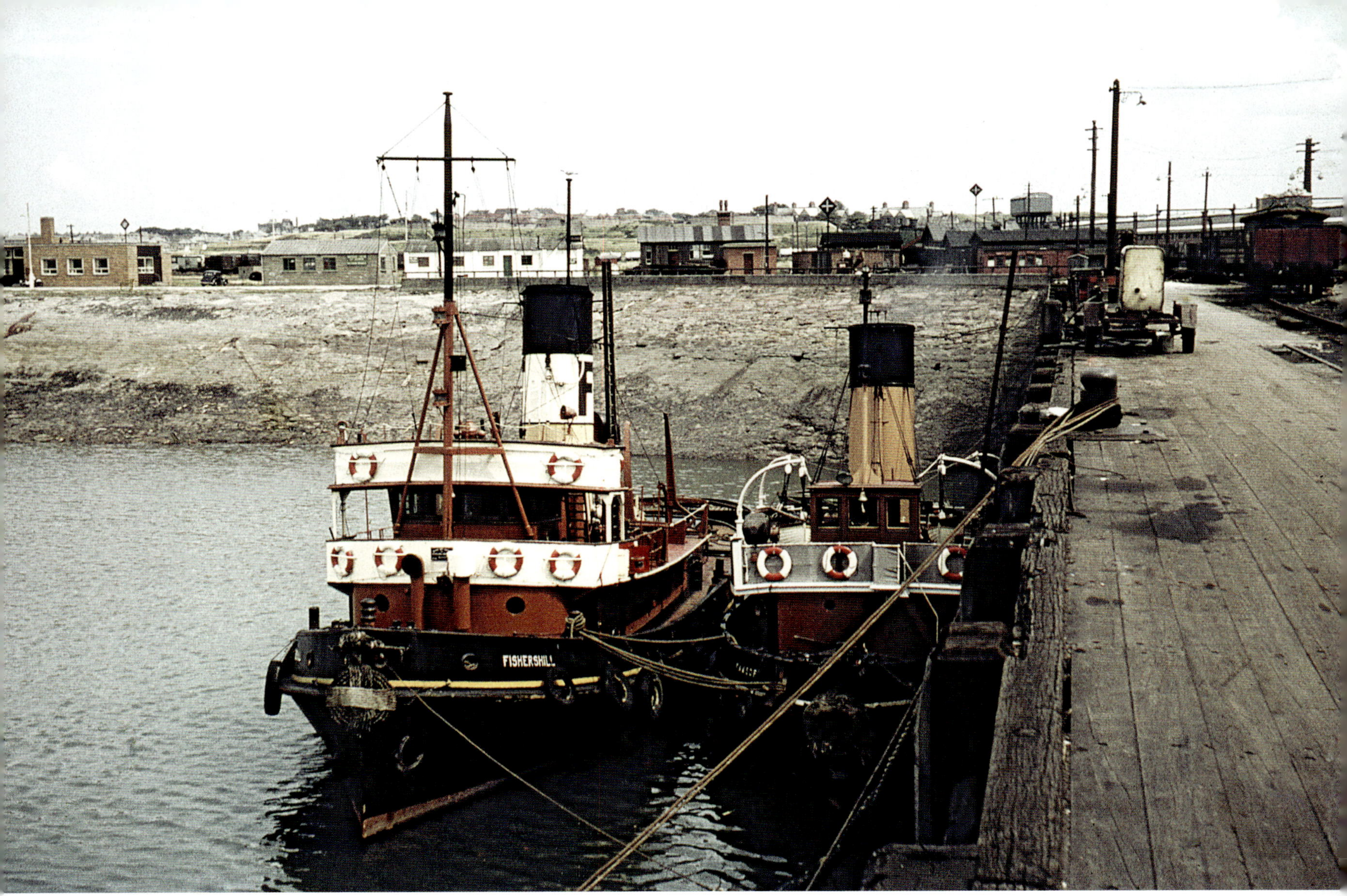

The BR tug *Ramsden* moored alongside *Fishershill* in 1960 at what would become the car ferry berth ten years later. *Fishershill* was built in 1946 as *Empire Hilda* for the Ministry of War Transport but sold in 1949 to James Fisher & Sons. This Barrow-based firm had engaged in sea transport since the days of sail and their ships were usually named after rivers. They used the port of Heysham both on Fisher business and sometimes chartering vessels to BR. *Solway Fisher* appeared in BR livery on the Belfast cargo service in the late 1970s. *(Peter Sunderland)*

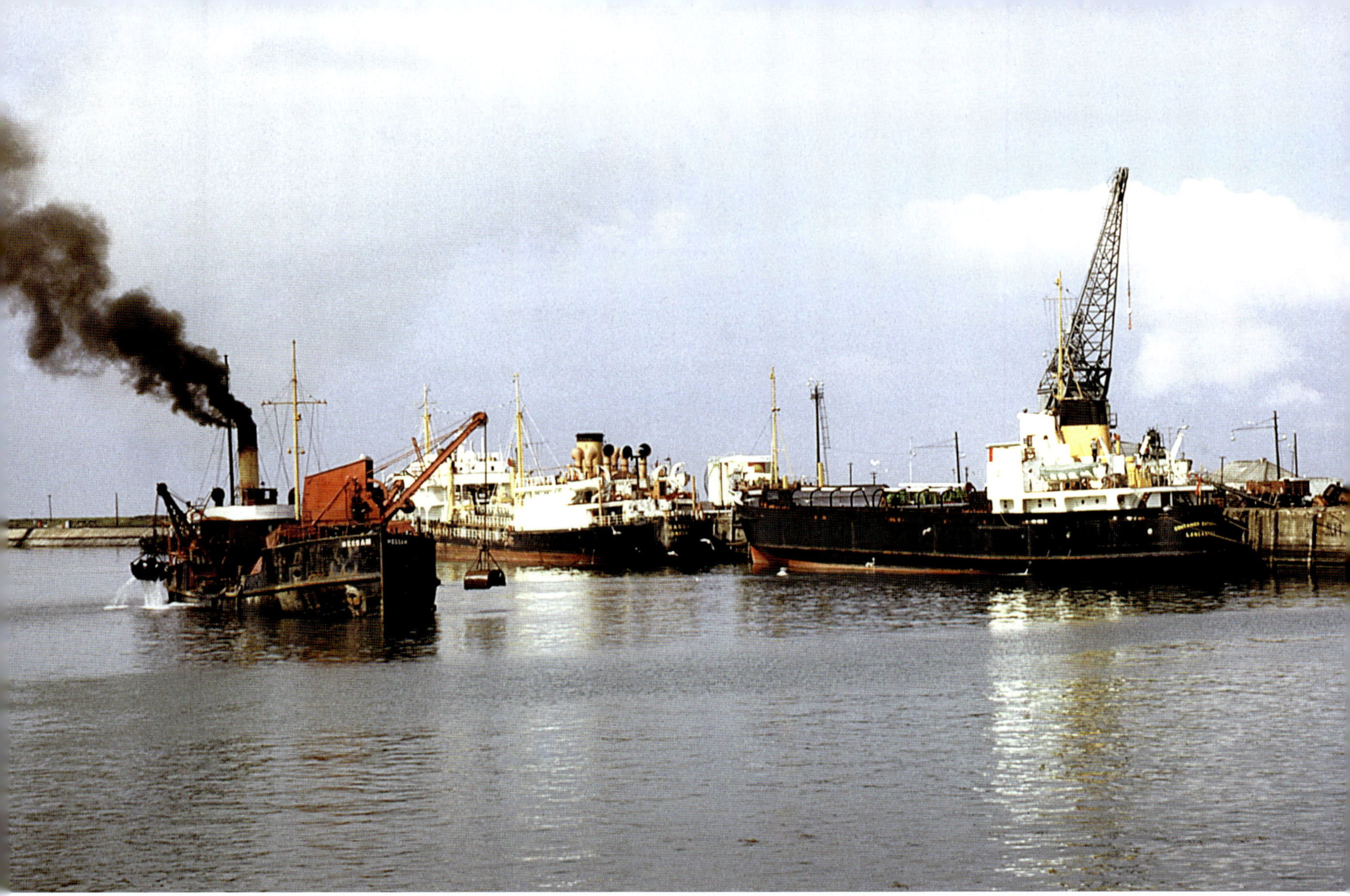

The harbour at Heysham needed continual dredging. Dating from 1908, the Midland Railway's dredger *Hassam* was still at work in September 1963. On the right, beneath the tall crane, is *Container Enterprise*. This and *Container Venturer* were built in 1958 to work between Heysham and Belfast carrying the type of container which was then gaining limited use on BR. Both vessels were withdrawn in 1978 when the route became roll on – roll off. *(Peter Sunderland)*

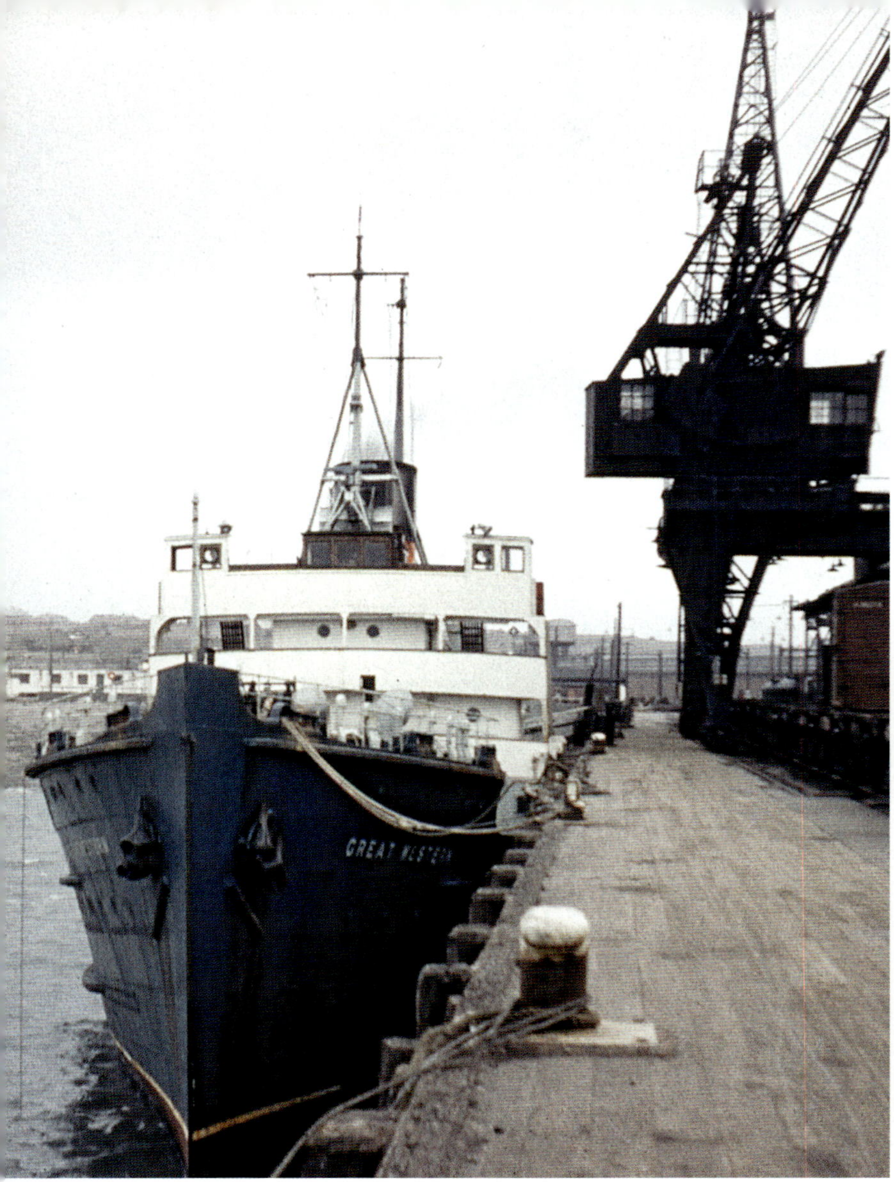

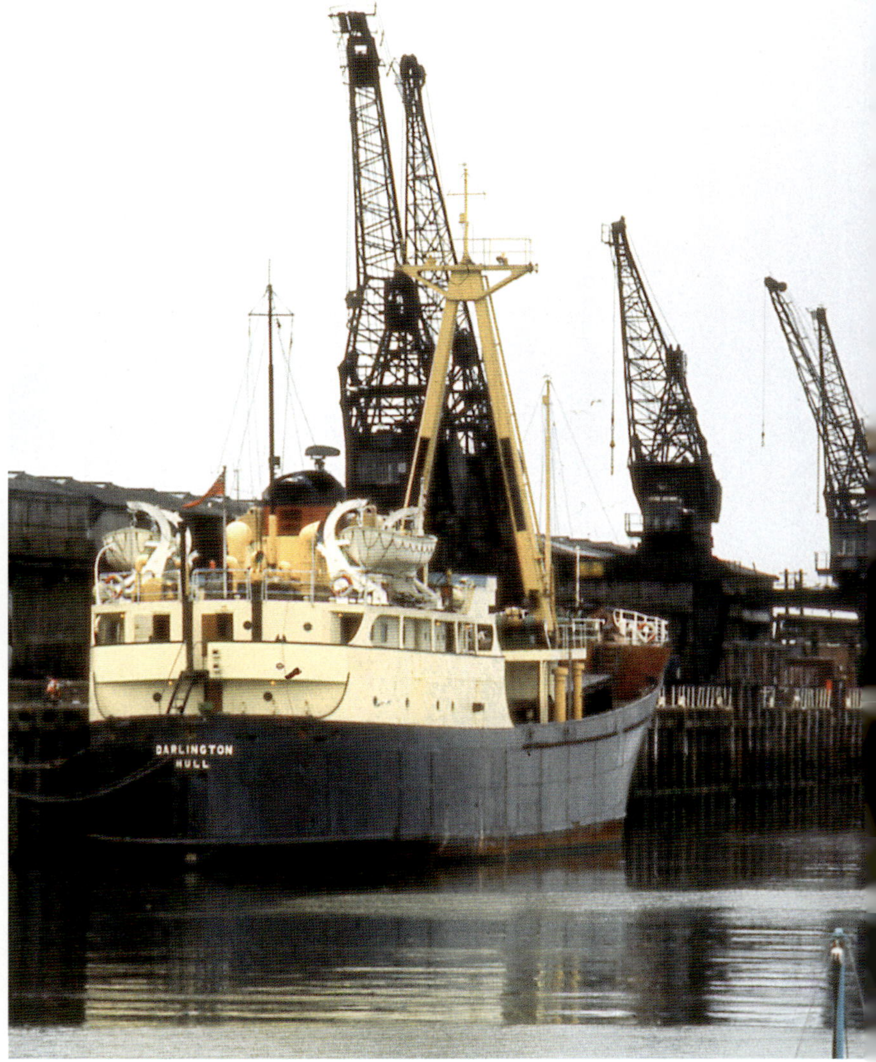

Ships were sometimes brought in from other BR ports to support the Belfast cargo service. *Great Western*, seen at Heysham in April 1967, was a coal-fired steam ship built in 1934 for Rosslare to Waterford. It ceased carrying passengers in 1959 but continued on that route until 1966. It then did some relief work until withdrawn for scrap later in 1967. *Darlington* was a motor vessel built in 1958 for Continental services from Hull. It is seen at Heysham in July 1968 in the livery of Associated Humber Lines, the body set up in 1935 to manage LMS and LNER shipping interests at Goole, Hull and Grimsby. *(Peter Sunderland)*

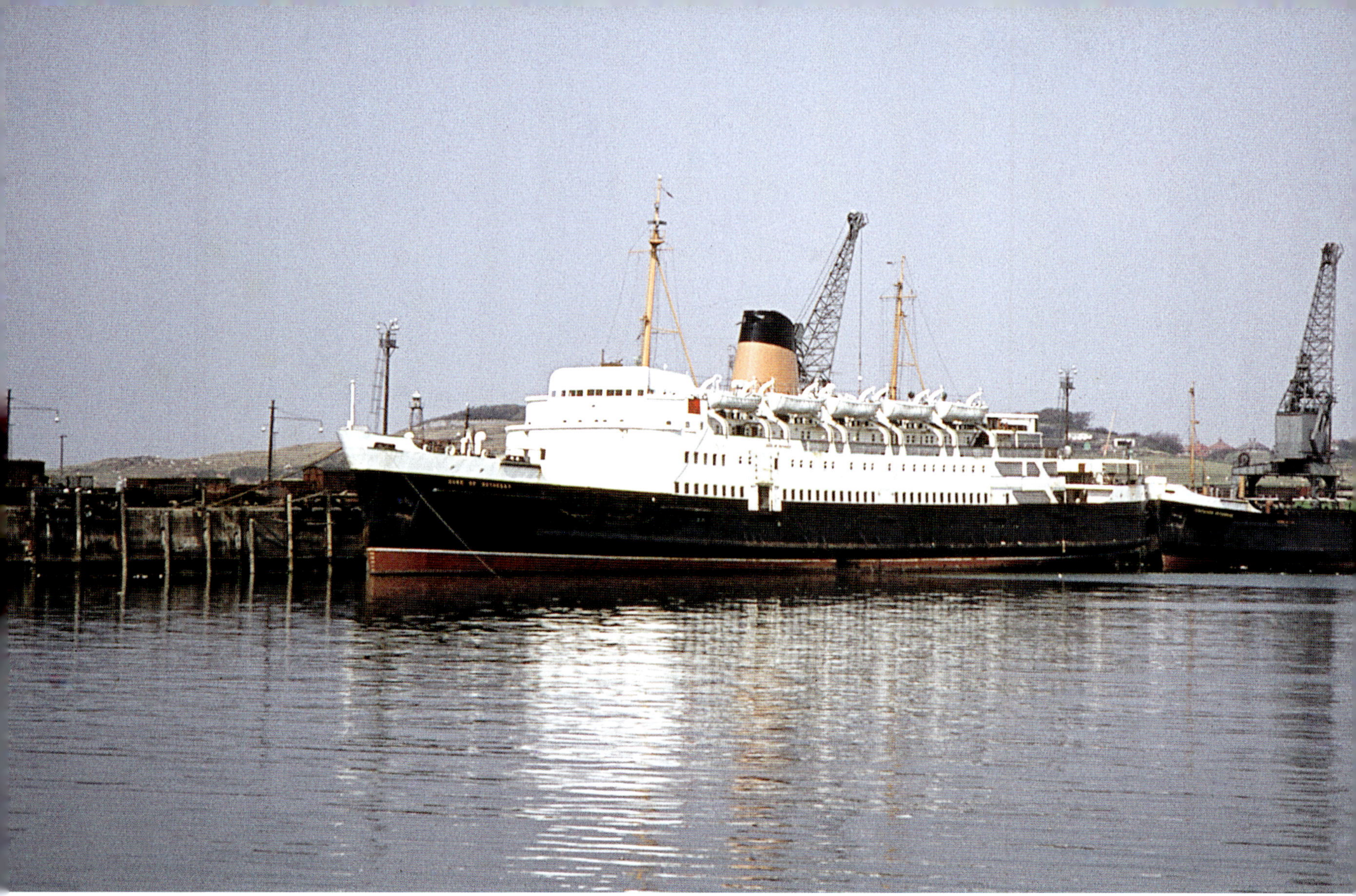

Duke of Rothesay at Heysham in 1966. The following year it was taken to Cammell Laird for conversion into a car ferry for the Fishguard to Rosslare route. The main deck was gutted to make space for the cars, taking away most of the overnight cabins. It served at Fishguard until 1971 and was then a relief vessel until sale for scrap in 1975. The remaining two 'Dukes' continued at Heysham, with occasional relief brought in from elsewhere, until the decision was made to convert the route to car ferry operation. *(Peter Sunderland)*

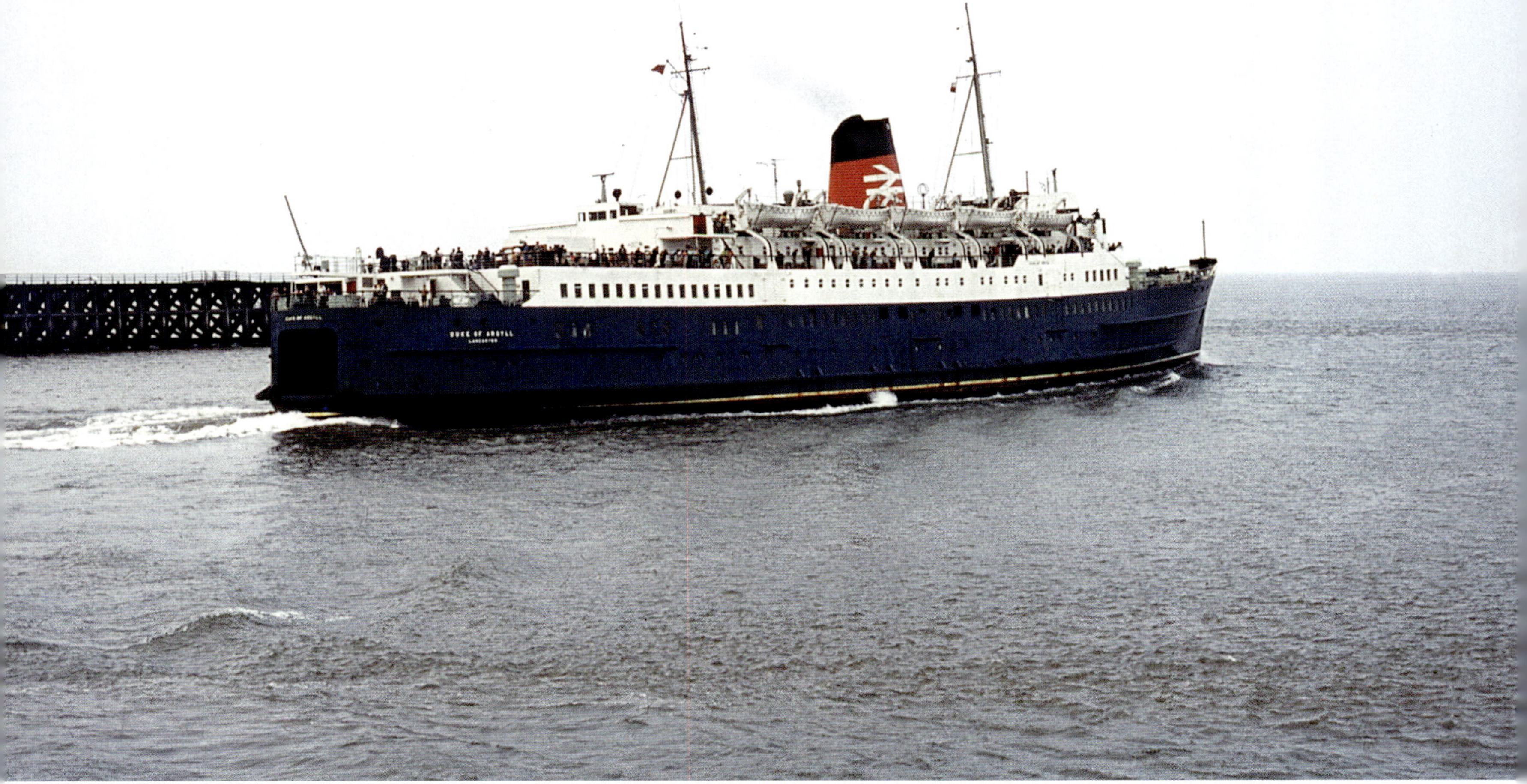

Duke of Argyll leaving Heysham for Belfast on 27 July 1971 as a stern loading car ferry. During winter 1969/70, *Duke of Argyll* and *Duke of Lancaster* had returned to Harland & Wolff for conversion. A new berth was commissioned at Heysham alongside a new three-platform railway station. Alterations were also made at Belfast Donegall Quay. The investment was short lived. The route closed to passengers on 5 April 1975. *Duke of Argyll* was then sold for further service in Greece. It lasted there until 1994, ten years longer than the last turbine steamer in British waters. *(Peter Sunderland)*

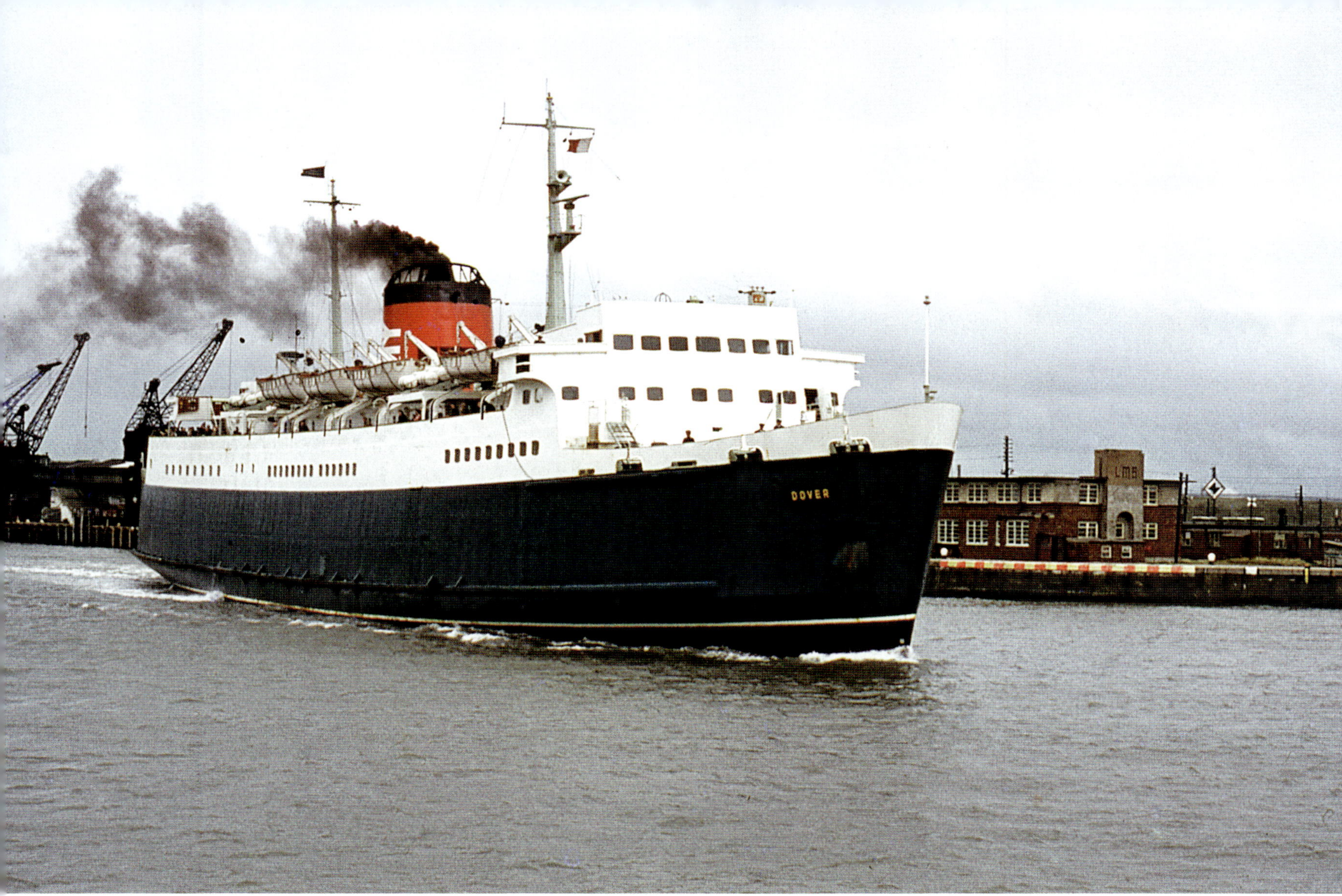

To build on its investment at Heysham, BR introduced a thrice weekly car ferry from Dun Lcoghaire in June 1970. This brought a Holyhead based vessel to Heysham. *Dover* was, jointly with *Holyhead Ferry 1*, the last turbine steamer built for BR in 1965. It was renamed *Earl Siward* in 1977 but lasted with BR only until 1981. It then had two years` service in Greece before becoming a nightclub in Newcastle, then a wreck in Middlesbrough before demolition in 2018. *(Peter Sunderland)*

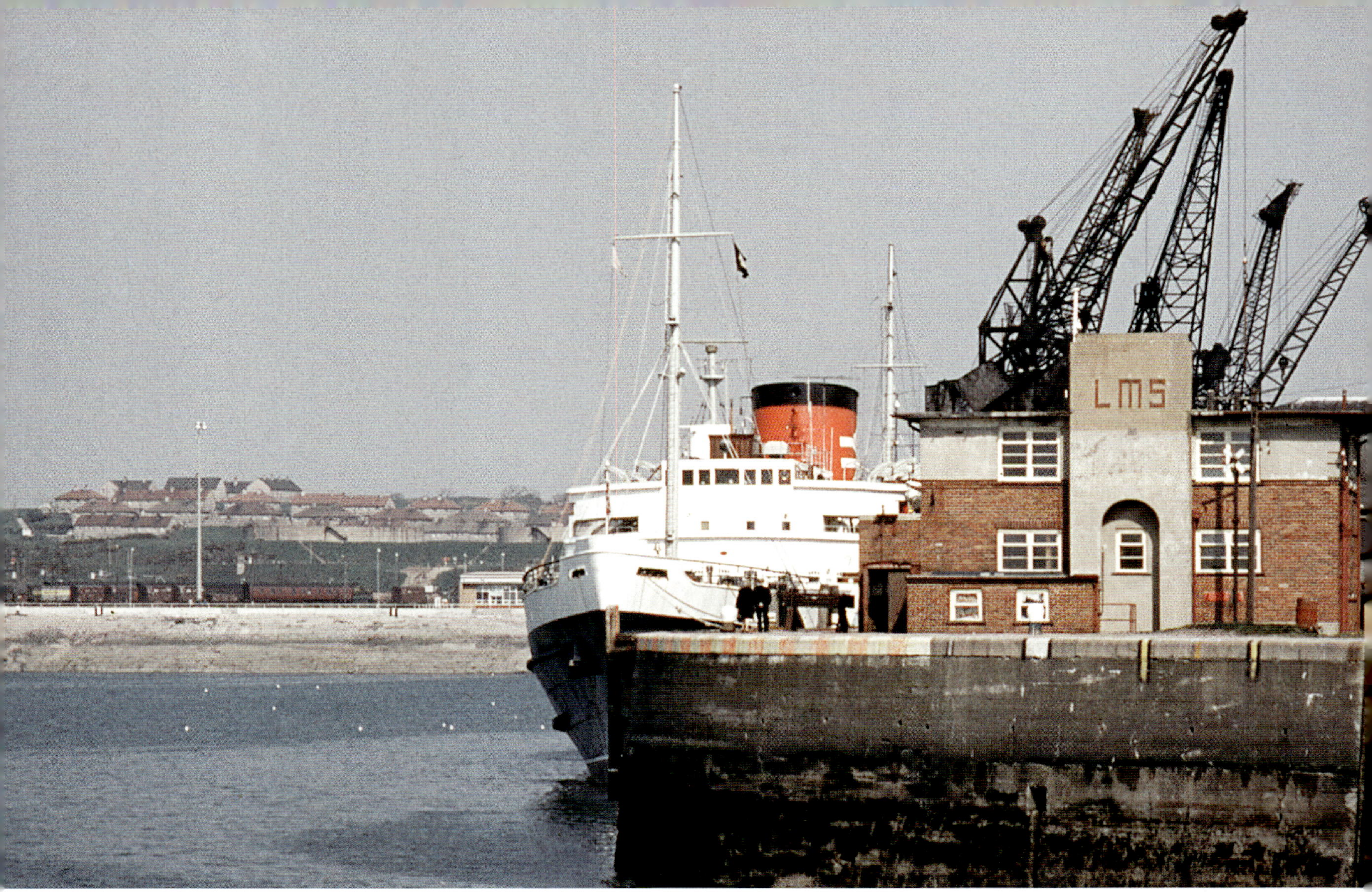

Even before the Dun Laoghaire car ferry had started, Heysham found itself handling sailings to Dun Laoghaire when the 'Irish Mail' was diverted from Holyhead after severe fire damage to the Britannia Tubular Bridge had severed rail access across the Menai Strait to the port. From 25 May 1970, the 'Irish Mail' from London Euston was diverted to Heysham where it was met by *Cambria* or *Hibernia* sailing overnight to Dun Laoghaire. These were motor vessels built for the Holyhead to Dun Laoghaire mail service in 1948. *Cambria* is seen at Heysham on 2 May 1971, alongside the former LMS Harbour Master's office. *(Peter Sunderland)*

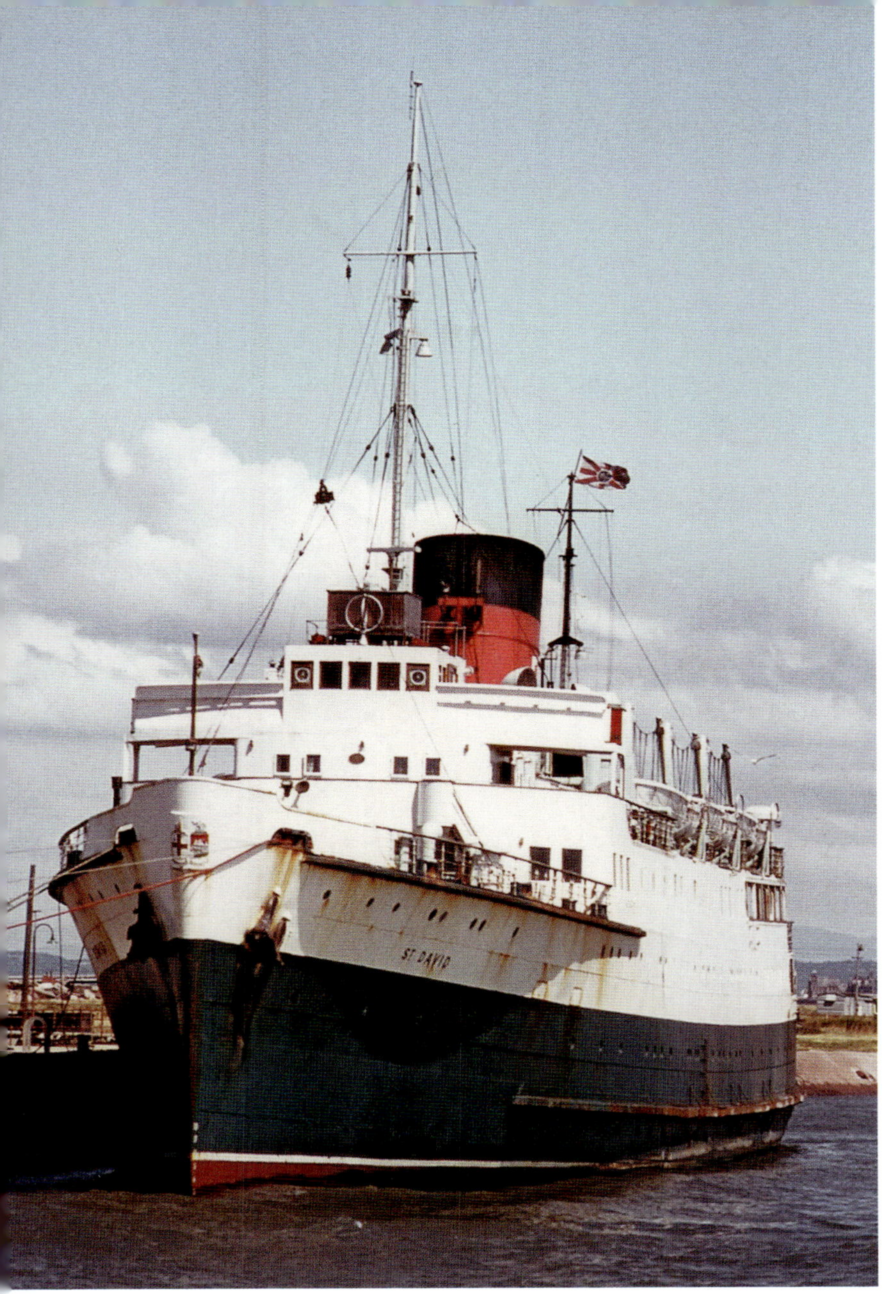

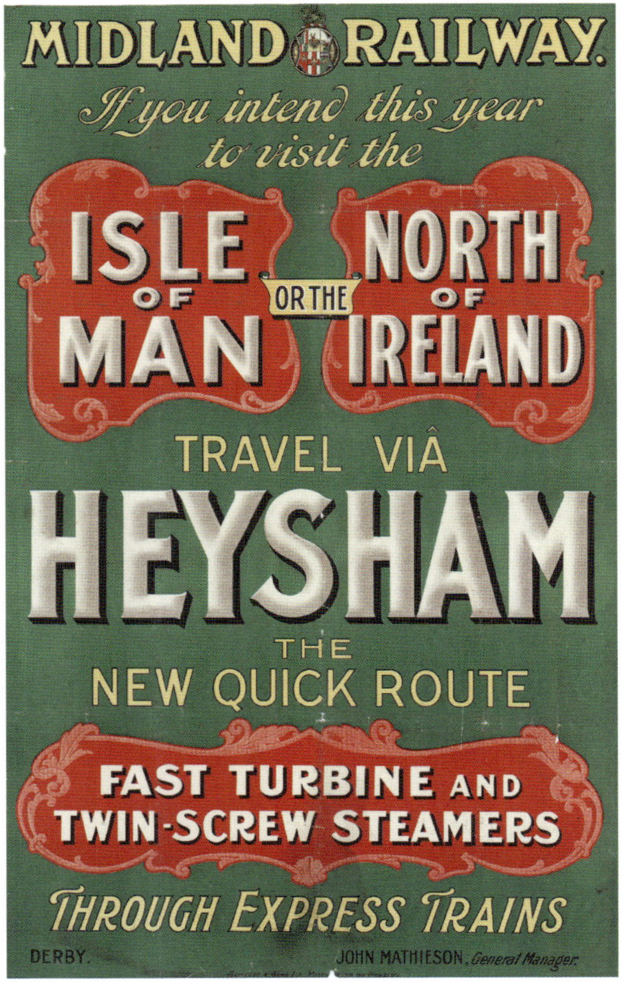

Whilst the LMS was ordering diesel ships for Holyhead, the Great Western had remained loyal to steam when it built *St David* for Fishguard to Rosslare in 1947. By 1970, *St David* had been replaced on its traditional route and was relieving at Holyhead. On 6 August, this role brought it to Heysham with the 'Irish Mail' from Dun Laoghaire. The bow carries the Great Western coat of arms and the funnel the insignia of the Fishguard & Rosslare Railways and Harbours Company. *St David* was withdrawn in 1971. The 'Irish Mail' reverted to Holyhead when the Britannia Bridge reopened in January 1972. *(Peter Sunderland, Poster: Midland Railway Study Centre)*

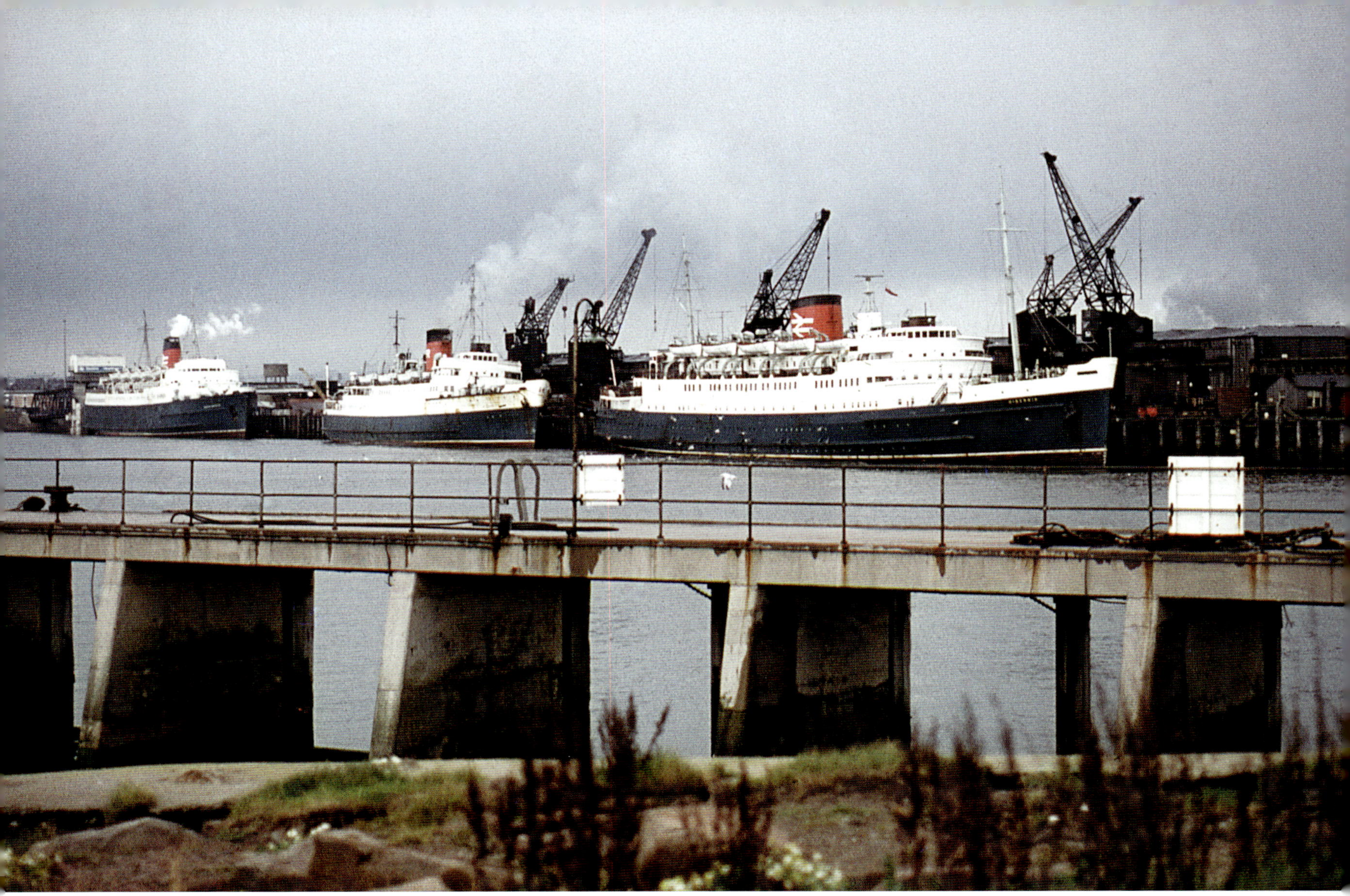

Thanks to the Dun Laoghaire services, scenes like this could be had at Heysham on certain days during 1970 and 1971. *Duke of Lancaster* is on the car ferry berth by the new station, *Hibernia* is at the old station and *St David* is in between. Wisps of steam distinguish the two turbine steamers from the motor vessel. The Dun Laoghaire to Heysham car ferry only ran for two summers. *Duke of Lancaster* relieved at Holyhead from 1975 until 1978, after which it became a floating amusement arcade at Mostyn, North Wales, where it is still rotting away, four decades later. *(Peter Sunderland)*

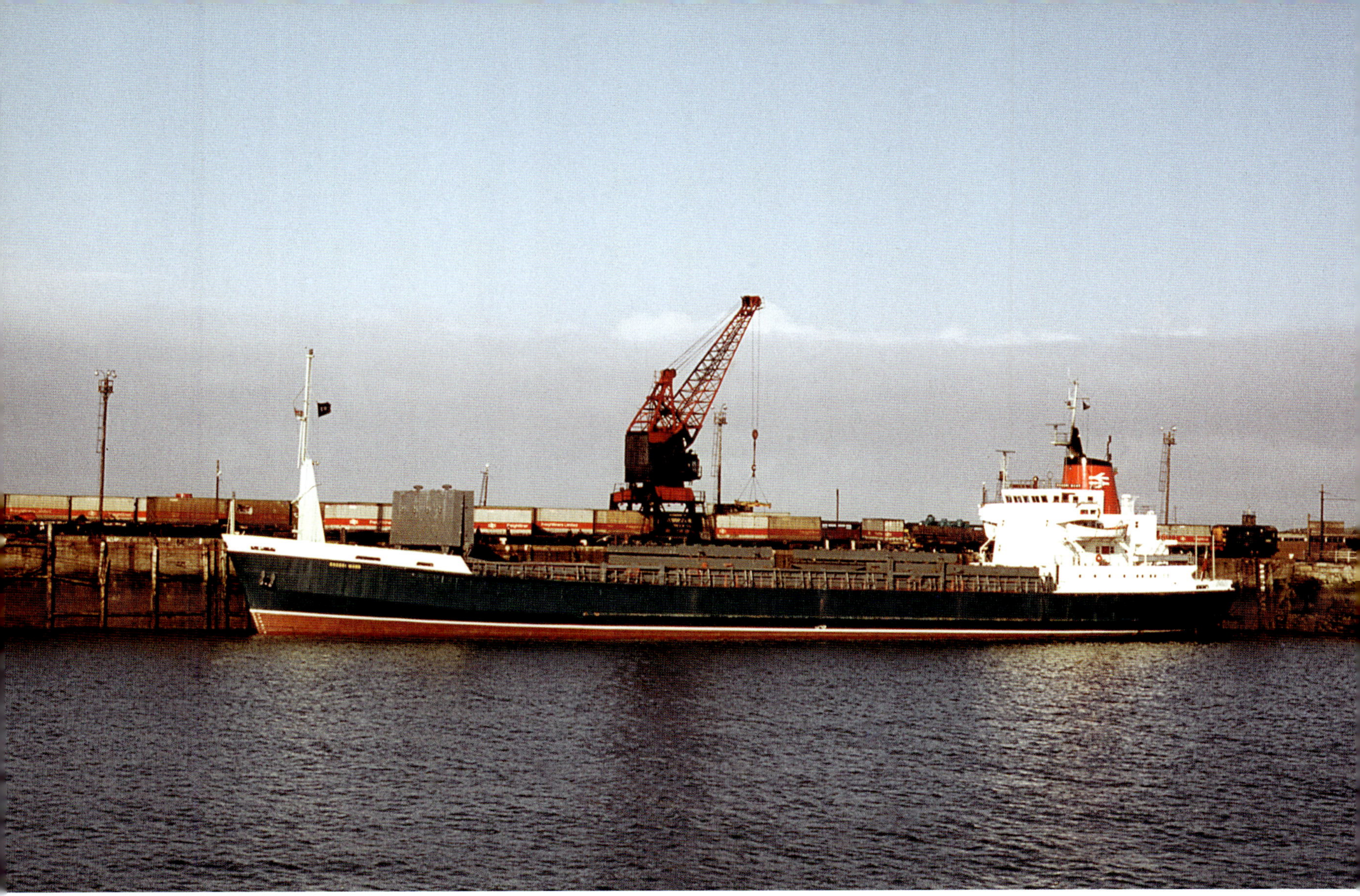

Also diverted by the Britannia Bridge fire, *Rhodri Mawr* and *Brian Boroime* had been built in 1970 to extend BR's freightliner service to Dublin and Belfast via Holyhead. They were cellular ships designed to carry standard containers stacked on top of one another. *Rhodri Mawr* is seen here loading containers on the Heysham North Quay in March 1971. Holyhead would have had gantry cranes for this operation. Both vessels returned to the Welsh port when the bridge reopened in 1972 and were eventually sold to Greece in 1989. *(Peter Sunderland)*

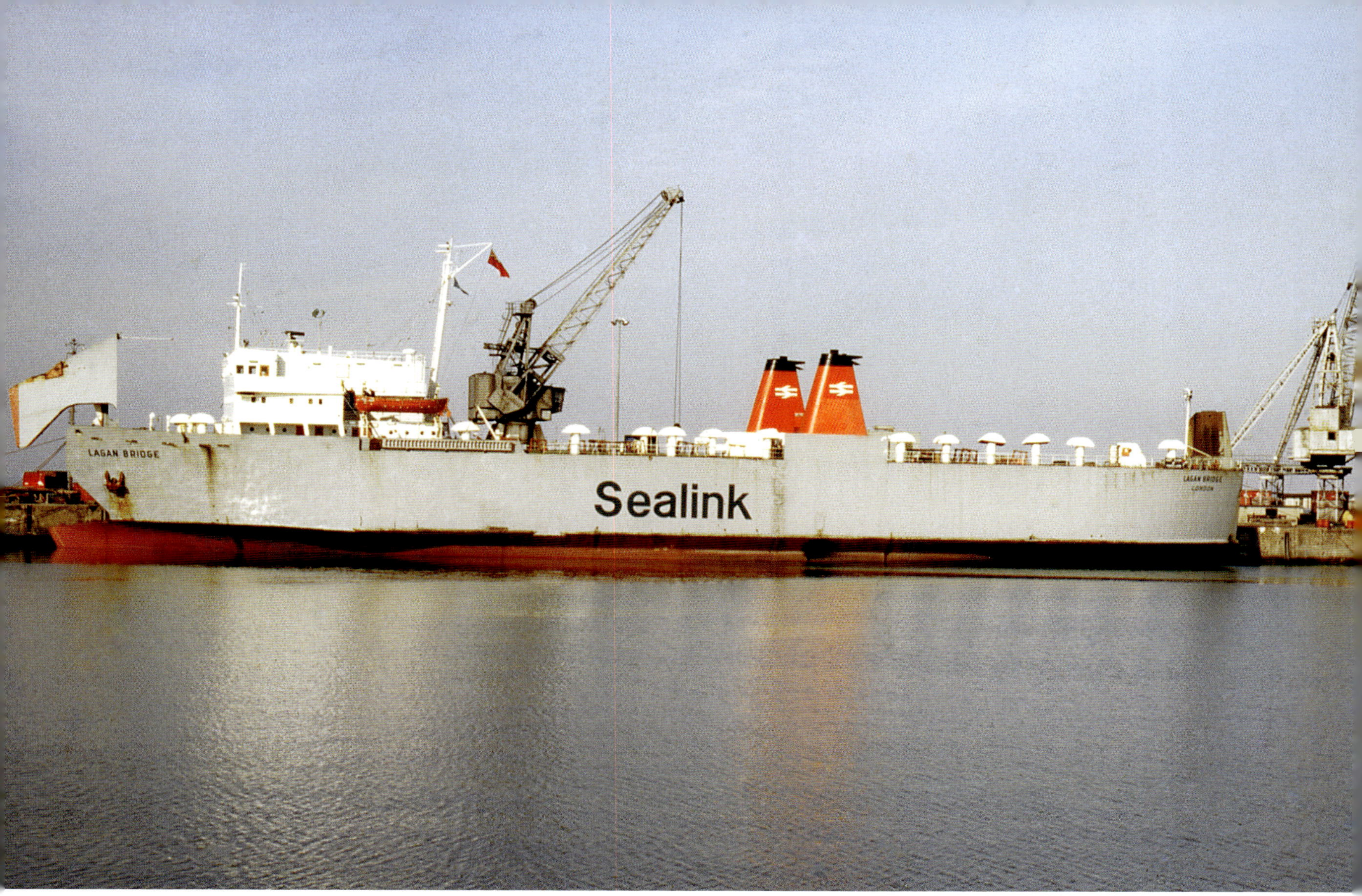

Lagan Bridge on the North Quay during 1980. After the 1975 passenger closure, BR continued with a freight service to Belfast. This became roll on – roll off in 1978 with the commissioning of a further link span for lorries. Early in 1980, BR chartered two larger vessels which they named *Lune Bridge* and *Lagan Bridge*. They then closed the route completely in December of that year. Sealink had been a brand name for the BR shipping Division since 1970. The Port of Heysham was included in the sale to Sea Containers when Sealink was privatised in 1984. *(Peter Sunderland)*

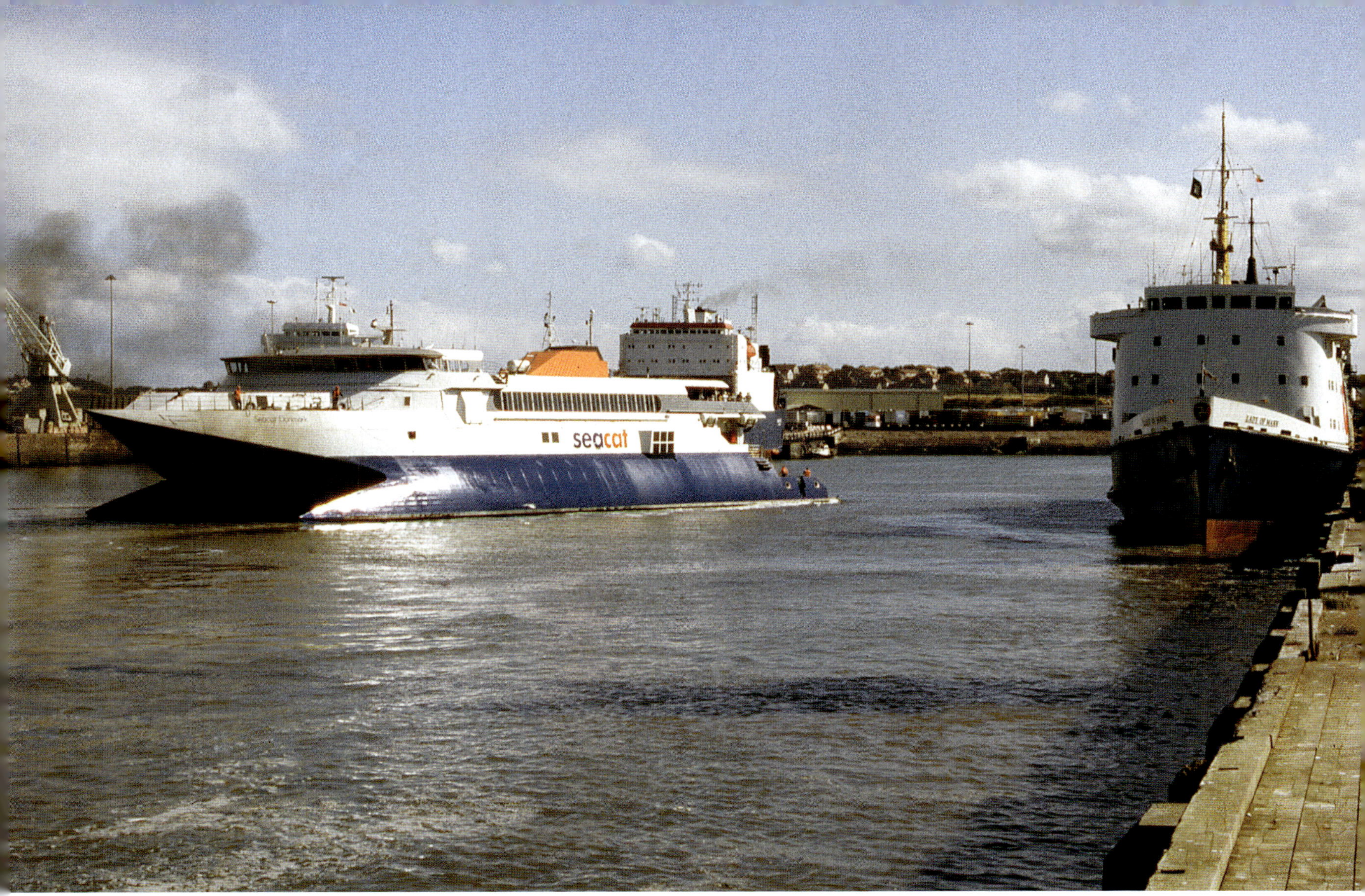

Seacat Danmark arriving from Belfast on 28 August 1999. In March that year, Sea Containers had started a seasonal passenger and car ferry service to Belfast using a fast craft which could do the crossing in four hours. A connecting train from Lancaster was introduced in 2000 but the venture ceased in August 2002. To the right is *Lady of Mann*, built for the Isle of Man Steam Packet Company in 1976 and sold to Greece in 2005. The Port of Heysham was sold to the Mersey Docks & Harbour Company, now part of Peel Ports, in 2001. *(Stuart Baker)*

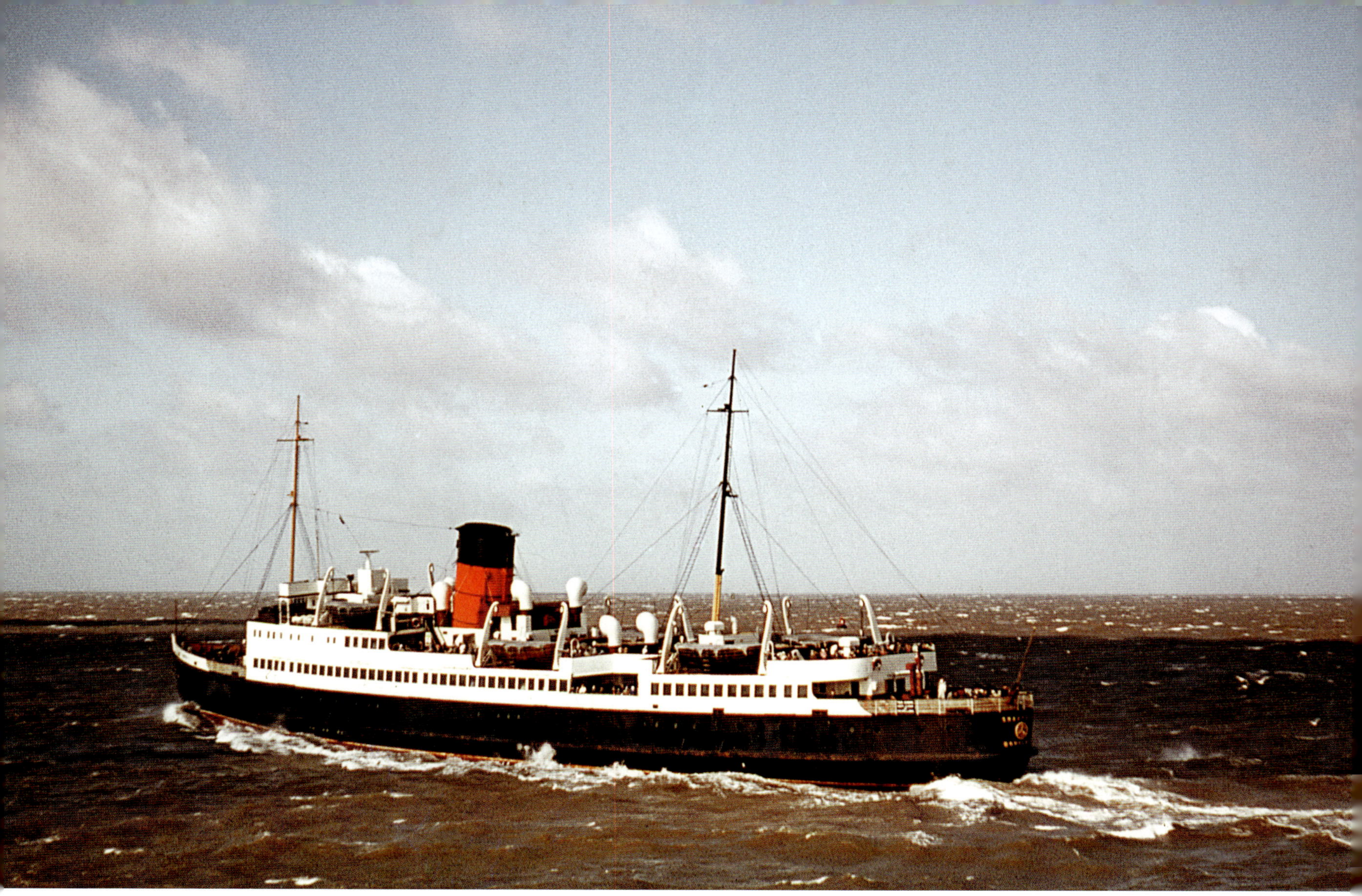

Having steamed out of Heysham stern first, *Snaefell* is now making course for Douglas, Isle of Man, in 1962. The route had been opened by the Midland Railway in 1904, employing the turbine steamer *Manxman*. The service ran daily for about four months of the year, connecting with an 'Isle of Man Boat Express' from Leeds and Bradford. In 1928, the LMS ceded the route to the Isle of Man Steam Packet Company who had been operating from Liverpool since 1830. They also ran seasonal services from other ports, including Fleetwood. *(Peter Sunderland)*

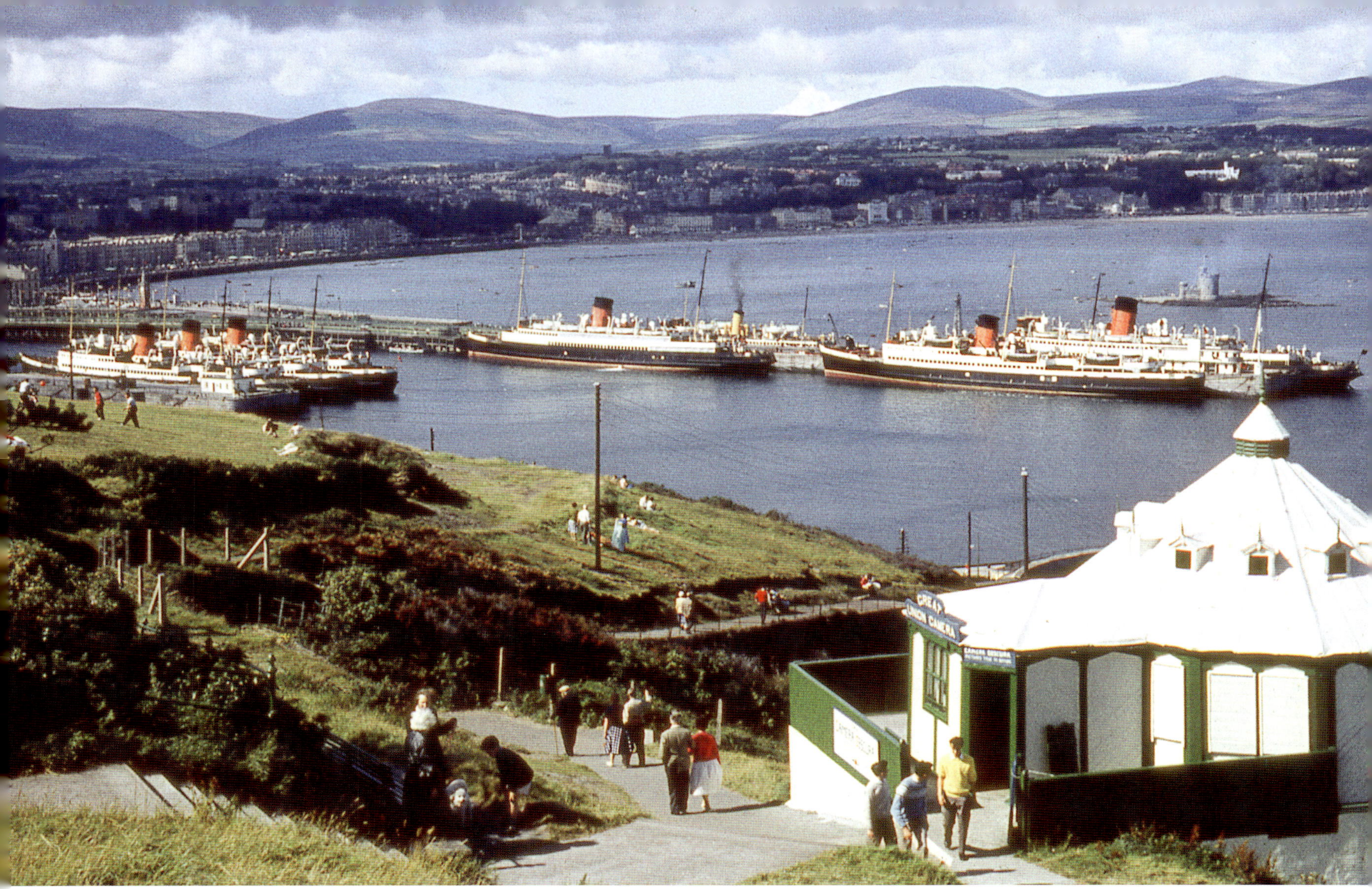

Summer traffic to the Isle of Man, including day excursions, was considerable although, post Second World War, Heysham's share was nothing like what it had been earlier. On an afternoon in August 1960, seven turbine passenger steamers have arrived in Douglas from various English, Welsh, Scottish and Irish ports. From eft to right: *Snaefell*, *Mona's Isle*, *Manxman*, the 1927 *Ben-my-Chree*, *St. Seiriol* of the Liverpool & North Wales Company, *Tynwald* and the 1930 *Lady of Mann*. At this time, the Isle of Man Company's fleet included eight passenger steamers. The other two, *King Orry* and *Mona's Queen*, must have been at sea. They also had three cargo ships - two steam and one diesel. *(Peter Sunderland)*

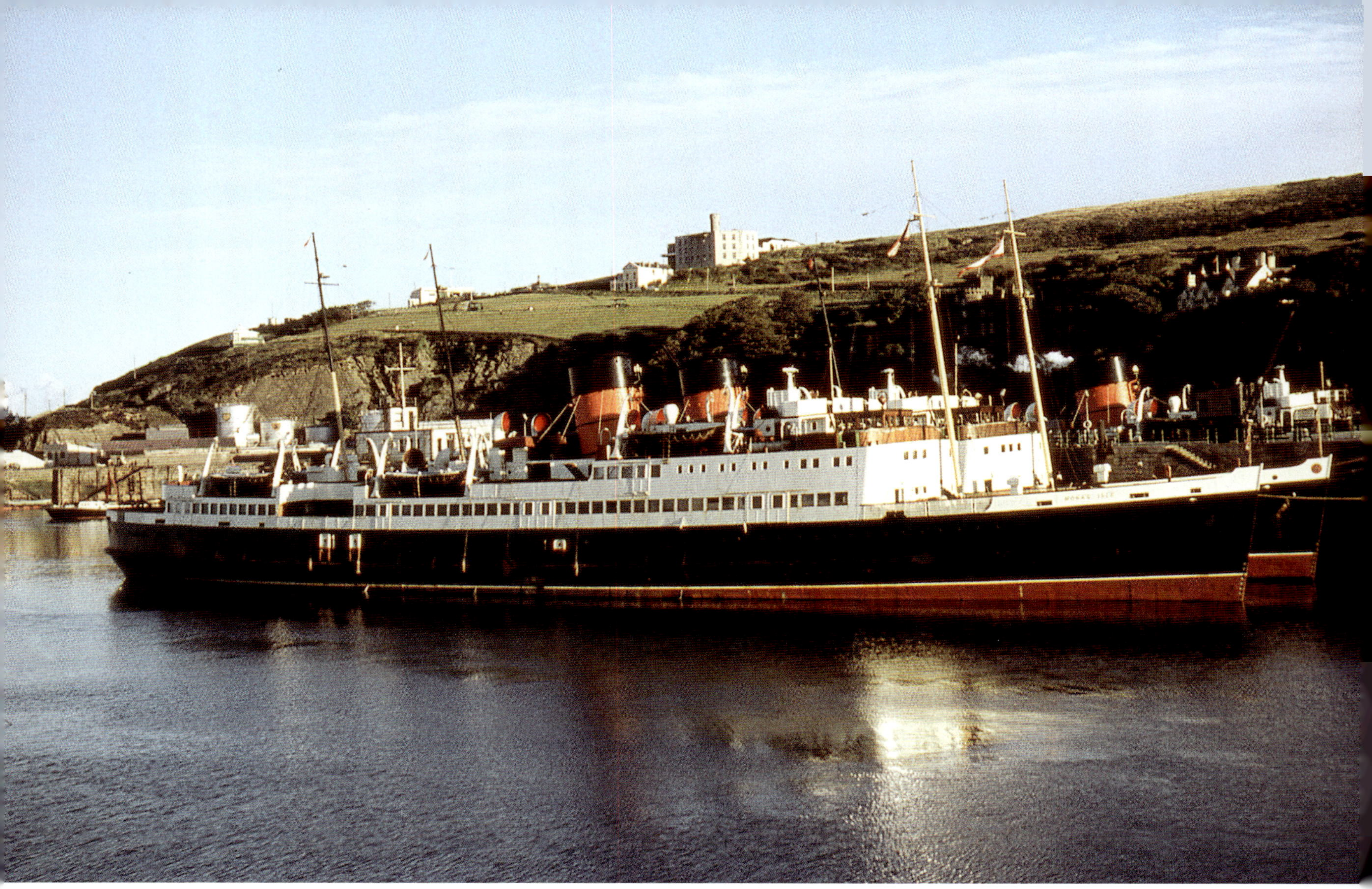

Isle of Man sailings from Heysham were suspended during the Second World War. They were not revived until 1953 and, even then, they were only scheduled for a dozen or so days a year. A connecting train ran from Lancaster and Morecambe, utilising a DMU after withdrawal of the electrics in January 1966. *Mona's Isle*, seen at Douglas in 1960, worked the last crossing to Heysham on 28 August 1974. The Company blamed the impending closure of Heysham Station for withdrawal of the Belfast service. Built in 1951, *Mona's Isle* was the fifth to carry the name of the original Steam Packet Company vessel of 1830. It was withdrawn in 1980. *(Peter Sunderland)*

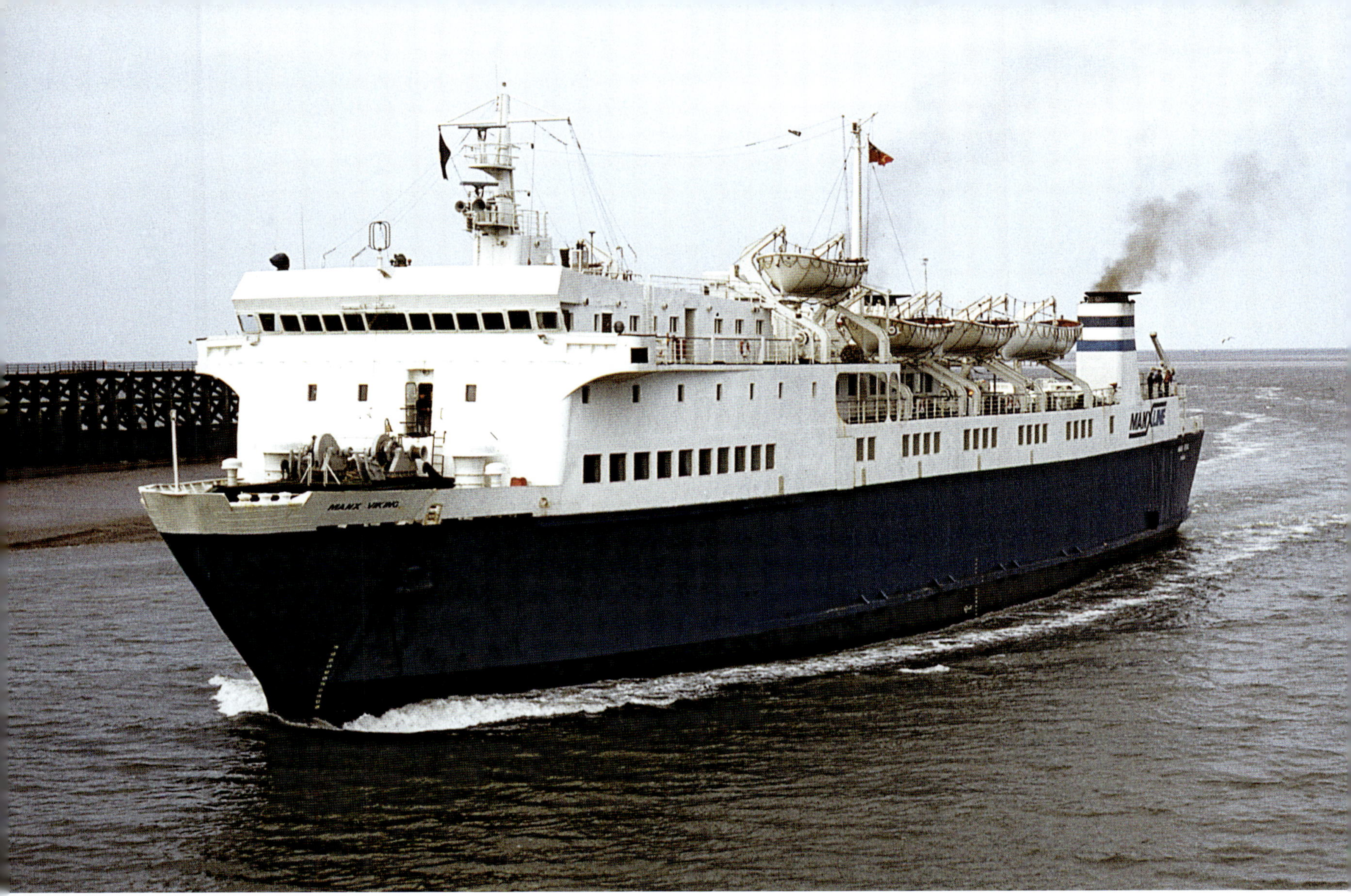

A new multi-purpose service began in August 1978. After a difficult start, it became the main year round route to the Isle of Man. *Manx Viking*, the two-year old former *Monte Castillo*, is seen arriving at Heysham on 17 June 1979 in Manx Line livery. It suffered problems of unreliability and the venture would most probably have collapsed if Manx Line had not been taken over by Sealink, then still part of British Railways, in 1979. Soon, *Manx Viking* was sporting BR livery but with an Isle of Man crest on the funnel in place of the double arrows. *(Peter Sunderland)*

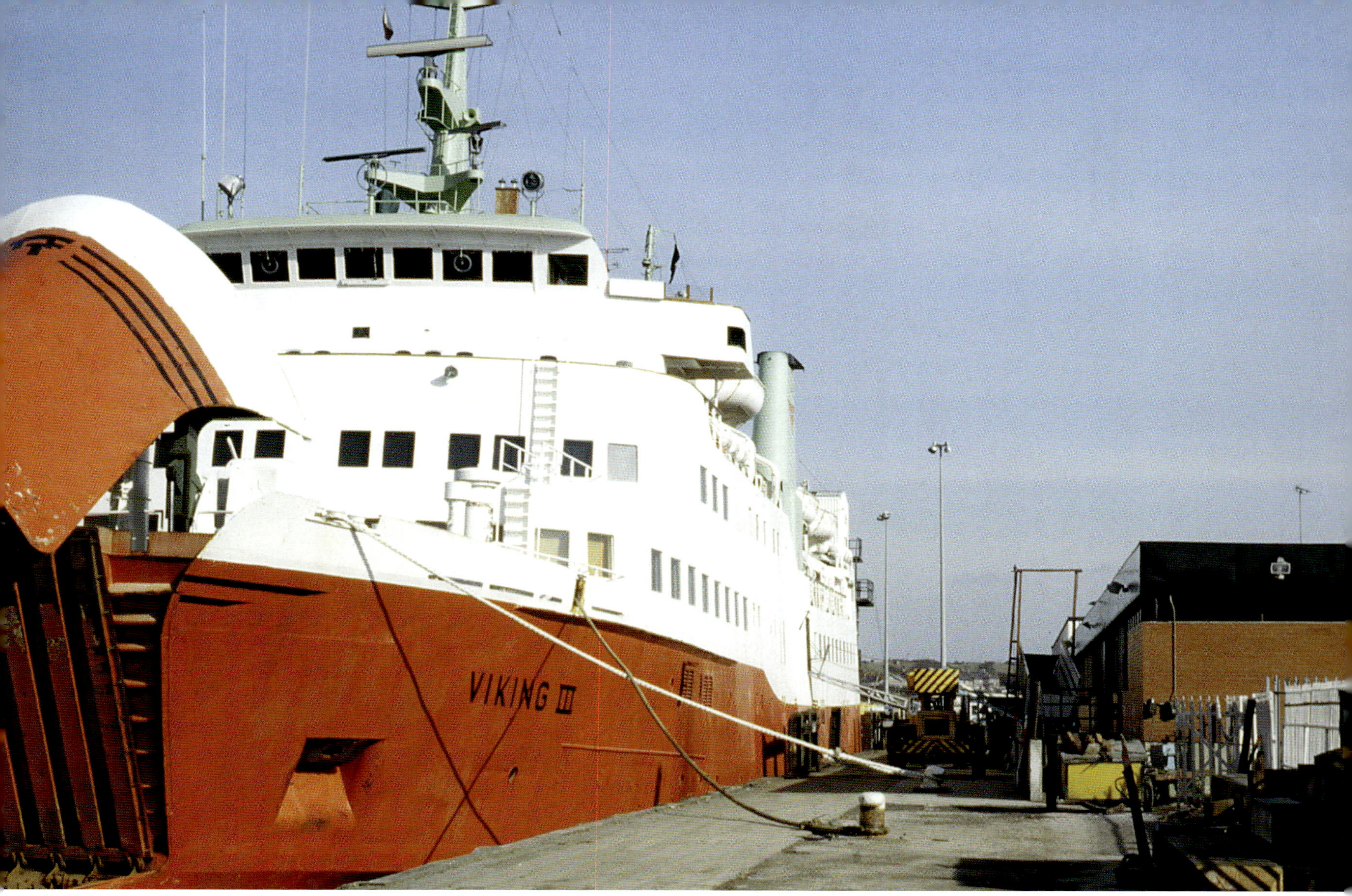

Townsend Thoresen's *Viking III* at Heysham on 3 March 1980. When *Manx Viking* was out of action, Sealink could bring one of its own vessels to cover or, in this case, charter one from Townsend Thoresen. The venture became a success, largely at the expense of traffic from Liverpool. By 1984, the Isle of Man Steam Packet Company was in serious trouble and had to be rescued by the newly privatised Sealink. They invested in the Steam Packet Company with a condition that Heysham should replace Liverpool as the main English port. *(Peter Sunderland)*

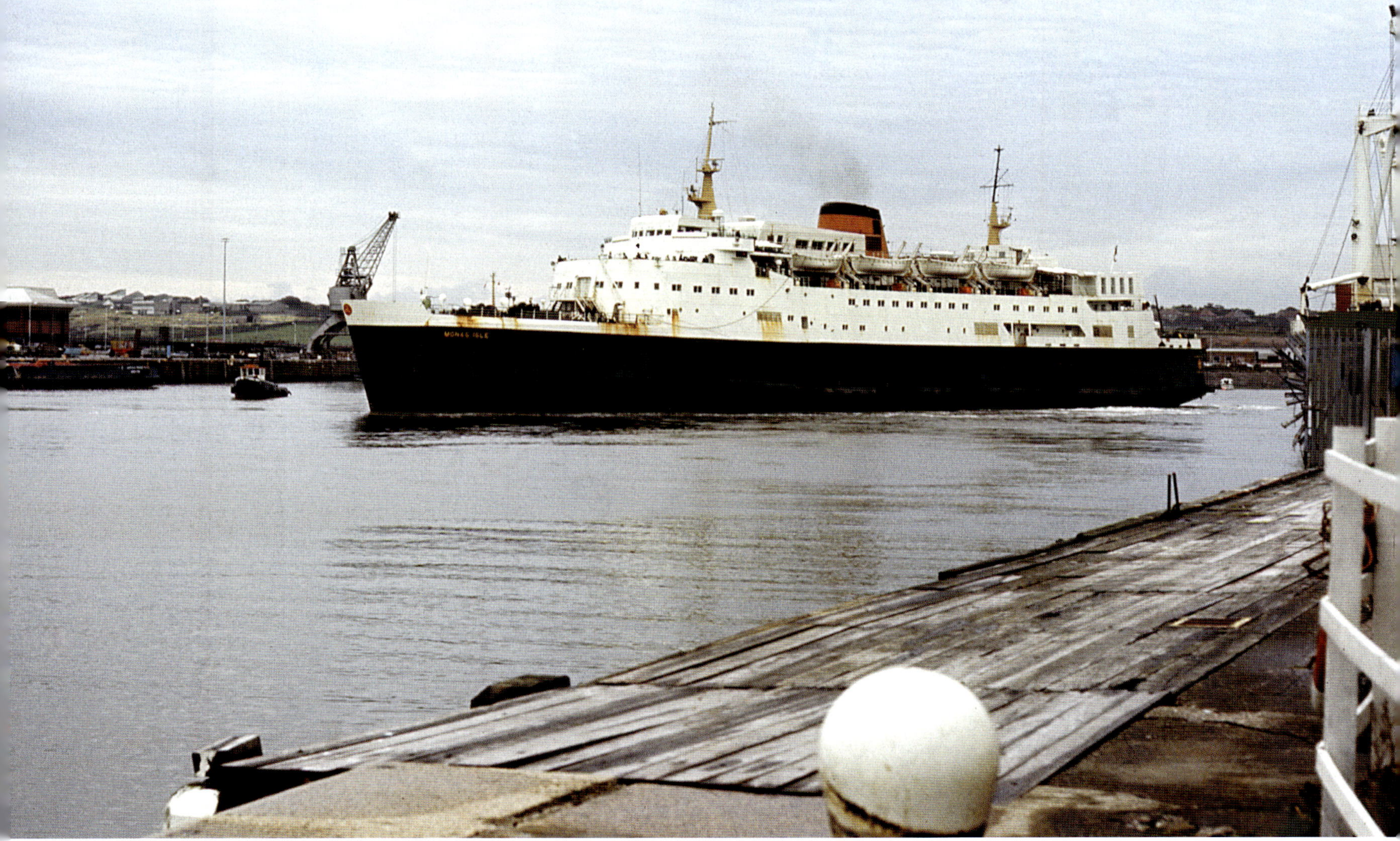

The rescued Steam Packet Company bought a new flagship - the former *Free Enterprise III* of Townsend Thoresen - which became the sixth *Mona's Isle*. It proved unsuitable, lasting only from April to October 1985. It is seen entering Heysham in August that year, stern first having turned outside, a manoeuvre which it found rather difficult. Sealink hastily identified a replacement in their own *Antrim Princess* from Stranraer – Larne which became the sixth vessel to carry the name *Tynwald*. *(Peter Sunderland)*

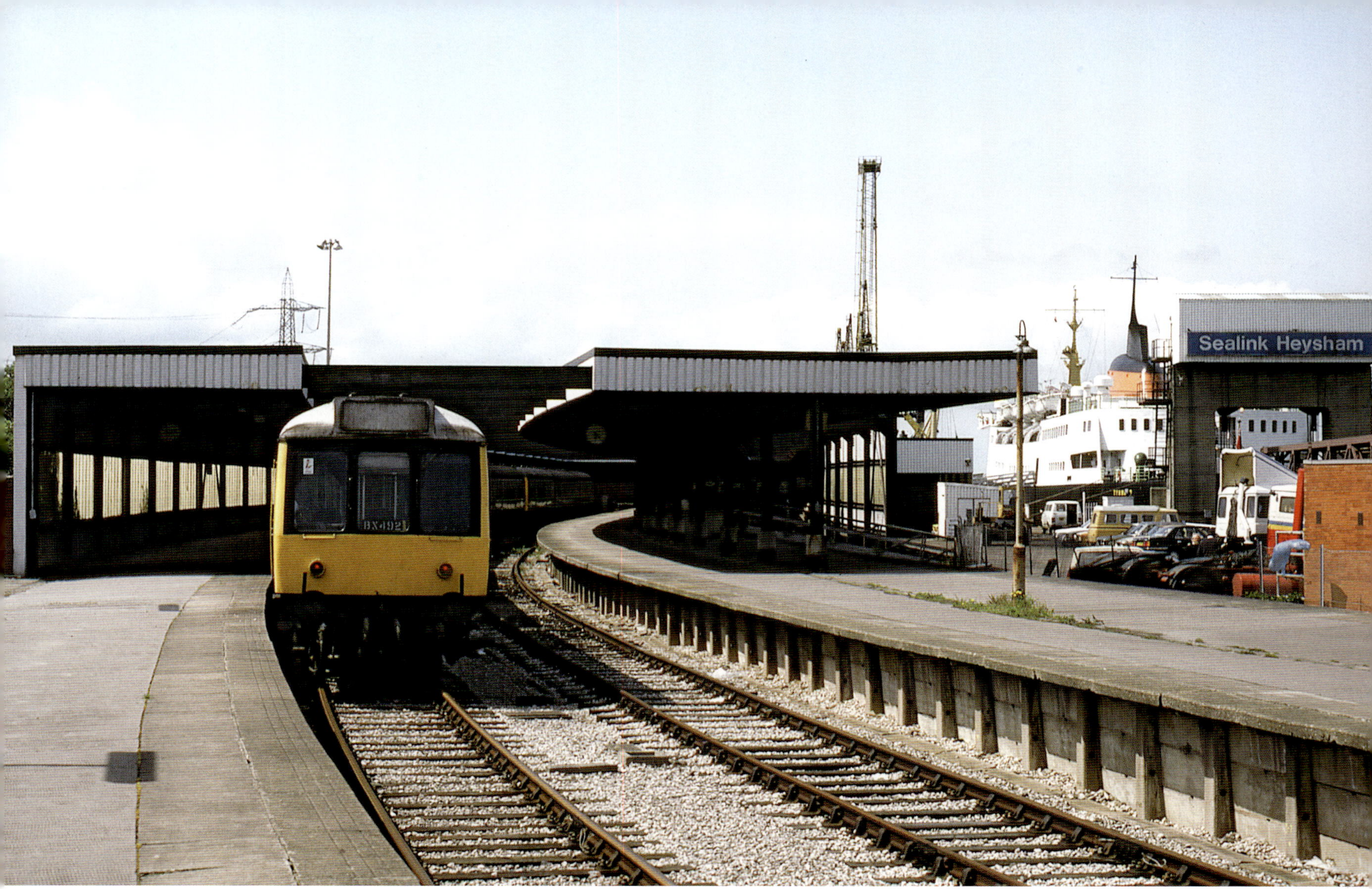

When the Manx Line service started, a bus was provided from Lancaster Castle. Eventually, on 11 May 1987, Heysham Station reopened for just one train a day. Class 108 power car No. 51935 is seen here at the rear of the train five days after the reintroduction of the service from Lancaster, on 16 May 1987. *Tynwald* provides the onward connection. At this stage, the 1970-built station was still largely intact. It has since been reduced to just one bare platform. Built in 1960, car 51935 was withdrawn in 1992 and preserved on the Severn Valley Railway. Sadly, however, it was scrapped in 2008 following an arson attack. The white cab roof confirms that it was based at Buxton at the time of this view. *(Tom Heavyside)*

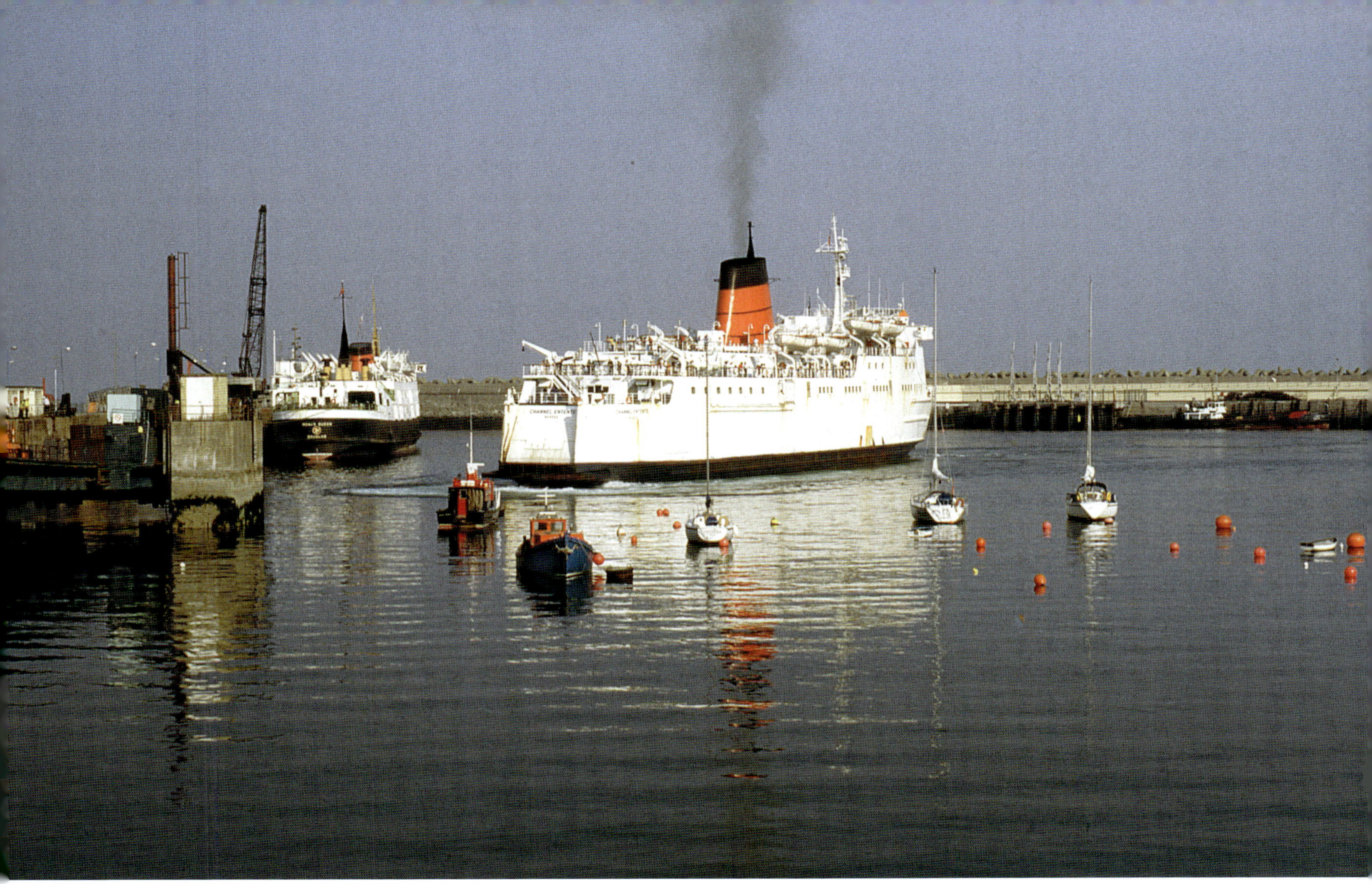

Tynwald was replaced in 1990 by the former Cross Channel train ferry *St Eloi*, then briefly named *Channel Entente*. It is seen arriving at Douglas from Heysham on 2 August 1990. Later that year, it underwent a major overhaul from which it emerged as *King Orry*. It was sold in 1998 to Moby Lines, of Italy, for whom it operated until 2017 as *Moby Love* between Piombino and Portoferraio. To the left is the 1972 *Mona's Queen*, the Isle of Man Company's first diesel passenger ship, which was withdrawn in September 1990. Since 1998, Heysham to Douglas has been in the hands of the purpose-built *Ben-my-Chree*, the sixth to carry the name, which departs daily at 2.15 a.m. and 2.15 p.m. The early morning service is mainly for freight. *(Stuart Baker)*

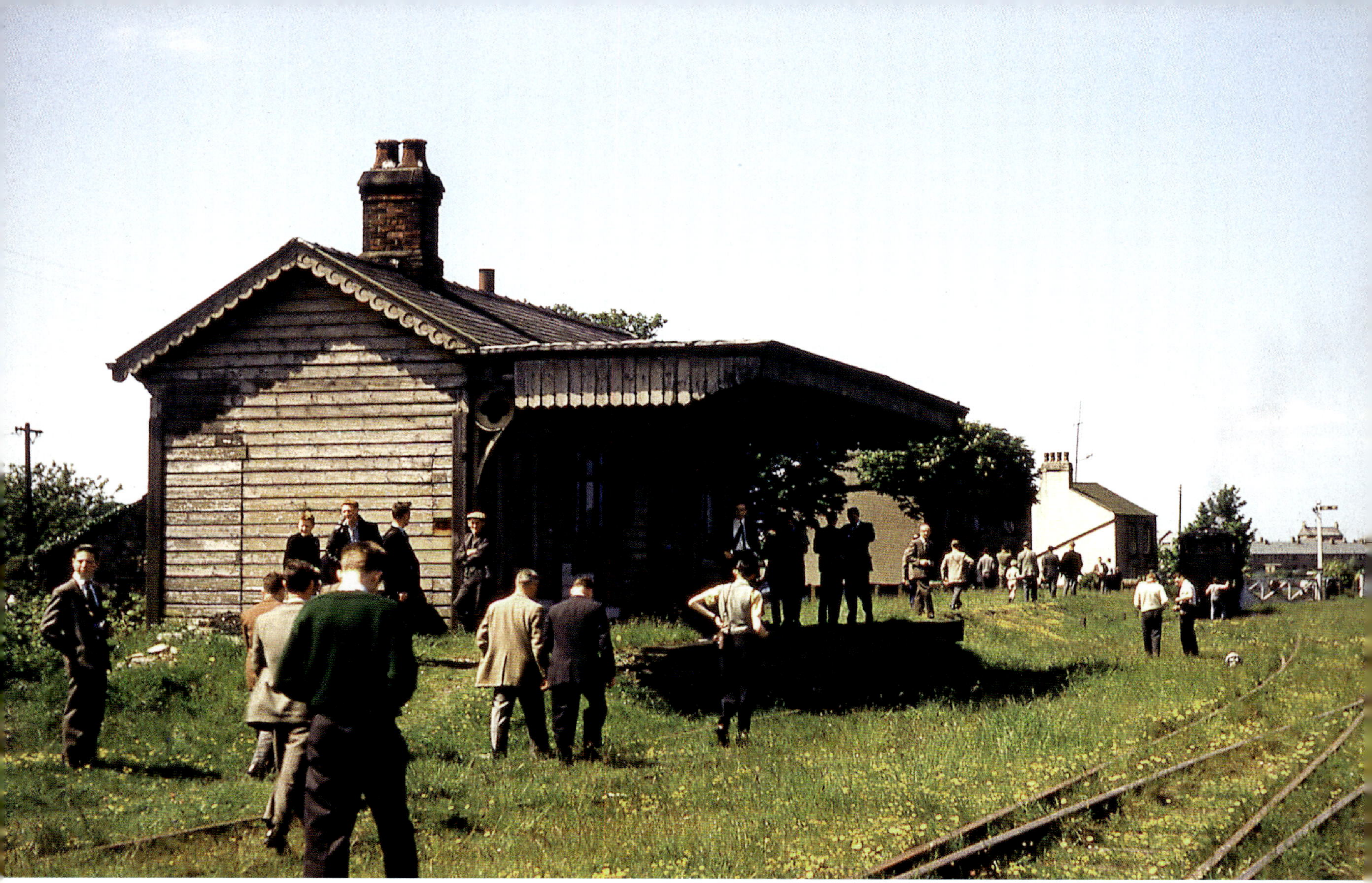

Glasson Dock is a small port on the River Lune, downstream from Lancaster. The five-mile single track branch was opened by the London & North Western Railway in 1883. The passenger service was withdrawn in 1930 - a consequence of the LMS Road Transport Act 1928. This had allowed the railway company to invest in Ribble Motor Services who substituted trains with five buses a day from Lancaster Castle. However, Glasson Dock remained open for parcels and freight until 7 September 1964. With its single platform having been cut back, the station is seen being thronged by participants from the 'Northern Fells Railtour' on 29 May 1960. This view is towards the end of the line and the dock itself. *(J. C. W. Halliday)*

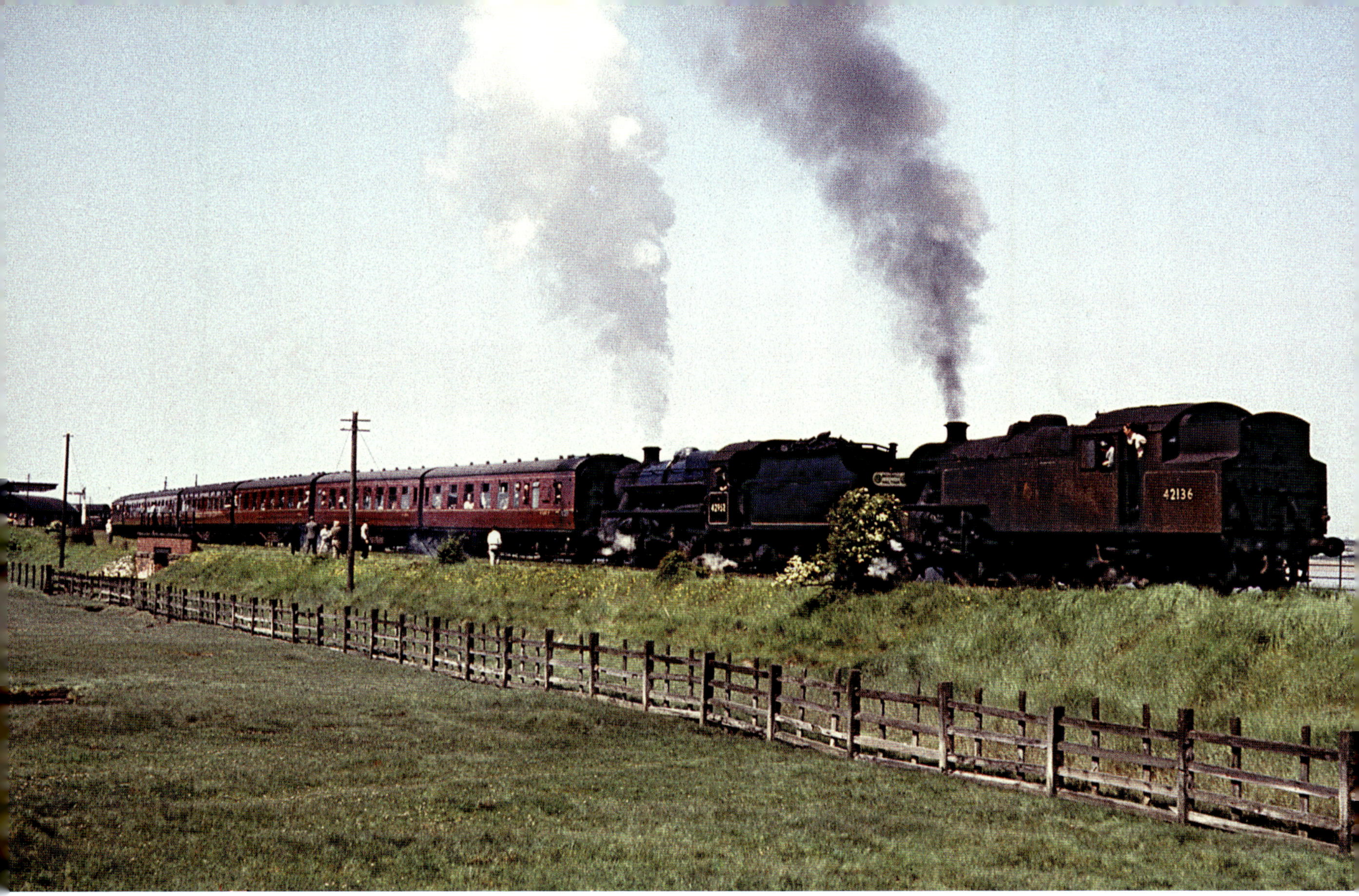

Fairburn 2 – 6 – 4T No. 42136 and Stanier 2 – 6 – 0 No. 42952 are ready to leave Glasson Dock with the next stage of the 'Northern Fells railtour.' Organised by the Stephenson and Manchester Locomotive Societies, this covered a number of goods only and soon to be closed routes. From Glasson Dock it reached Penrith via Lancaster Castle, Caton, Clapham and Ingleton. It then found its way to Lakeside (Windermere) via Kirkby Stephen East, Tebay, Hincaster Junction, Sandside and Ulverston before returning to Morecambe Promenade. *(Peter Sunderland)*

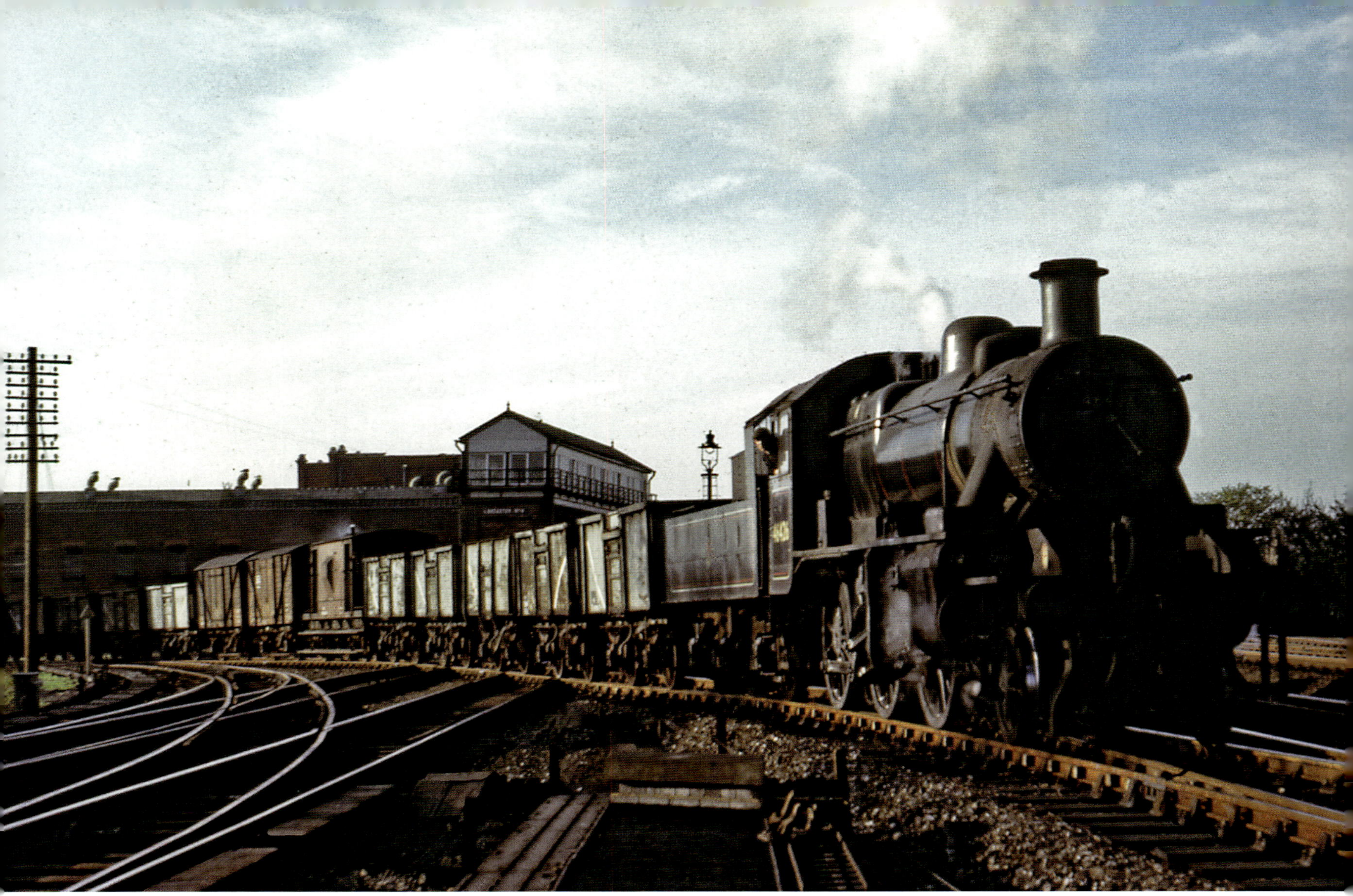

Ivatt Class 2 No. 46426 brings a freight off the Glasson Dock branch at Lancaster No. 4 box in 1963. The four boxes at Lancaster Castle were named, rather unimaginatively, No. 1, No. 2, No. 3 and No 4 from south to north. All were closed in favour of Preston power box on the first weekend of 1973, along with Morecambe South Junction. Hest Bank was reduced to a gate box. Lancaster No. 4 had 144 levers to control the northern exit from the station, the merging of the through lines with the platform lines and the junctions for Glasson Dock and Green Ayre. *(Colour-Rail)*

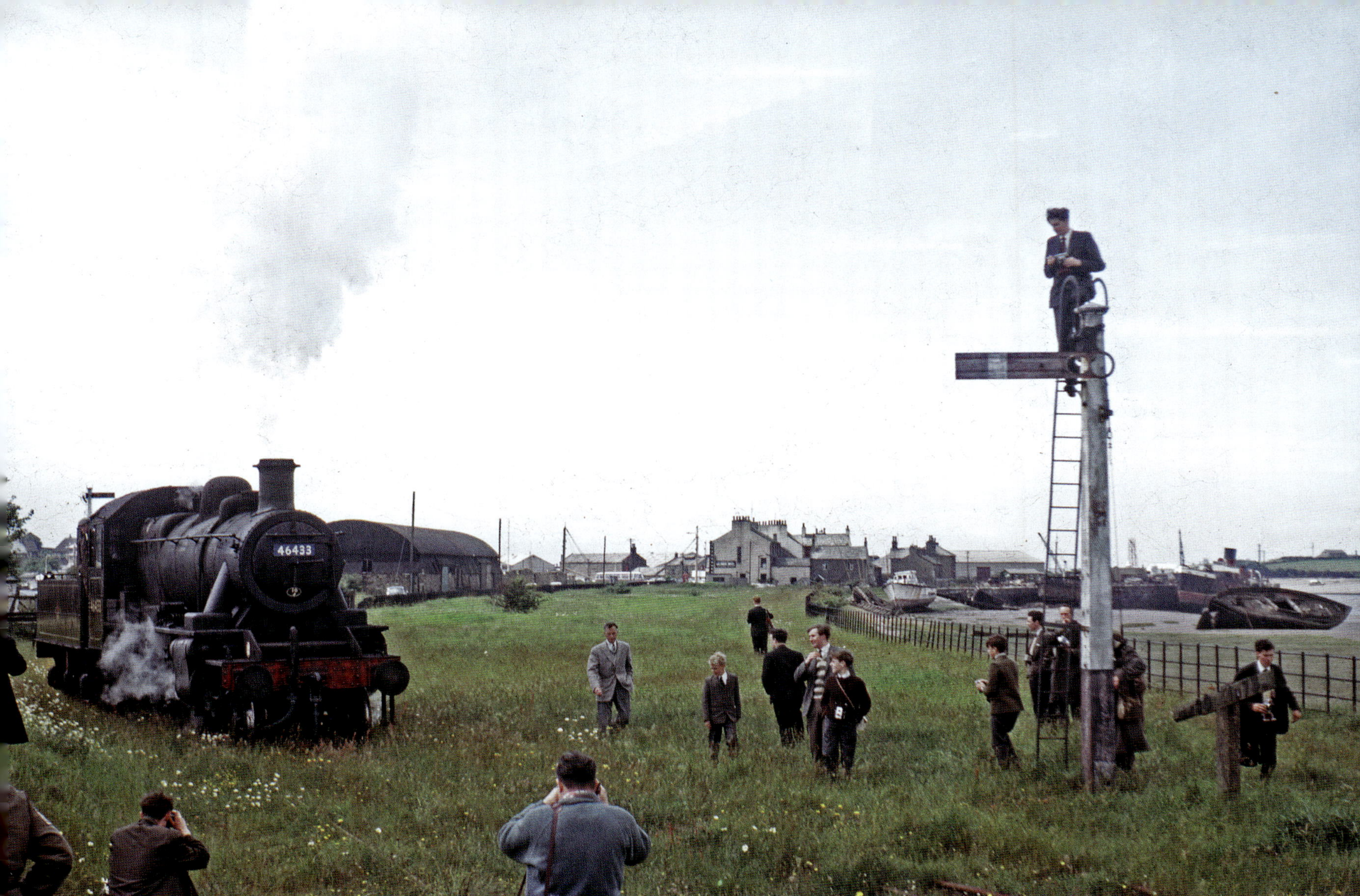

With complete closure just weeks away, vegetation has already taken over the Glasson Dock terminus. The Railway Correspondence & Travel Society organised a farewell trip from Lancaster Castle on 20 June 1964 with Ivatt Class 2 No. 46433 hauling six brake vans. The more industrial part of the branch, nearer Lancaster, lingered on until 1969 by which time the remaining traffic to the power station and Lune Mills had dried up. Walkers and cyclists can now use the final three miles of the branch alongside the Lune Estuary. *(RCTS Archive)*

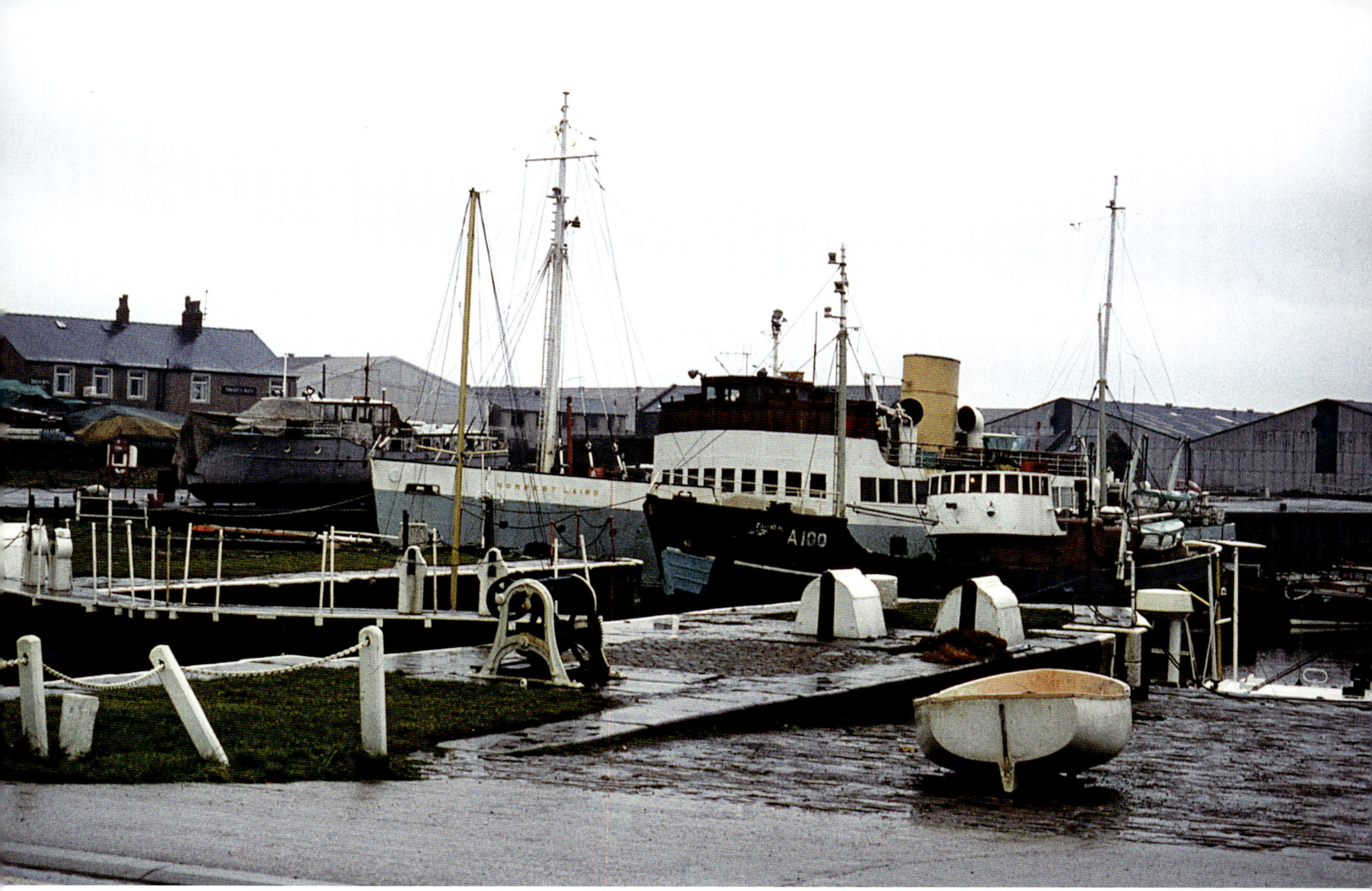

There was never any passenger shipping at Glasson Dock but, early in 1971, MacBrayne's *Locheil* arrived there under arrest. Renamed *Norwest Laird*, it had been purchased for a failed Fleetwood to Isle of Man service. Built in 1939, *Locheil* had earlier been the star of *McCutcheon v MacBrayne (House of Lords, 1964)* which we accountancy students had to learn. It had sunk in West Loch Tarbert on 8 October 1960 taking McCutcheon's Ford Popular car with it. The ship, unlike the car, was re-floated and repaired. It continued to serve MacBrayne until 1969 and ended up as a floating pub in Bristol where it was scrapped in 1994. *(Peter Sunderland)*

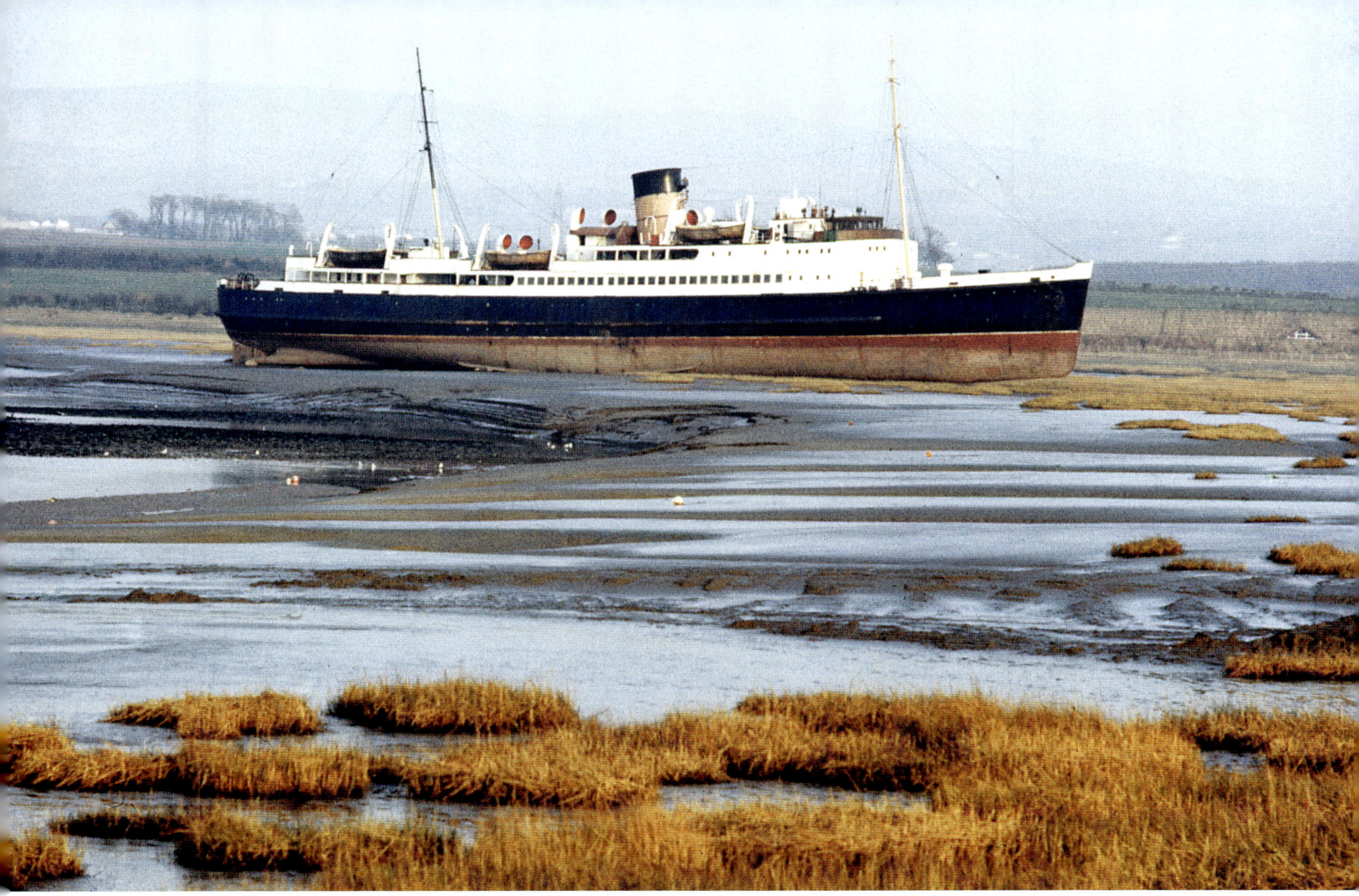

Five years later, another passenger steamer made an unconventional visit to Glasson Dock. Built in 1946 to replace its namesake lost at Dunkirk, the Isle of Man Company's fourth *King Orry* was the first of six almost identical turbine steamers which entered service between then and 1955. Withdrawn in August 1975 and sold to a scrap yard at Glasson Dock, *King Orry* broke loose in a storm on 2 January 1976 and ended up on mud flats in the Lune Estuary. It took until April to re-float and then re-sell it to a scrapyard in Kent. *(Peter Sunderland)*

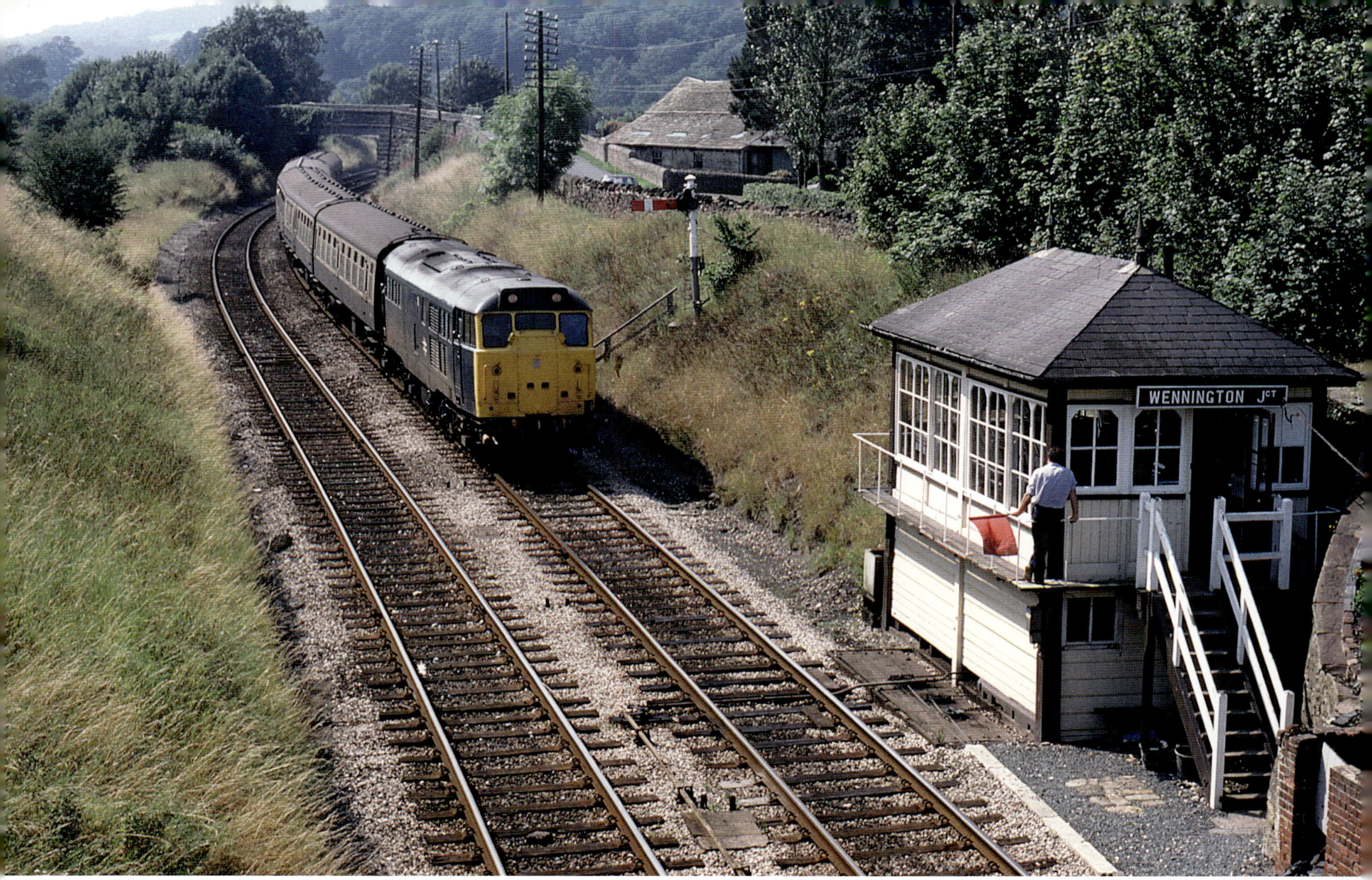

We now return to Wennington to take the post-1966 route to Lancaster, Morecambe and Heysham. Class 31 No. 31440 is approaching Wennington, still claiming to be a Junction, on 11 August 1984. The direct Lancaster line used to diverge opposite the second carriage. The signalling is much simplified from what we saw on pages 6 to 8. The box was still open at the time of this view. The signalman evidently needs to speak to the driver so he will have brought the train almost to a halt at the Home (historically, the Outer Home) which he will then have pulled off slowly. The loco, originally D5628, was built in 1960 and allocated new to Ipswich. It was withdrawn following accident damage in 1987 and scrapped shortly afterwards. *(Tom Heavyside)*

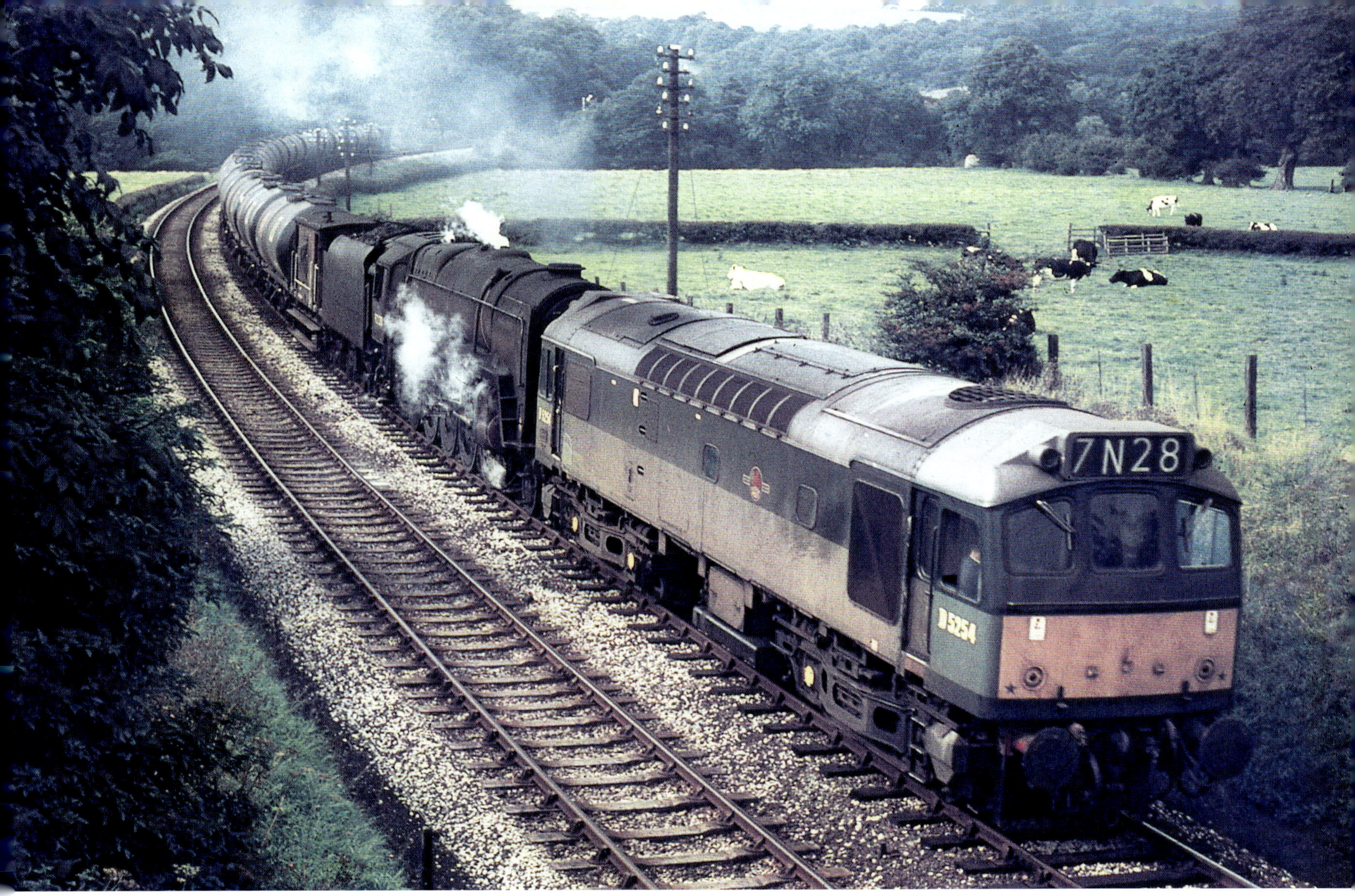

Transition from steam to diesel: Sulzer Type 2 diesel D5254 pilots BR Standard 9F No. 92128 on the Heysham Moss to Haverton Hill ammonia tanks train as it approaches Wennington from Carnforth on 16 September 1967. Up to June 1967, this train would have gone via Lancaster Green Ayre without the need to run round at Morecambe. The steam loco was withdrawn for scrap two months later after a ridiculously short life of only 10 years. The diesel managed 18 years of service from 1964 until 1982, by which time it had become 25104. *(Martin Bairstow collection)*

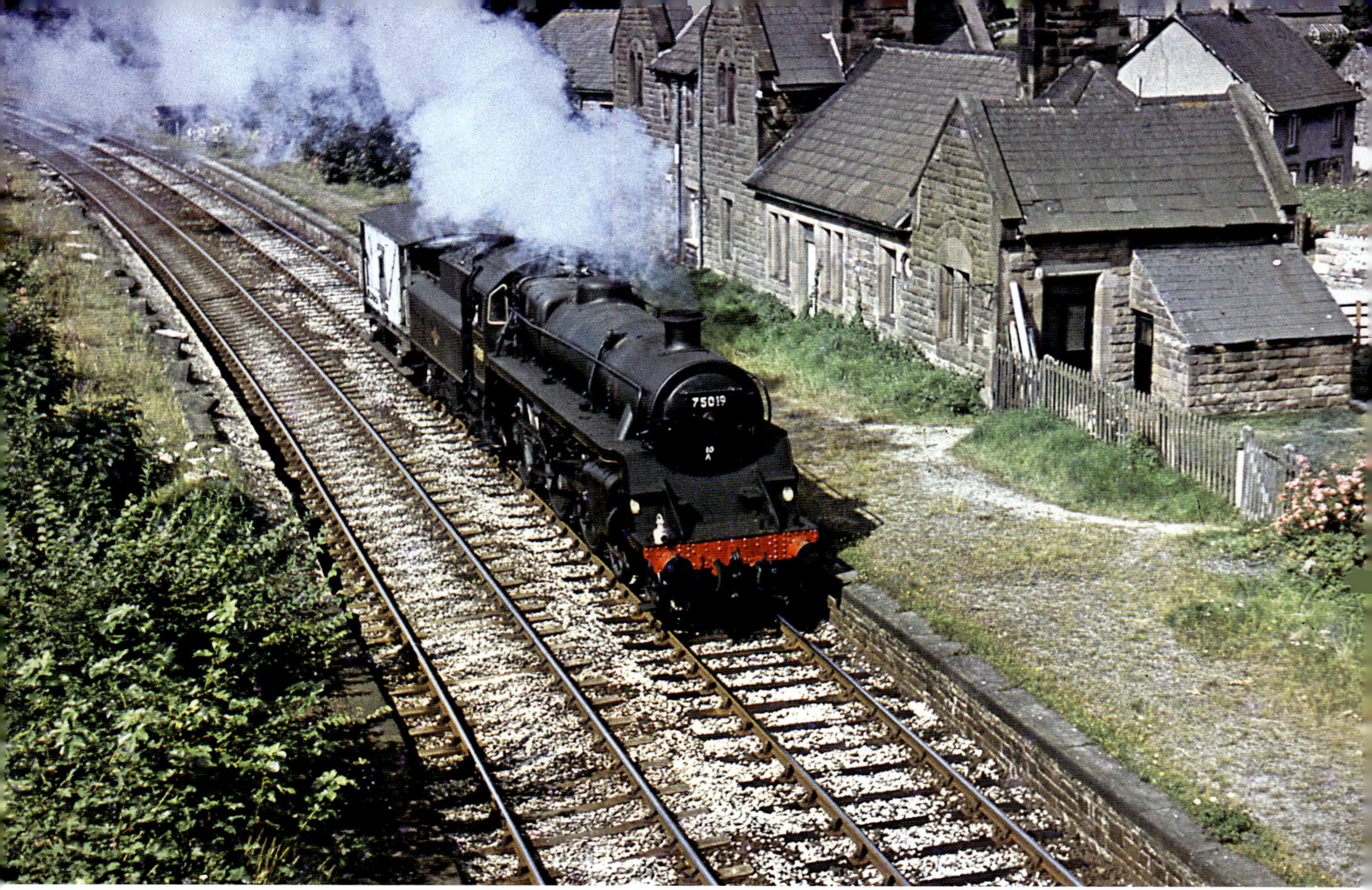

Standard Class 4 No. 75019 trundles through Borwick with a brake van on Friday 2 August 1968, the penultimate day of timetabled BR steam. The loco is clean having worked the Carnforth to Skipton leg of a 'Farewell to Steam' special the previous Saturday. Borwick Station had closed, along with neighbouring Arkholme, in September 1960, leaving no stops between Wennington and Carnforth. The main building survives as a private residence, as does an almost identical structure called Station Cottage about 100 yards off the right of the photo, parallel to - but not on - the railway. A possible explanation is that the station was built before the alignment of the railway had been finalised. *(Colour-Rail)*

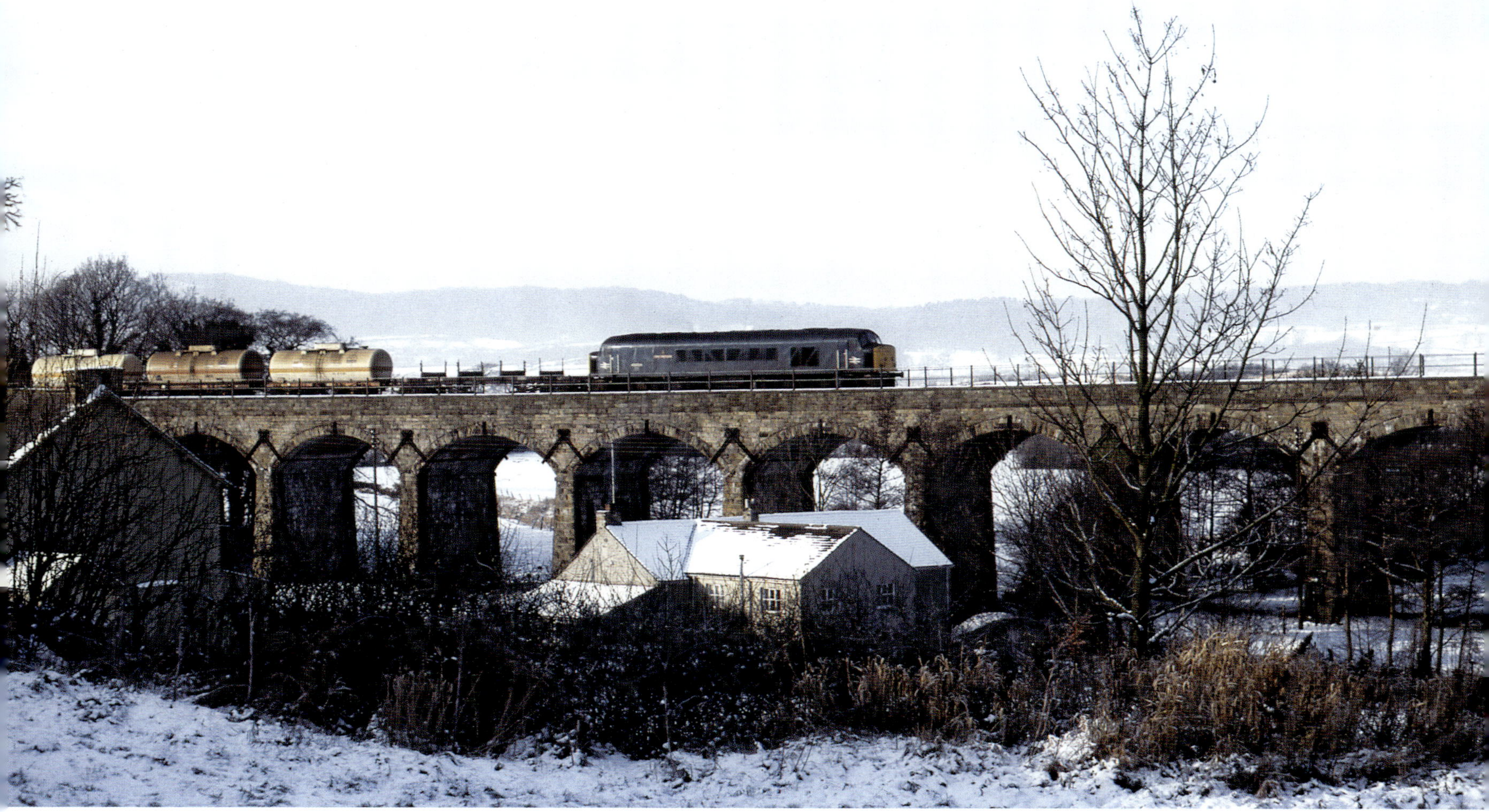

'Peak' Class 45 diesel 45004 *Royal Irish Fusilier* (formerly D77) crosses the 11-arch Capernwray Viaduct, between Carnforth and Borwick, with the Heysham Moss to Haverton Hill tanks on 12 December 1981. This working lasted from 1939 until 1986. Until 1965, it was routed after Skipton via Ilkley, Otley, Arthington, Harrogate and Ripon. Since 1986, there has been no regular freight traffic between Carnforth, Wennington and Settle Junction. The loco was built at Crewe Works in 1960 and withdrawn for scrap in 1988. *(Gavin Morrison)*

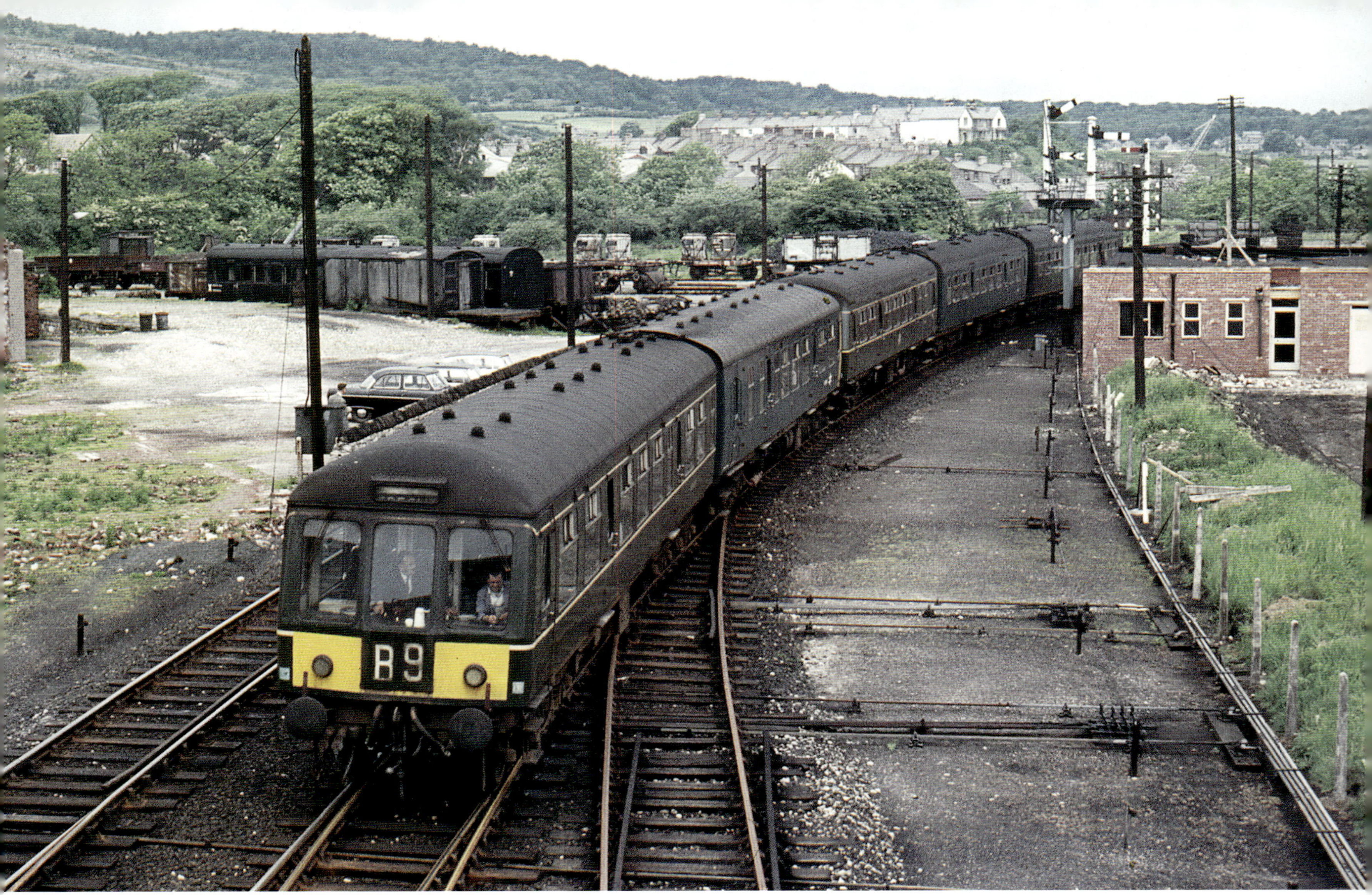

A two-car Class 108 Derby DMU leads a three-car Metro Cammell set into Carnforth in about 1967. The second and fourth coaches are in the drab all over blue livery which was replacing the far more attractive lined green at the time. The Morecambe-bound train is signalled into the through platform. The leading coach is on the facing point which, in earlier times, would have given access to the Leeds bay where the train would have terminated - the Morecambe portion having parted company at Wennington. Five-coach trains on the route are long gone. Today's passengers normally have the pleasure of just a two-car unit on Leeds – Morecambe services but, occasionally, only a single car Class 153 is provided. *(RCTS Archive)*

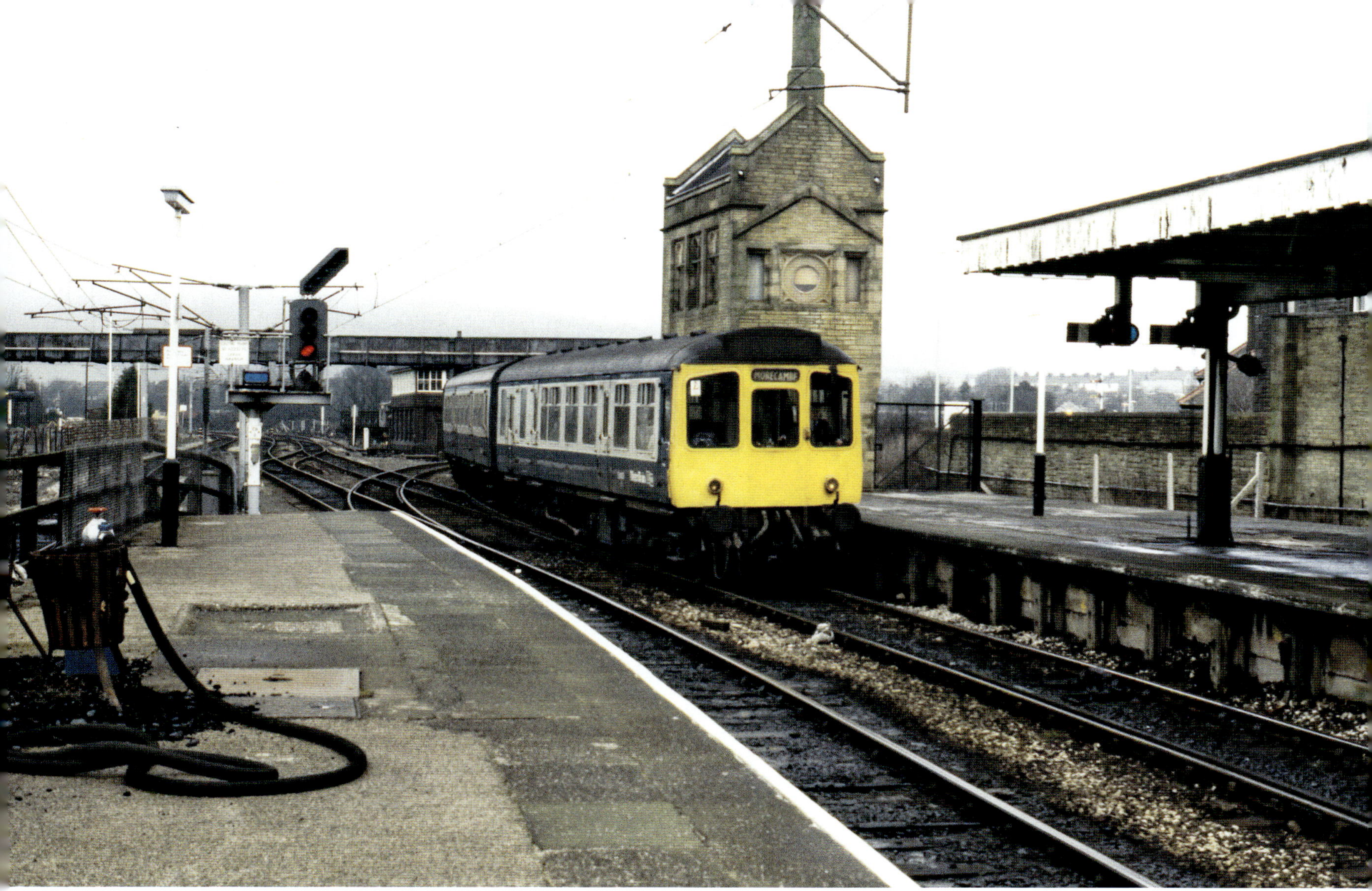

Class 110 DMU car No. 51809 leads a Leeds – Morecambe service into Carnforth in March 1989, just three months before its withdrawal for scrap. These three-car units were built in 1961 by the Birmingham Railway Carriage & Wagon Co for the Calder Valley service between Leeds Central, Bradford Exchange and Manchester Victoria. The centre trailers had been removed in the early 1980s but this train has one taken from a Metro Cammell set. Before 1966, Leeds trains started from the bay platform on the right. The tall building is the 1882 signal box which was closed in 1903 in favour of the one visible in the V of the junction. *(Graeme Phillips)*

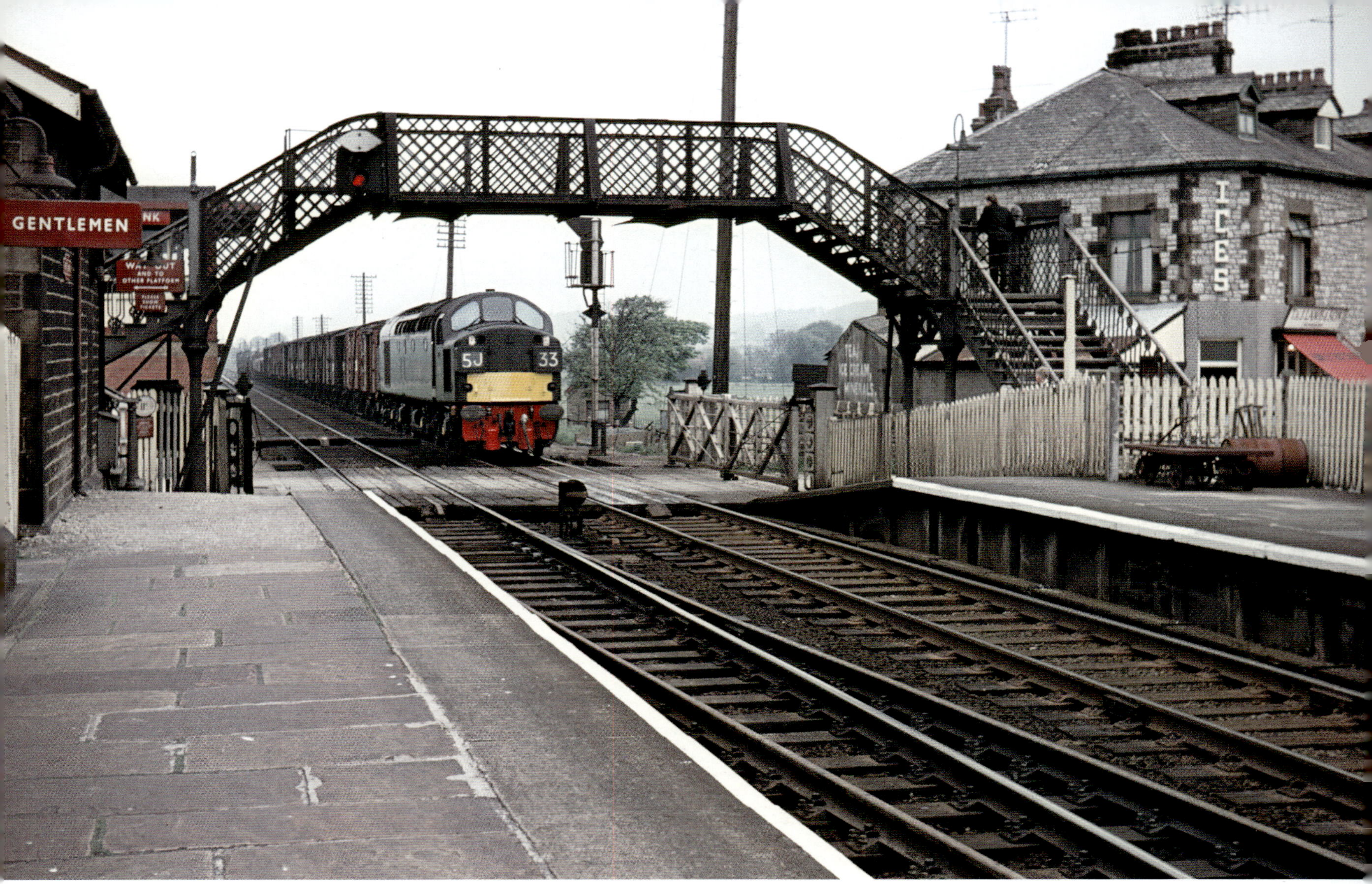

A fine view under the footbridge towards Carnforth at Hest Bank sees an English Electric Type 4 heading south with a freight in 1967. This example was one of 20 in the 200-strong class fitted with split head code boxes. These were numbered between D325 and D344. The diverted Leeds – Morecambe trains did not stop at Hest Bank which closed in February 1969. They would have had to stop at the signal box to collect the token to Bare Lane but the system changed to a direction lever in about 1967. This may have been in response to the appearance of regular DMUs on the single track north curve of the Morecambe branch. The flat roof signal box dated from 1958 when it replaced an LNWR box further south at the actual junction. *(M. Pinder/Alan Whitaker collection)*

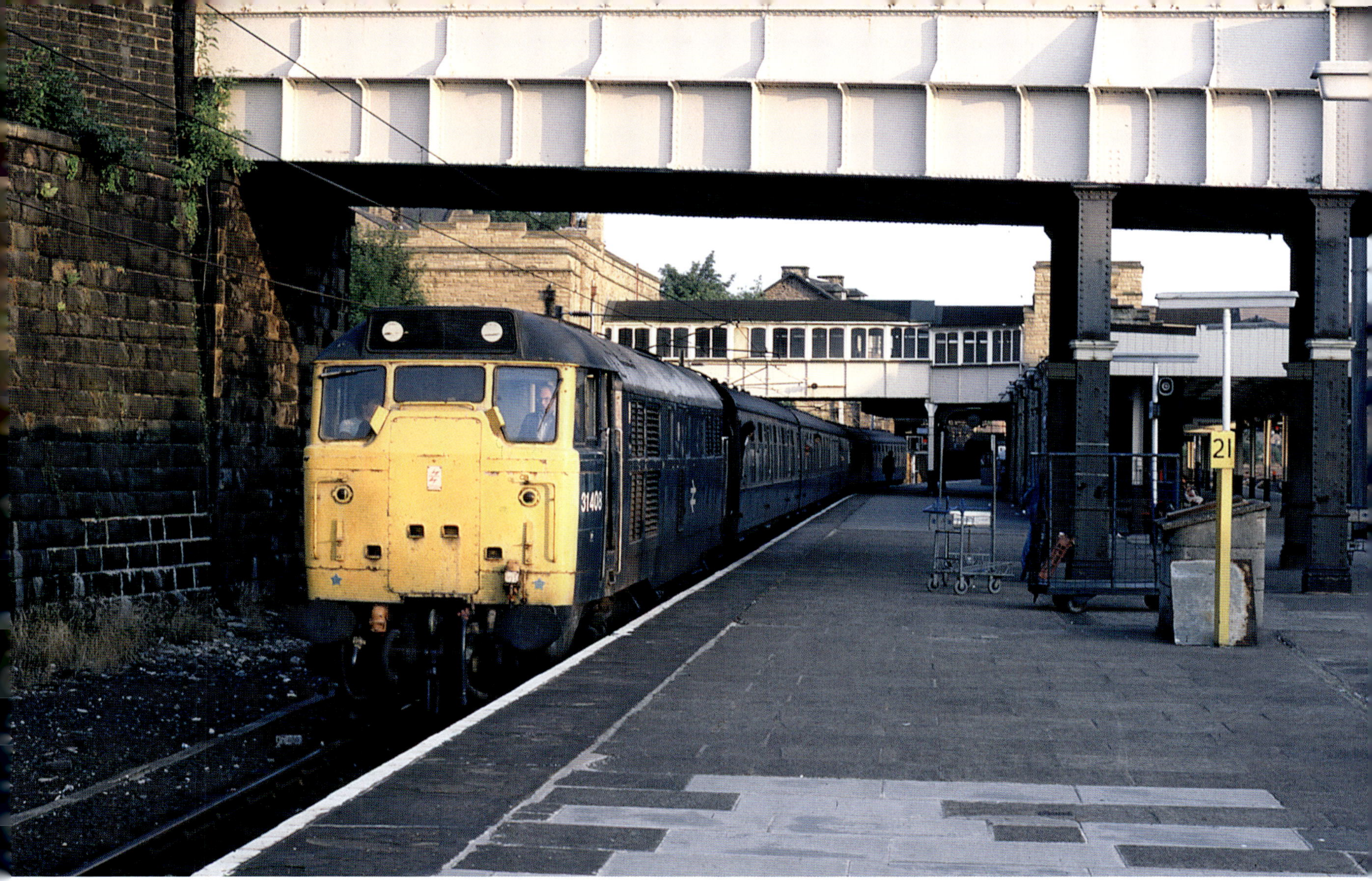

31408 is preparing to depart for Leeds from Platform 5 at Lancaster Castle on 11 August 1984. In 1982, BR had finally decided that having Leeds to Morecambe trains miss Lancaster wasn't very clever and had diverted some trains to call and reverse there. By 1984, the service comprised four DMUs a day, calling at all stations to Morecambe via the Hest Bank to Bare Lane curve and three loco-hauled semi fasts to Lancaster only. Since 1987, virtually all trains have served Lancaster, with some continuing to Morecambe. The once electrified Platform 5 at Lancaster Castle station was wired again as part of the West Coast Main Line electrification extension programme in 1974 but there is no track in Platform 6 opposite. *(Tom Heavyside)*

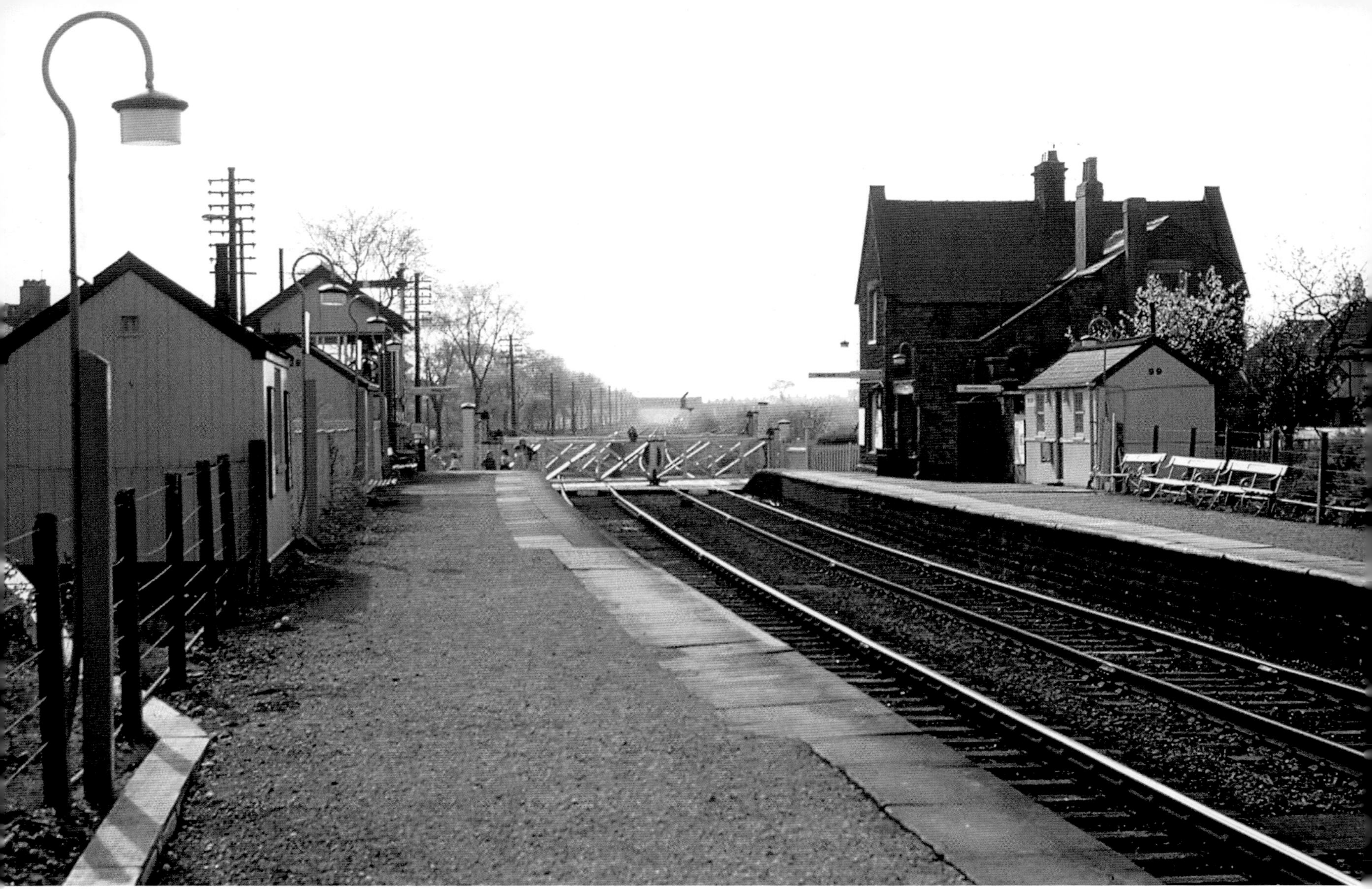

Bare Lane looking towards Morecambe in April 1974. This is the one station which benefitted from the 1966 re-routing. It had previously seen only a sparse service between Lancaster Castle and Morecambe. This was increased but not to anything like the half hourly frequency provided by the withdrawn electrics. It also gained the Leeds trains. Since 1994, trains in either direction have been able to run on either track, potentially leaving passengers on the wrong platform and cut off by the level crossing. Recently installed electronic displays should now alleviate this. The signal box was demolished in 2014. *(Alan Young)*

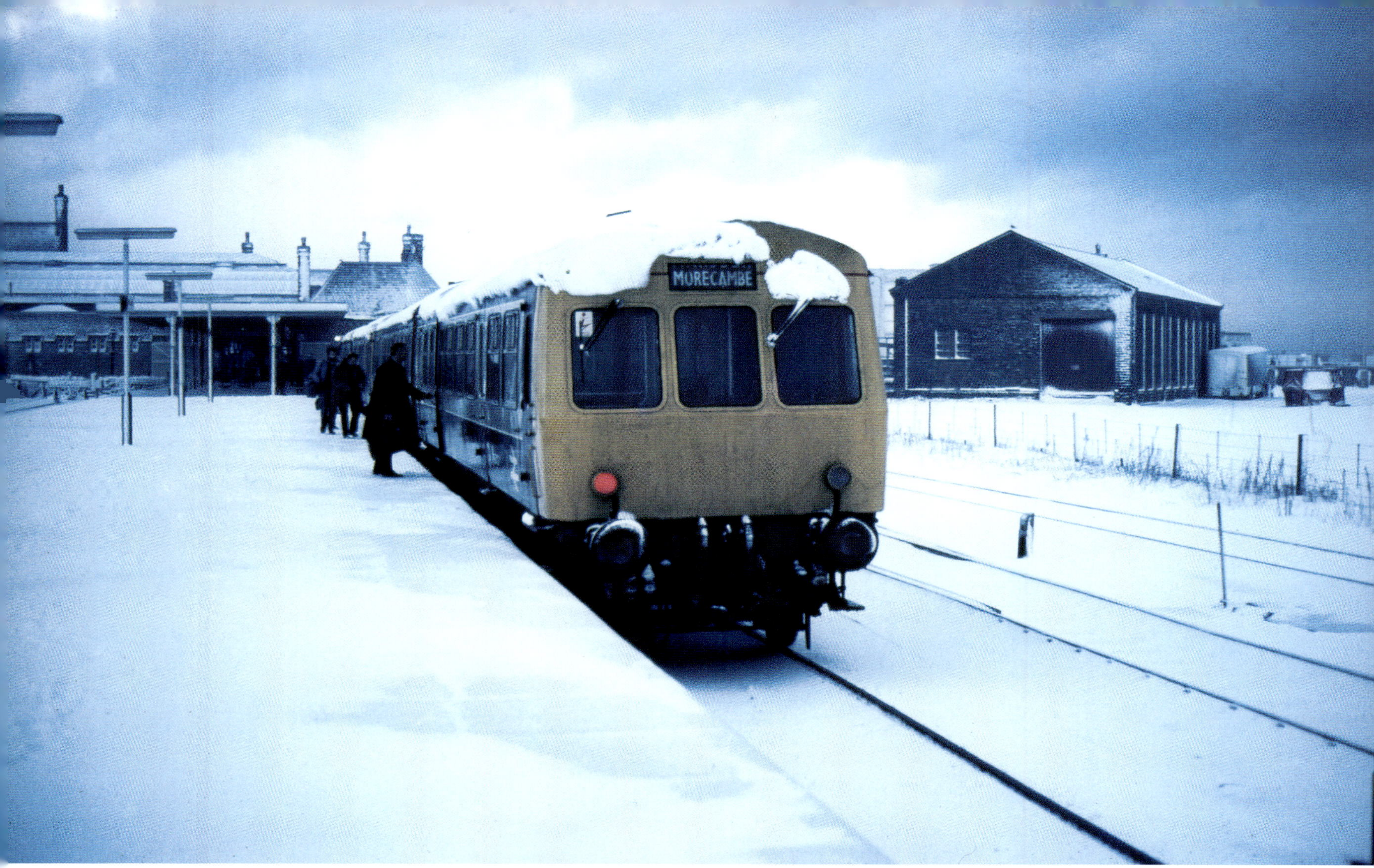

Winter has descended on Morecambe Promenade station as the 7.12 a.m. to Lancaster prepares to leave, running two hours late. Power car 50227 and driving trailer 56070 make up the two-car Metro Cammell set on 14 December 1981. Dating from 1957, the power car lasted until 1988. By that time, Class 142 and 144 four-wheel 'Pacer' units had taken over most of the Leeds workings, as well as the locals to Lancaster, and these remained dominant for the next 30 years. The impressive Promenade Station, which had been progressively reduced to a shadow of its former grandeur, closed in February 1994 after 87 years of service. The line was then cut back ¼ mile to a new simplified two-platform terminus built on the site of the pre-1907 station. The imposing Midland Railway goods warehouse to the right of the DMU survived well into the 1990s, although the yard had closed in 1967. *(Peter Cooper)*

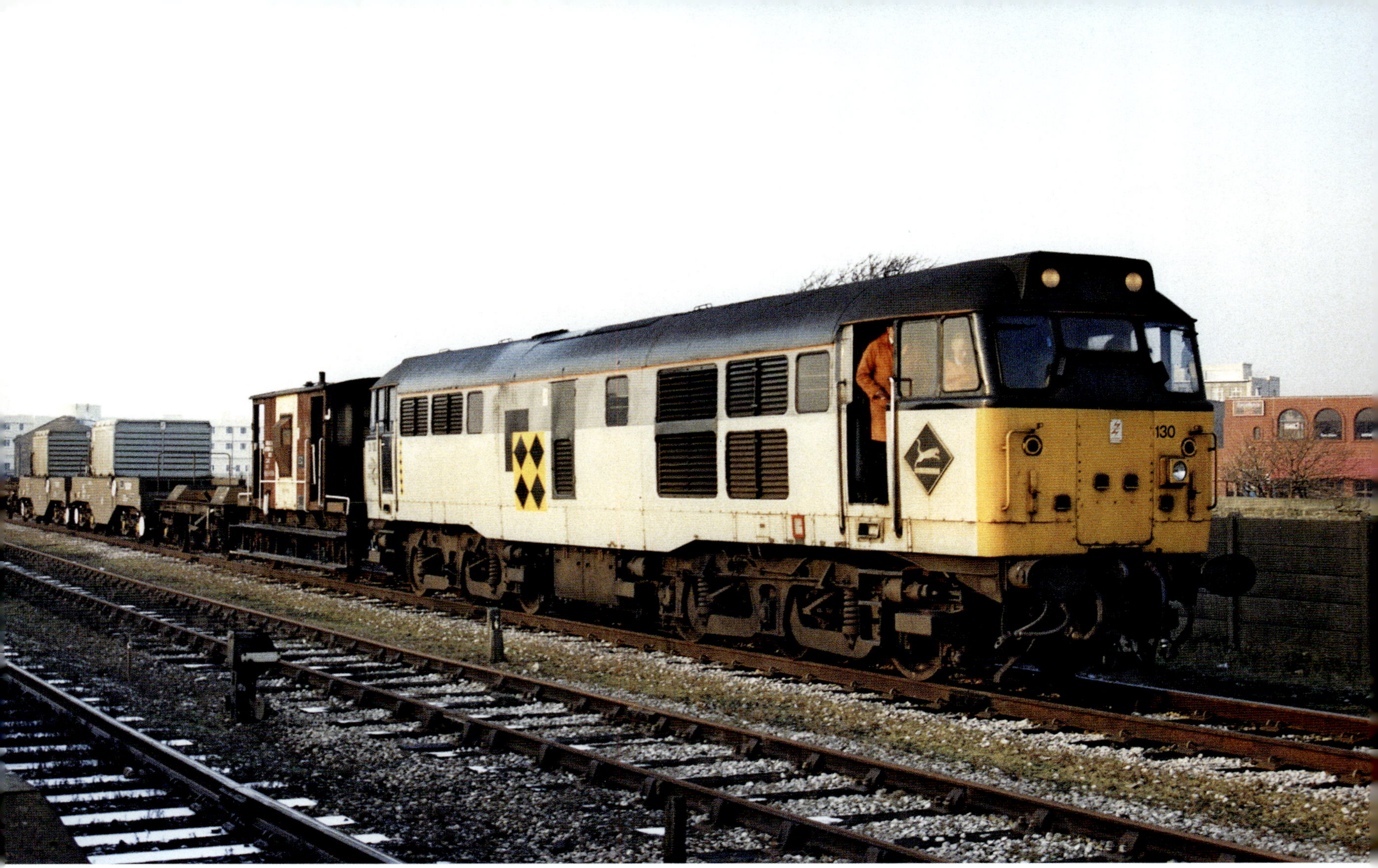

Sporting British Rail's relatively short-lived Trainload Freight Coal Sector branding, 31130 has run round at Morecambe Promenade with the Sellafield to Heysham nuclear flasks on 9 December 1991. This train has operated about once a week since 1986 and is the only freight on the line. The 1994 Morecambe Station has a run round loop but it is rarely used as the flasks now have a locomotive at each end, usually a pair of 3,800hp Class 68s. Reversal at Morecambe would not be necessary if BR had built the direct curve between the Bare Lane and Heysham lines for which they obtained statutory powers in 1965. The more modest 1,250hp Class 31 in this view was new as D5548 in 1959 and is now preserved on the Avon Valley Railway. *(Alan Whitaker)*

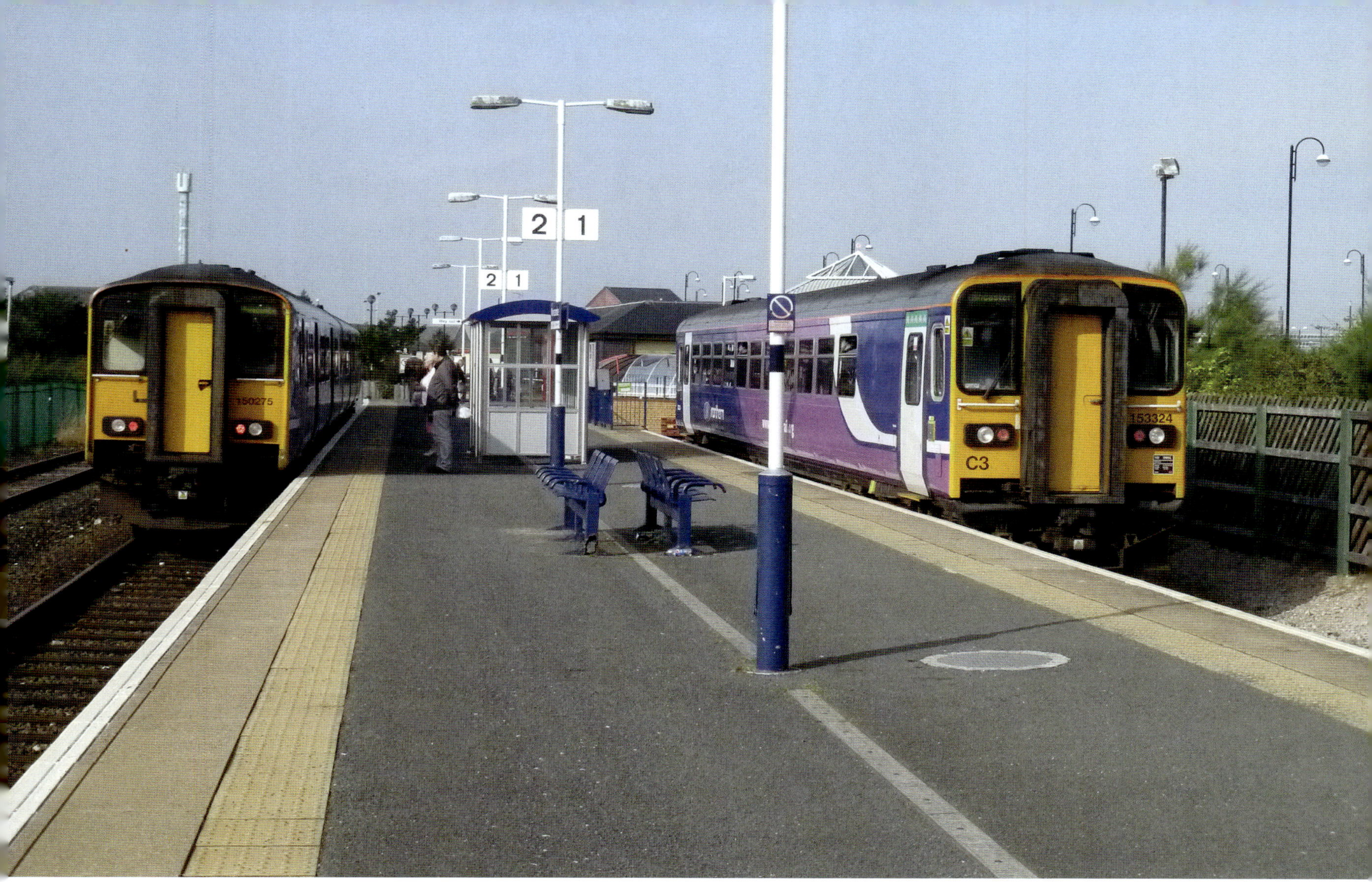

The location of the current Morecambe terminus is almost exactly on the site of the station featured on Page 1. When the line was cut back to this new island platform facility in 1994, the layout was simplified, with the double track from Bare Lane worked as two single lines and no cross over at Morecambe. Trains arriving in Platform 1 have no option but to return towards Bare Lane. Those for Heysham must use Platform 2. Access to the branch is by a ground frame operated by the driver. This view, captured on 19 September 2015, shows two-car 150275 on Platform 2 awaiting its return to Leeds while single car unit 153324 occupies Platform 1, having arrived from Lancaster. *(Martin Bairstow)*

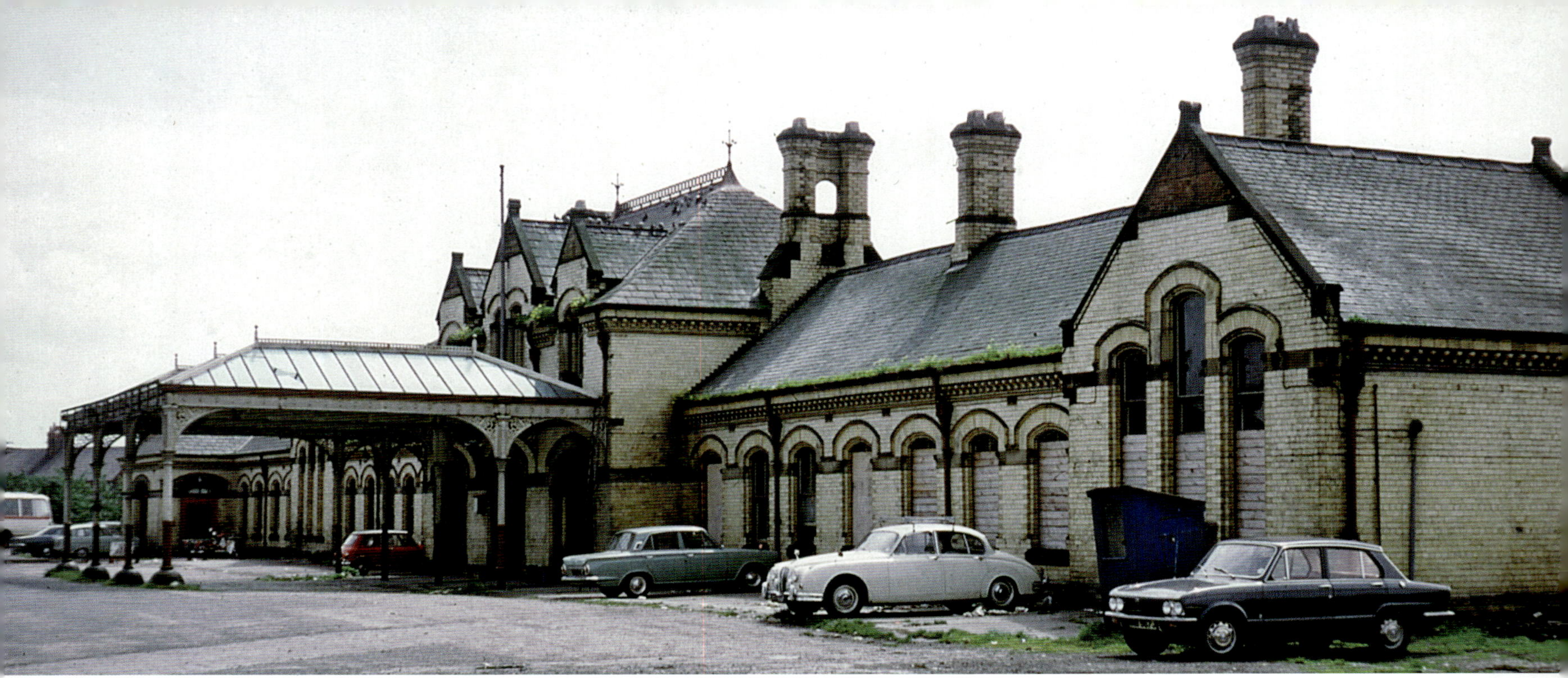

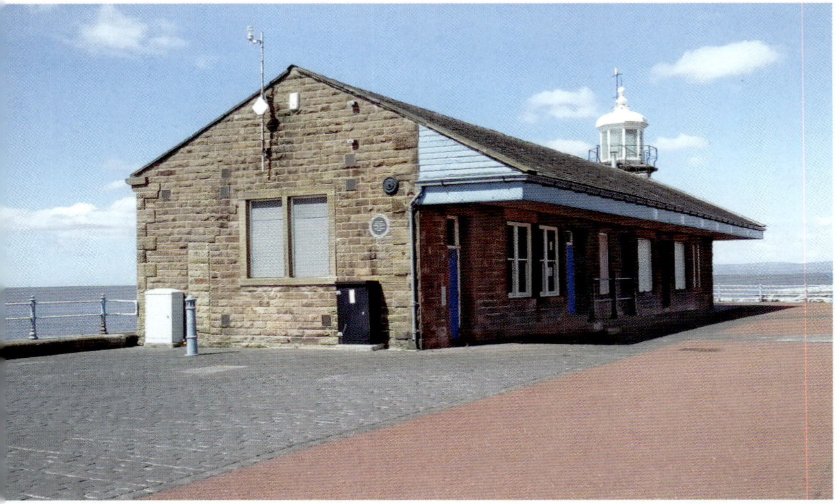

Left: Dating from the early 1850s, this building on the Stone Jetty was part of the Morecambe Pier Station at which trains met the steamers for Ireland. The Railway Company sailings to Belfast were transferred to Piel, near Barrow, in 1867 but Laird Line continued to connect Morecambe with Dublin and Londonderry until Heysham opened in 1904. Morecambe Harbour then became a scrapyard, disposing of more than 50 ships over the next 25 years, including the paddle steamers *Ben-my-Chree* and *Mona's Isle* of the Isle of Man Steam Packet Company. The yard closed in the early 1930s, making way for construction of the grand Art Deco Midland Hotel which opened in 1933, replacing the smaller North Western Hotel which had dated from the opening of the railway. The Stone Jetty was the outer wall of the harbour. In its commercial and scrapyard days, there was also a wooden pier on the east side. Both piers carried railway tracks. When the horse tramway opened along the Promenade in 1887, it had to cross ten lines and sidings leading to the harbour. This view dates from April 2018. *(Alan Whitaker)*

Above: Opened in 1886, the former London & North Western Station at Morecambe Euston Road, seen here in a dilapidated state in June 1972, had closed to passengers on an all year round basis in 1958 but was revived each summer until 1962. It was then used for parcels and as carriage sidings until the tracks were removed in 1965. The goods yard continued to receive traffic until October 1972, five years longer than the former Midland Railway yard adjacent to Promenade Station. *(Roger Hepworth)*

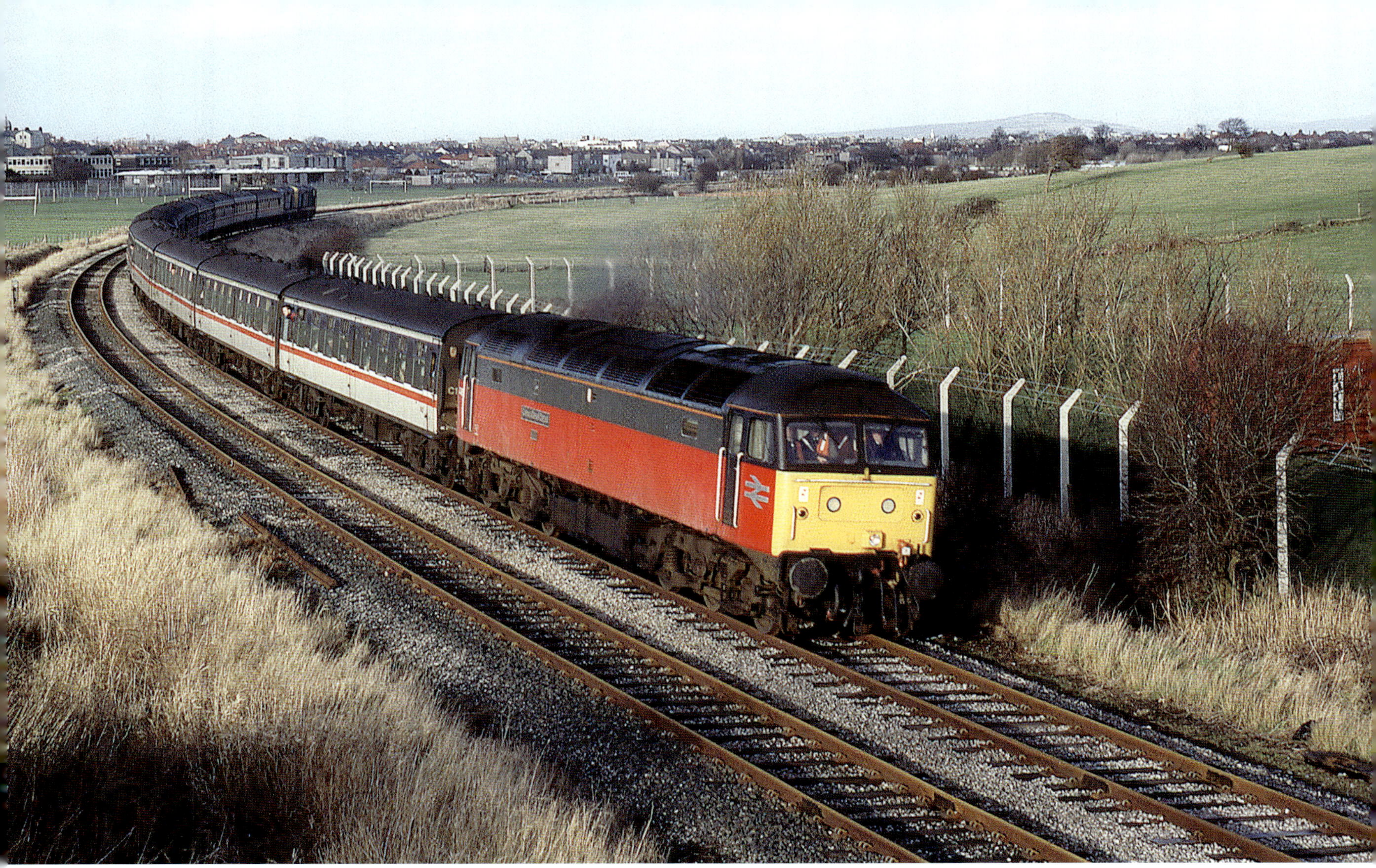

The 'Lune Ranger' railtour on 15 February 1992 saw Class 47 No. 47489 pressed into service on a section of line it would rarely, if ever, have visited. The train is passing King George's Playing Fields, about half way between Morecambe and Heysham. At that time, the track was still double as far as Heysham Moss. It was singled as part of the new Morecambe Station arrangements in 1994. The loco was built at Brush Traction, Loughborough, as D1716 and entered service in February 1964, allocated to Oxley shed at Wolverhampton. After a respectable 43 years and eight months of service, it was withdrawn in October 2007 and sold for scrap. The Heysham line had been singled temporarily during the First World War when the railway companies were asked to make track available to be re-laid for additional sidings to serve new munitions factories. *(Tom Heavyside)*

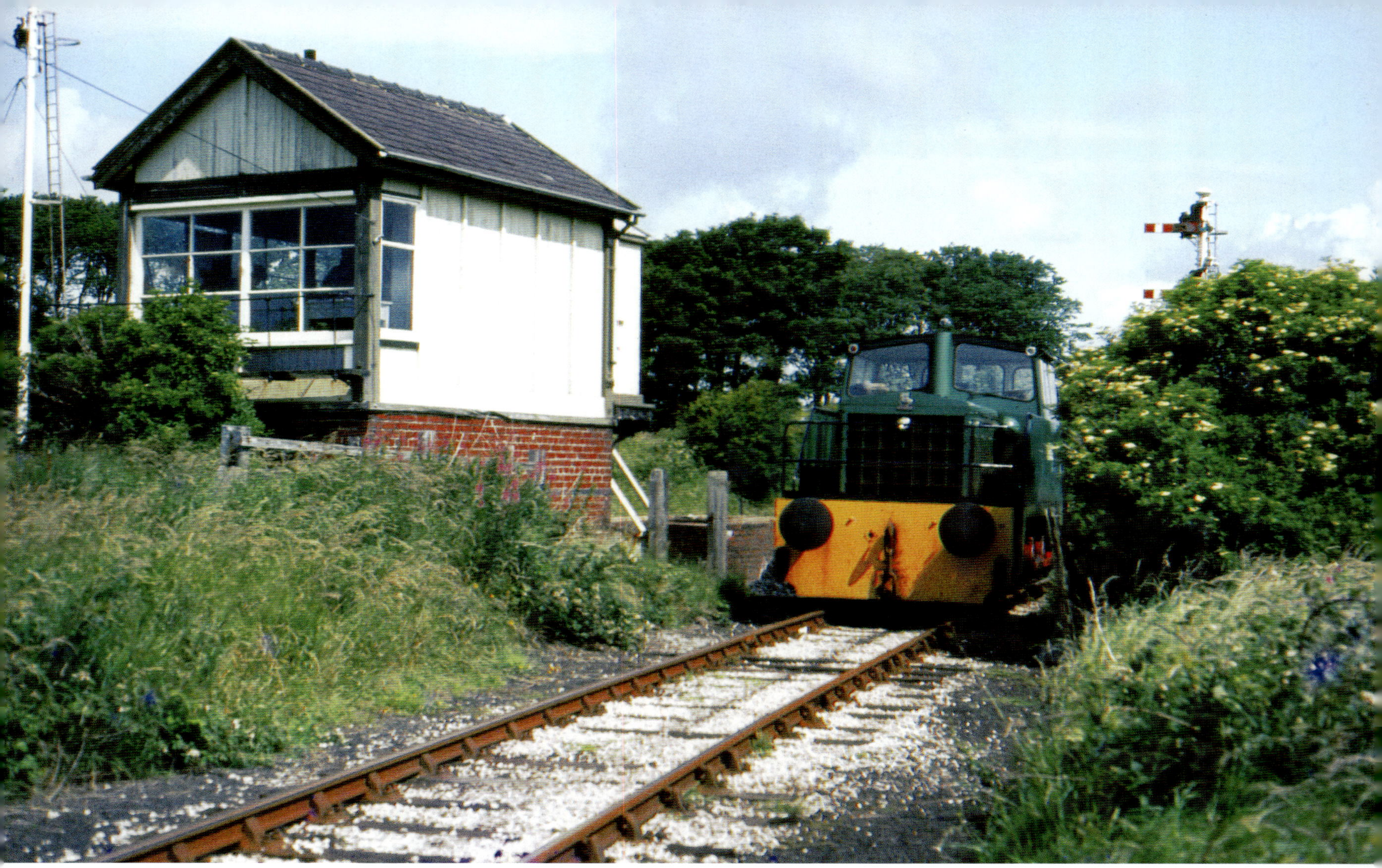

Diesel – hydraulic 0 – 6 – 0 *King* waits at Heysham Moss for the arrival of the ammonia tanks from Haverton Hill, Teesside, on 13 May 1982. The view is towards Morecambe. The signal box was commissioned on 3 December 1939 to serve the ICI sidings. These closed in 1986 and the box was destroyed in an arson attack in January 1987. After this, there was a spring-loaded point where the double line from Morecambe gave way to the single track to Heysham. The loco was a Sentinel Vanguard built by Thomas Hill, of Rotherham, to replace the Bagnall 0 – 6 – 0 fireless steam loco which had served from 1952 until 1970. Up to 2,000 people were employed at the Shell and ICI complex. In 1957, staff were asked how many would commute by train if a halt was provided at Heysham Moss but nothing came of the idea. *(Peter Cooper)*

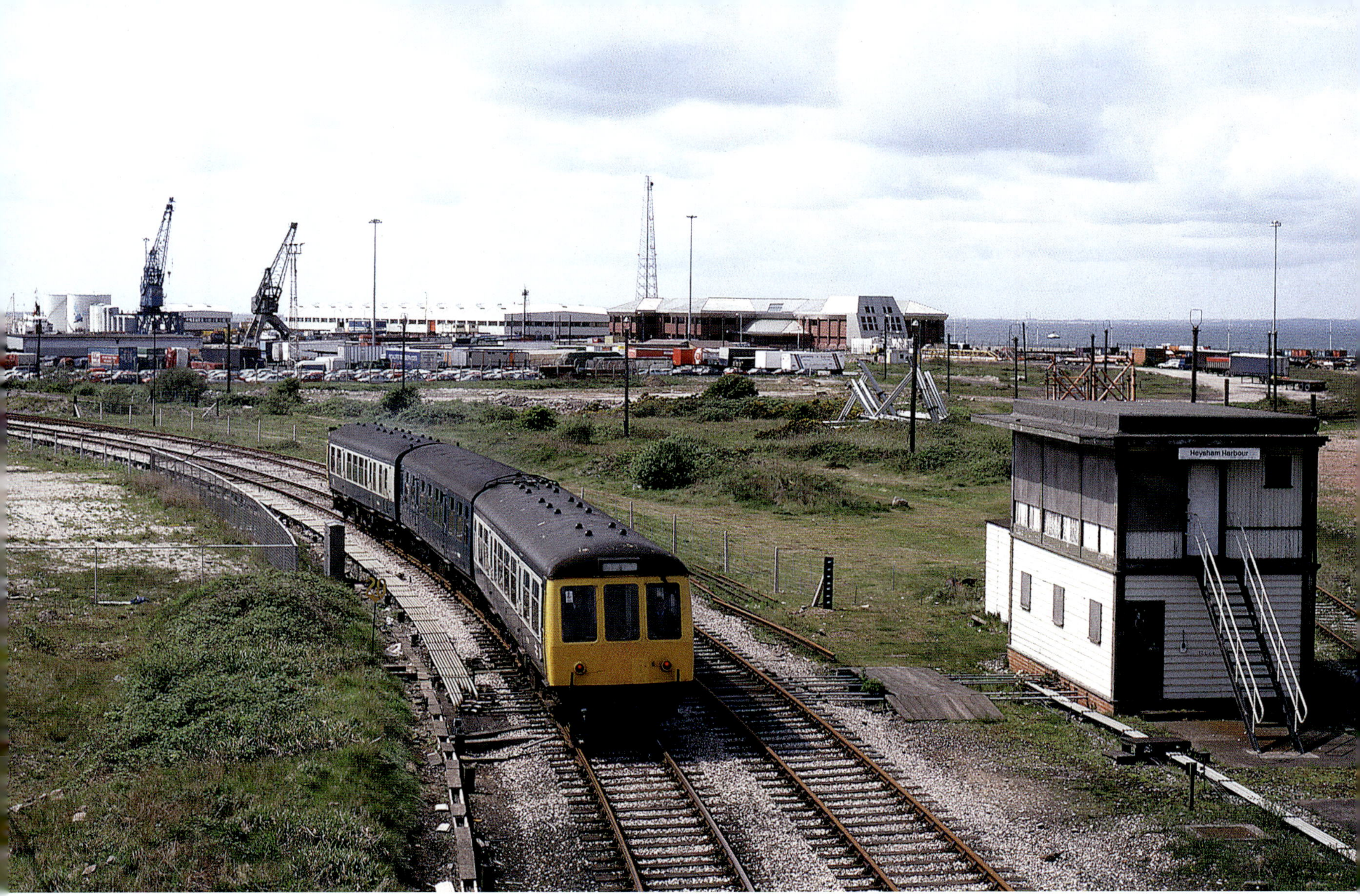

Today, Heysham Harbour is busier than ever before but none of the freight and only a modest number of Isle of Man passengers connect by rail. A Class 108 set with a Class 104 DMU centre trailer arrives with the daily service from Lancaster shortly after its resumption in May 1987. The signal box was commissioned in 1970 to replace two Midland boxes. It was reduced to ground frame status after only seven years when the section from Heysham Moss was singled. The box is now in operation at Lydney Junction on the Dean Forest Railway. *(Tom Heavyside)*

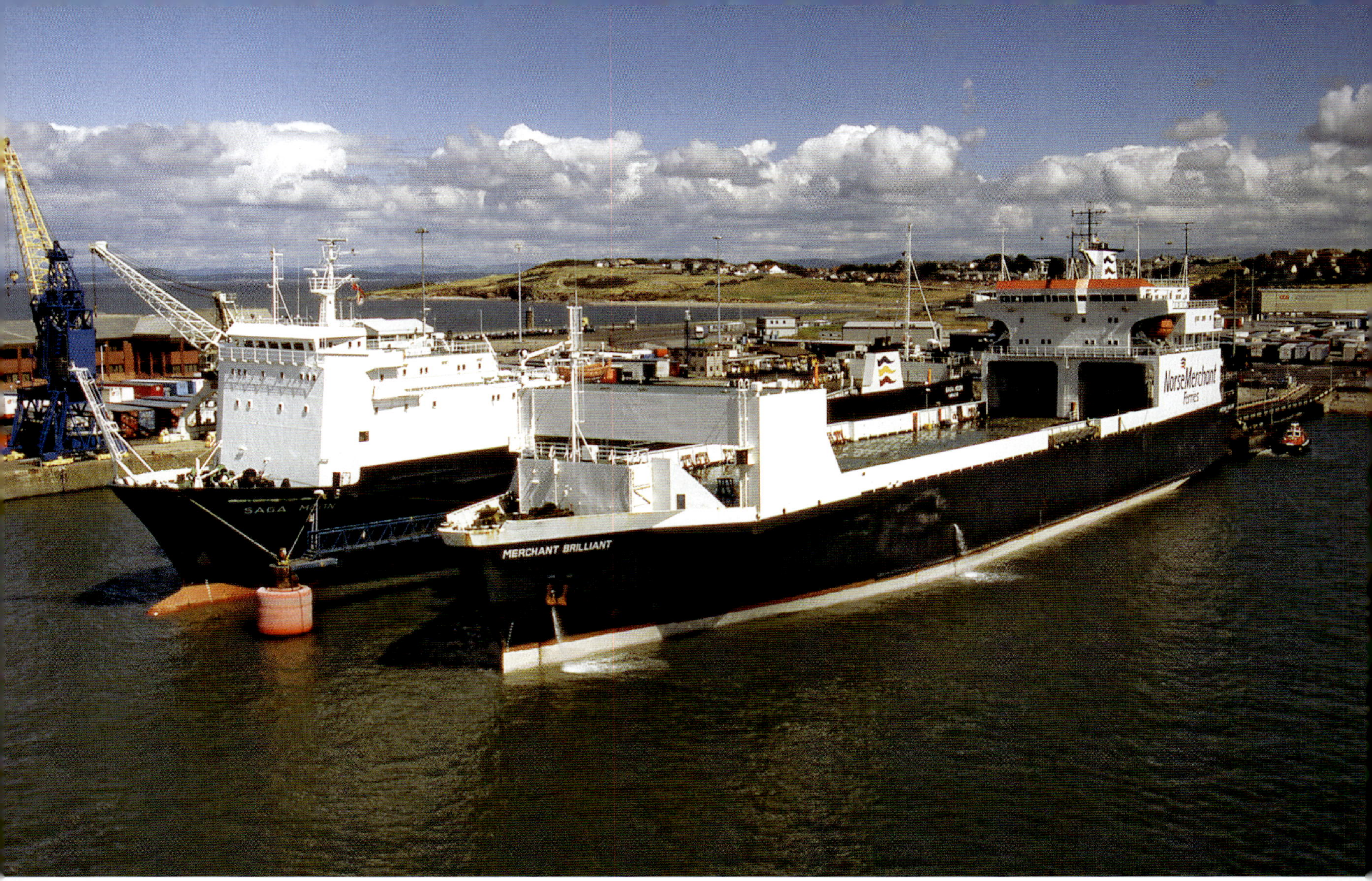

Roll on – roll off freight ferries *Saga Moon* and *Merchant Brilliant* at Heysham on 5 August 2001. The Belfast route was reopened in 1984 by Belfast Freight Ferries which has subsequently passed through the hands of Norse Merchant, Norfolk Line and DFDS. Since 2010, it has been part of Stena Line. Sailings operate overnight six days a week, with five more during the day. Traffic is mainly in unaccompanied road trailers but there is accommodation for 12 lorry drivers. Regular vessels are the 13,000 ton *Stena Hibernia* and *Stena Scotia* - two heritage Holyhead names but with the prefix. *(Martin Bairstow)*

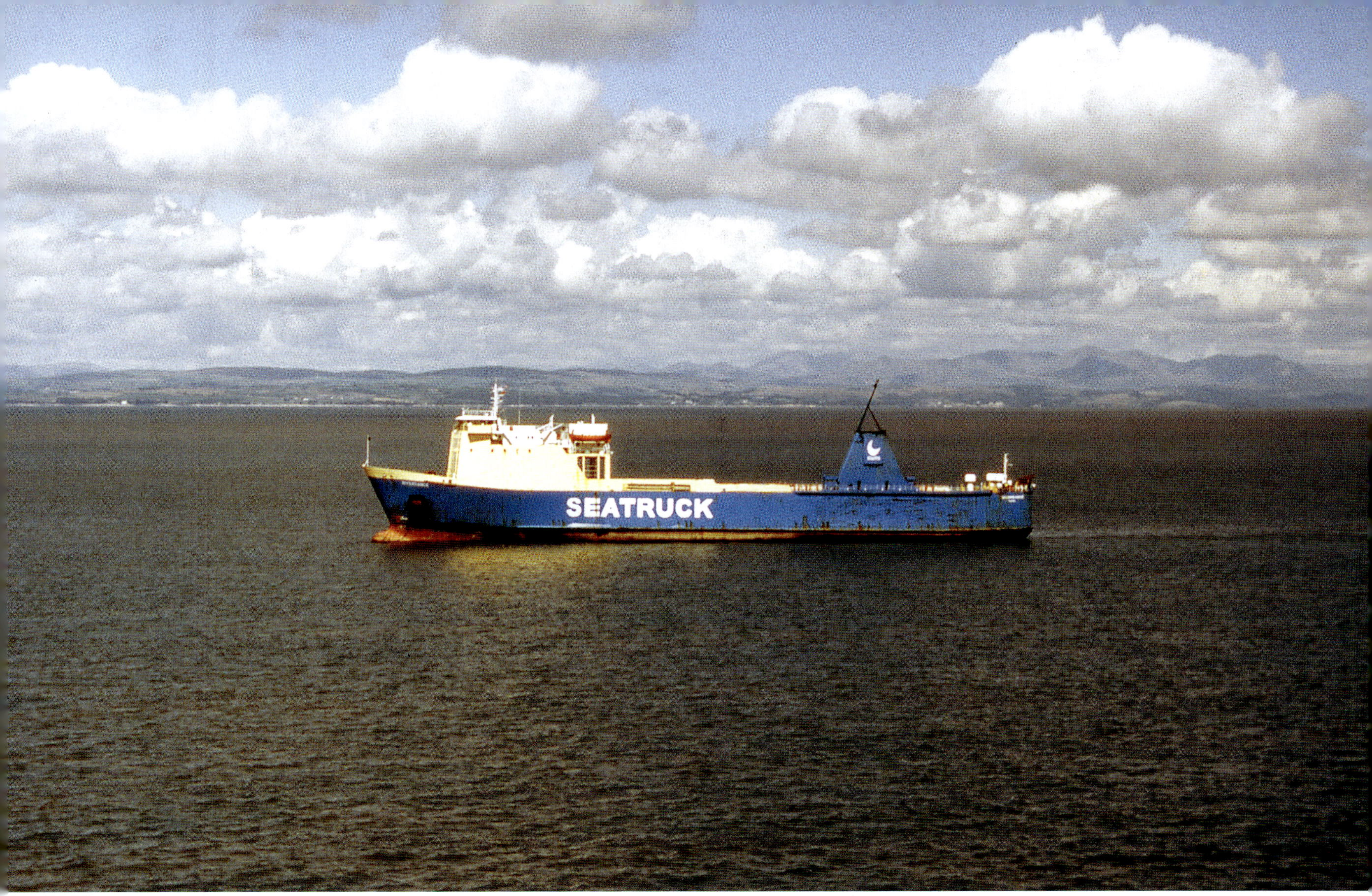

Having discharged its load, *Riverdance* is riding outside Heysham on 5 August 2001, waiting for a berth to become vacant again. Seatruck began in 1996 with *Riverdance* offering a freight service to Warrenpoint in Northern Ireland. The operation has developed and now has purpose-built ships sailing also to Dublin. *Riverdance* met a sad fate and had to be scrapped on the beach at Anchorsholme, near Blackpool, after being driven there by a freak wave on 31 January 2008. *(Martin Bairstow)*

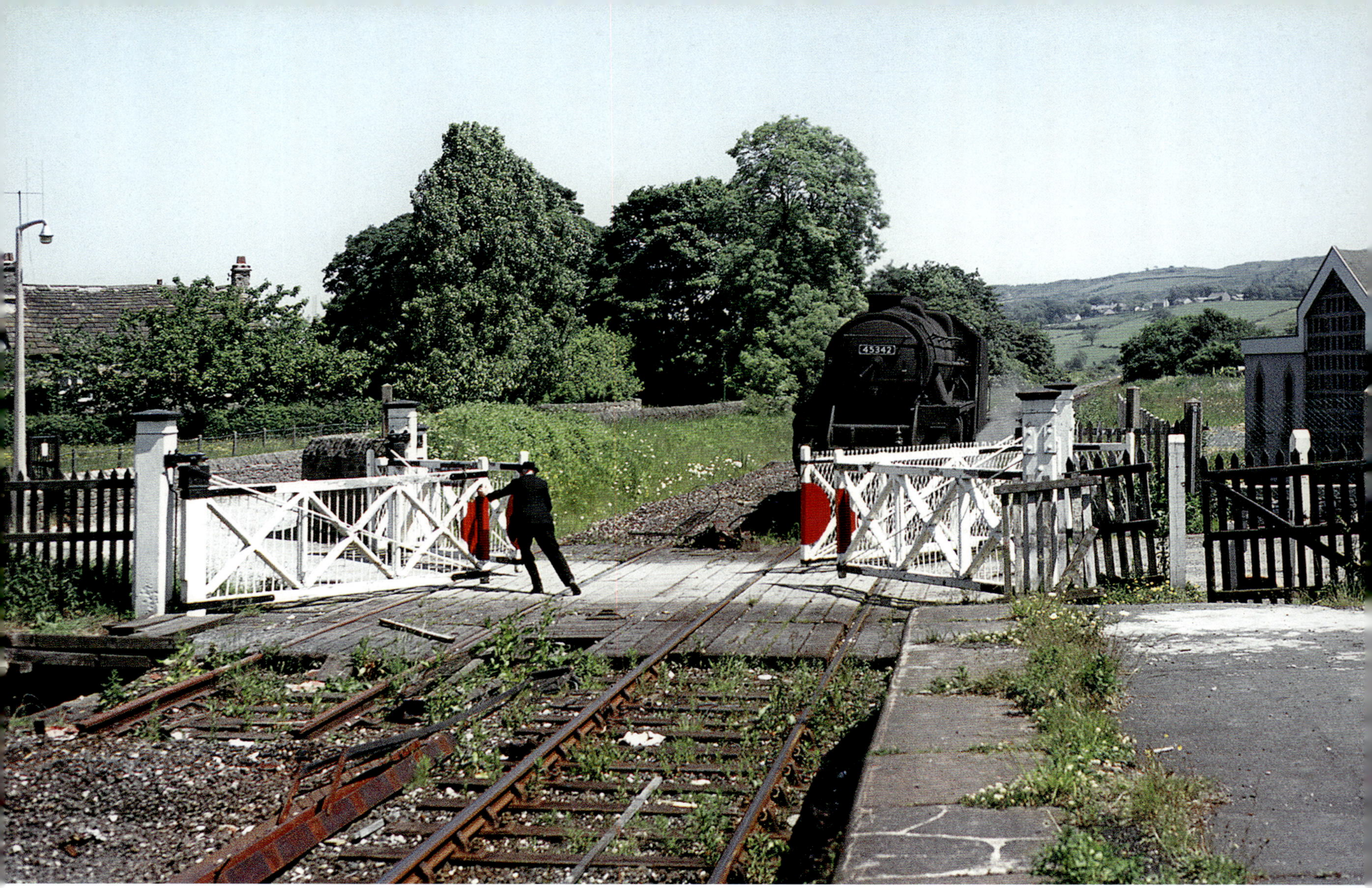

The end of the line. 'Black Five' No. 45342 spent part of its last few weeks in service helping to demolish the railway at Caton in July 1968. The loco was shedded at Carnforth right up to the end of steam on 3 August. Fellow 'Black Five' No 44898 had hauled the last scheduled train through Caton, a fully fitted freight from Heysham Moss to Leeds, on 3 June 1967. Two months later, the line was severed by flood damage between Wennington and Hornby. Demolition left a single track from the power station to Lancaster Castle and another from the gas works west of Scale Hall to Morecambe. These lasted until 1976 and 1970, respectively. *(Derek Phillips)*

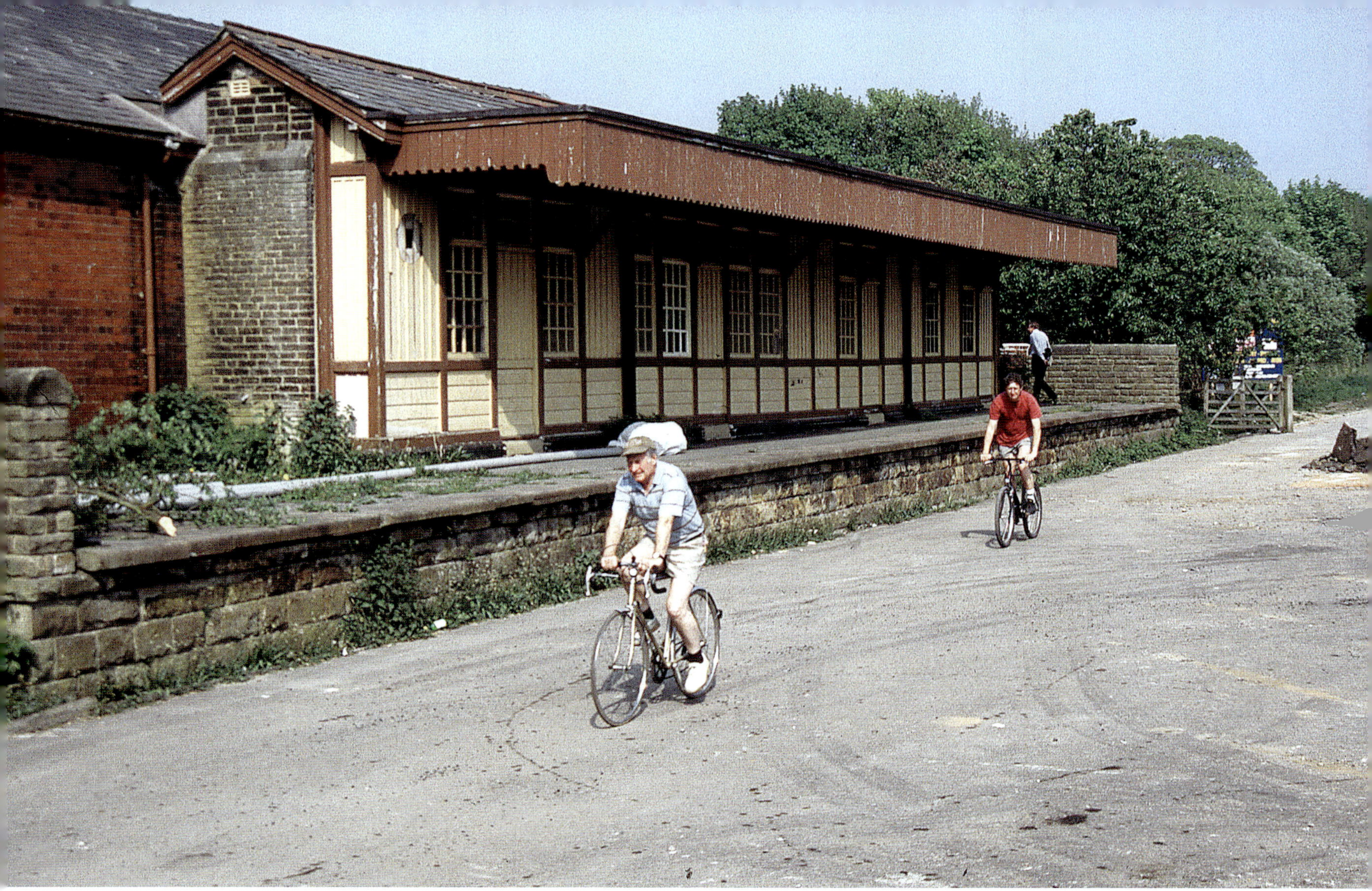

And finally, an 'Express' for Lancaster passing Halton on 9 May 2000. The abandoned route is now a footpath and cycleway from half a mile east of Caton all the way through to Morecambe. At first, there was a section of route missing in Lancaster because the Greyhound Bridge had become a highway. But in 2001, the Millennium Bridge opened for cyclists and pedestrians. The surviving part of Halton Station is used by the Lancaster University Boat Club. The building is not in 'Little' North Western style because it was rebuilt following destruction by fire on 3 April 1907 when sparks from the Heysham to St. Pancras 'boat train' ignited a wagon in the goods yard loaded with naphtha. *(Martin Bairstow)*

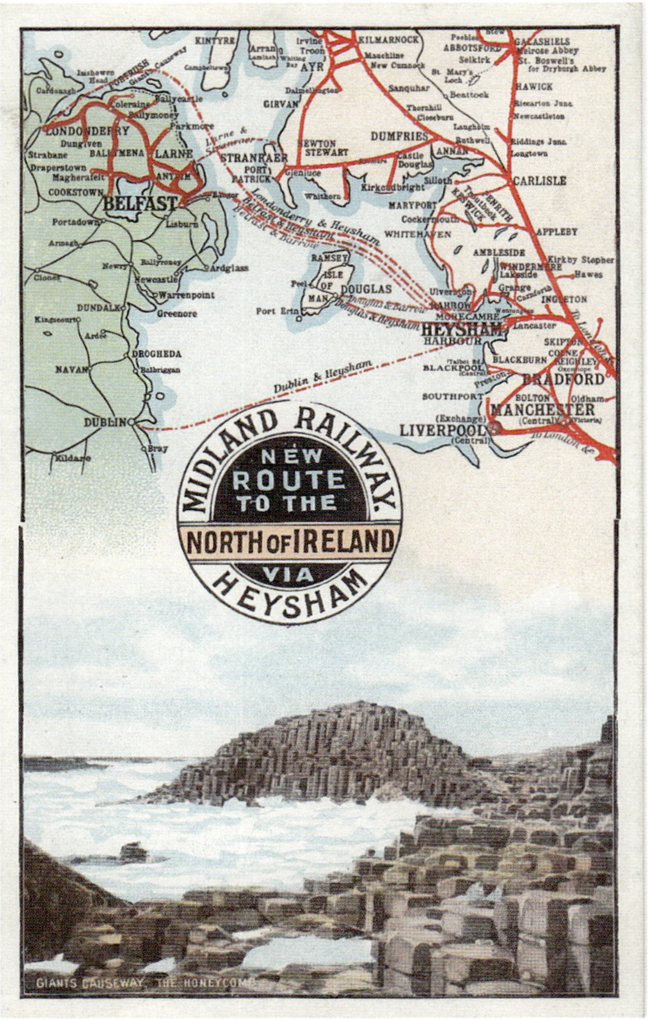

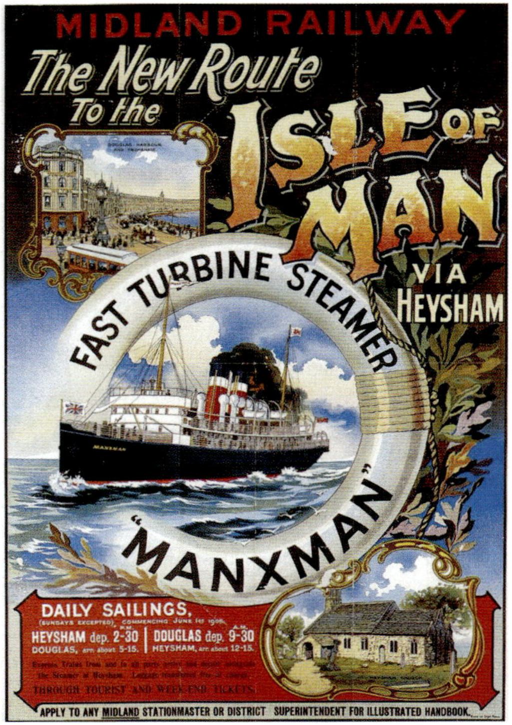

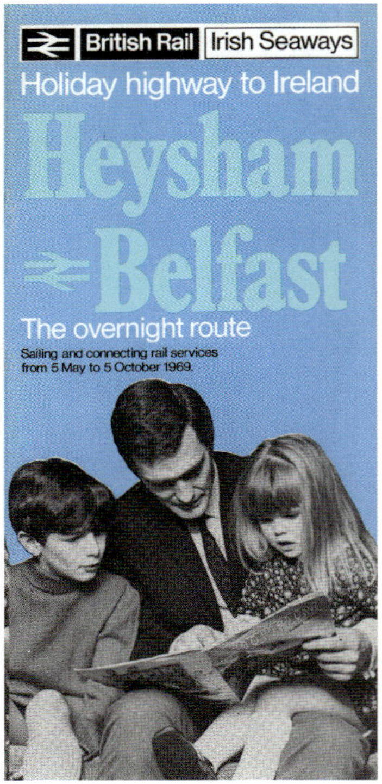

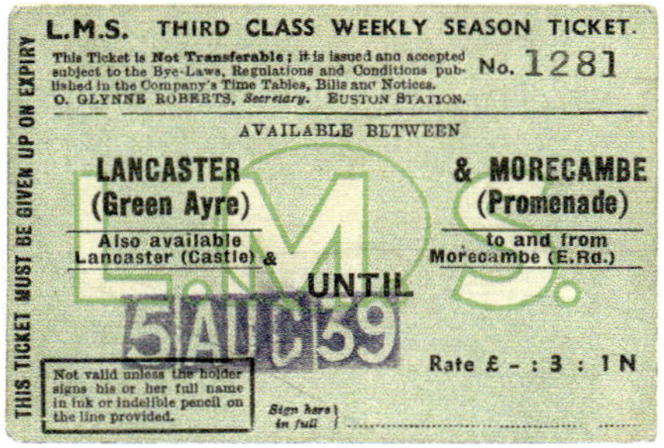

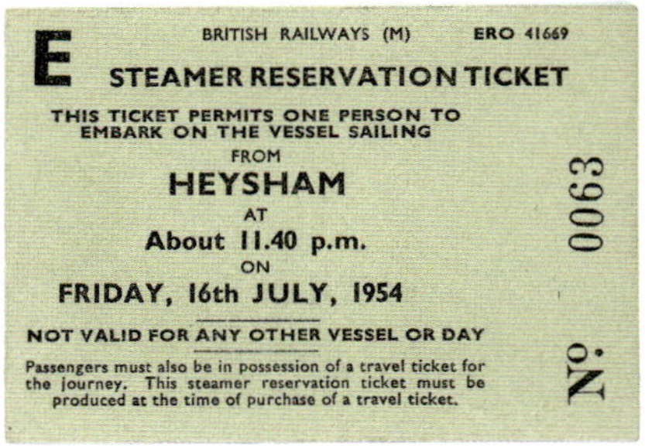

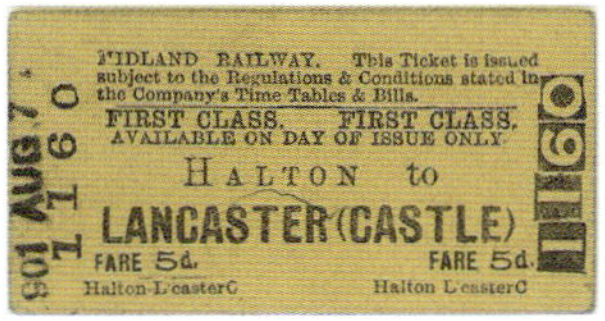

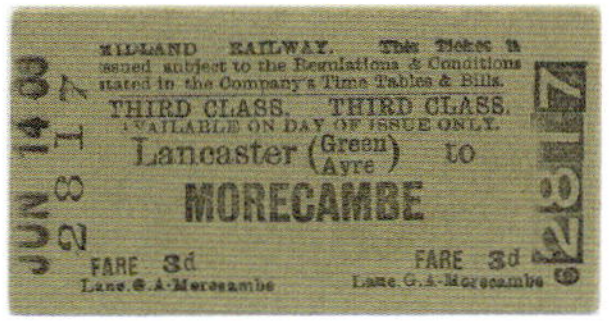

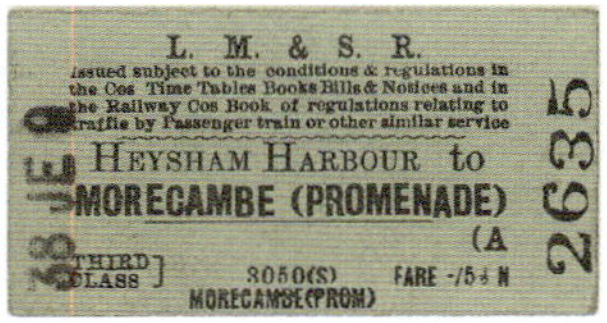

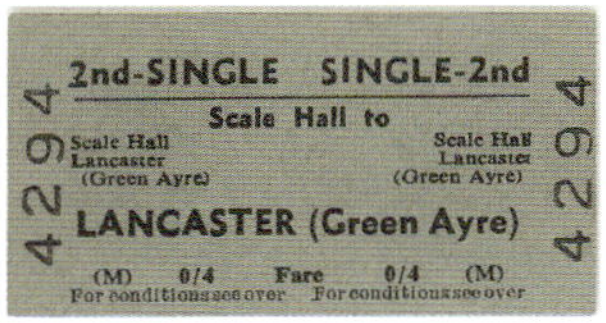

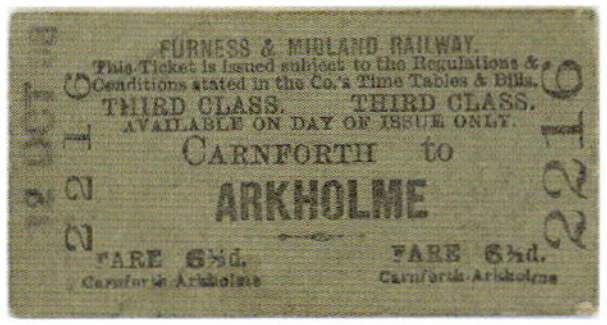

Publicity material and tickets from the Midland Railway Study Centre and Alan Whitaker collections.